LENGTHENING OUR STRIDE

LENGTHENING OUR STRIDE

GLOBALIZATION OF THE CHURCH

Reid L. Neilson & Wayne D. Crosby
Editors

RSC BYU
DESERET BOOK

Published by the Religious Studies Center, Brigham Young University, Provo, Utah, in cooperation with Deseret Book Company, Salt Lake City.

Visit us at rsc.byu.edu.

Printed in the United States of America by Sheridan Books, Inc.

Visit us at DeseretBook.com.

Cover and interior design by Madison Swapp.

ISBN: 978-1-9443-9424-0
Retail US: $27.99

Library of Congress Cataloging-in-Publication Data

Names: Neilson, Reid L., 1972- editor. | Crosby, Wayne D., 1966- editor.
Title: Lengthening our stride : globalization of the church / edited by Reid L. Neilson and Wayne D. Crosby.
Description: Provo, Utah : Religious Studies Center/ Deseret Book, [2018] | Includes index.
Identifiers: LCCN 2017030651
Subjects: LCSH: Church of Jesus Christ of Latter-day Saints--History--21st century. | Mormon Church--History--21st century. | Globalization--Religious aspects--Church of Jesus Christ of Latter-day Saints--History--21st century. | Globalization--Religious aspects--Mormon Church--History--21st century.
Classification: LCC BX8611 .L455 2018 | DDC 289.3/32--dc23 LC record available at https://lccn.loc.gov/2017030651

My brethren, I wonder if we are doing all we can. Are we complacent in our approach to teaching all the world? We have been proselyting now 144 years. Are we prepared to lengthen our stride? To enlarge our vision?

—President Spencer W. Kimball, Regional Representatives Seminar, April 1974

When I think of the concept of "lengthening our stride," I, of course, apply it to myself as well as urging it upon the Church. The "lengthening of our stride" suggests urgency instead of hesitancy, "now," instead of tomorrow; it suggests not only an acceleration, but efficiency. It suggests, too, that the whole body of the Church move forward in unison with a quickened pace and pulse, doing our duty with all our heart, instead of halfheartedly.

—President Spencer W. Kimball, MIA June Conference, June 1975

To R. Lanier Britsch (RLN)
and Marlin K. Jensen (WDC)

CONTENTS

PART 3: PEACEMAKING AND DIPLOMACY

PART 4: RELIGIOUS FREEDOM AND OPPRESSION

PART 5: GROWTH AND GLOBALIZATION

President Kimball called on Latter-day Saints to "lengthen our stride." (Spencer and Camilla Kimball walking. Courtesy of Intellectual Reserve, Inc.)

FOREWORD

WILLIAM F. ATKIN

History is a prologue of the future. Our vision today is the same vision we had when the International Society was started in 1989. Let me give you a bit of the history of the International Society so you will understand. Does anybody know John Harris? John was a friend of mine in Caracas, Venezuela (1980–82). We both left Venezuela in 1982, and I ended up in Taipei, Taiwan, in 1984. I remember sitting in sacrament meeting in Taipei, and in walked John. I was on the stand, and I saw him in the back. I thought, "What on earth is he doing here?" That was relevant to me, because I quickly learned when I went to Venezuela as a young attorney in 1980 that there was this whole group of returned missionaries who served their missions in Latin America that had progressed through graduate school and taken assignments with various employers in Latin America: the Mormon professionals of Latin America.

A number of years later, I was in Asia. I started to meet a network of professionals who had served their missions in Asia. And so I learned there was an Asia "Mormon Mafia." When John came in, he disrupted my whole view of the world, because I thought, "What are you doing here? You're supposed to be in Latin America." He probably thought the same thing when he saw me: "What are you doing here? You speak Spanish, not Mandarin. What are you doing in Taiwan?"

That was the spark of the idea: "Gee, wouldn't it be nice if all those 'Mormon Mafia' folks in Asia got to know all of the LDS corporate leaders in Latin America, and the two of them got to know all those serving in professional capacities in Europe?" That was the impetus behind the International Society.

In the spring of 1987, Brigham Young University professors Spencer Palmer and Ray Hillam came to Taipei, and they called me. Even though I had had classes from them, I did not know them personally. They said, "Could you get a group of the LDS professionals in Taiwan together for lunch so we can talk to them about BYU, the David M. Kennedy Center, and the international programs?" I said that I would be delighted to do that.

We did that, and afterward, they came over to our home for dinner and talked about it. We discussed the idea of having a way to network all of the Mormon professionals who were involved in international activities, whether it be academia, government, business, or law, etc. That was the beginning.

They said, "Why don't we meet next summer at BYU when you're home on leave?" They would pull together a group. In the interim, I had also met with Blaine Tueller, who was the special assistant to David M. Kennedy, ambassador-at-large for the Church. Blaine had much the same idea. He had been developing lists of members of the Church who were involved in international activities. That summer, we met together at the Kennedy Center on the BYU campus with probably twenty or twenty-five faculty members and started developing the idea of having a global group.

We created this Mormon community to (1) promote collegiality among members and friends of the Church who are involved or interested in international business, law, government, service, education, or other professional activities; (2) provide support for BYU international programs; and (3) promote shared professional interests and concerns of society members.

I am convinced that part of the future of the International Society is to help build Zion, and we all have the obligation as members of the Church to do so. In many ways, we do that in our local wards as we participate in the various ecclesiastical activities, but as we do that, the Lord is not compartmentalizing our lives—we can also do it in our professional and personal capacities. This is a quote I love from the Prophet Joseph:

> The building up of Zion is a cause that has interested the people of God in every age; it is a theme upon which prophets, priests and kings have dwelt with peculiar delight; they have looked forward with joyful anticipation to the day in which we live; and fired with heavenly and joyful anticipations they have sung and written and prophesied of this our day; but they died without the sight; we are the favored people that God has made choice of to bring about the Latter-day glory; it is left for us to see, participate in and help to roll forward the Latter-day glory.[1]

It is my hope that we as the International Society will catch the vision of how we in our professional lives and with our interest in the international world will be of assistance to the Lord in the building of his kingdom in the latter days.

NOTE

1. "The Temple," an editorial published in *Times and Seasons*, 2 May 1842, 775.

Spencer W. Kimball served as President of the Church from 7 July 1972 to 30 December 1973. (Courtesy of Intellectual Reserve, Inc.)

EDITORS' PREFACE

Thoughtful observers have noted that the doors of world history turn on small hinges. Likewise, when the Book of Mormon prophet Alma the Younger entrusted his son Helaman with the Nephite records in about 74 BC, he reminded Helaman "that by small and simple things are great things brought to pass; and small means in many instances doth confound the wise" (Alma 37:6). In our study of the sacred past of The Church of Jesus Christ of Latter-day Saints we have sought to identify and appreciate pivotal events—large and small—in the unfolding Restoration. One such moment occurred on 4 April 1974, when President Spencer W. Kimball delivered a landmark address on LDS proselytizing possibilities at a regional representatives seminar (see appendix 1).[1] He spoke on the future possibilities of the global Church for one hour and ten minutes—his sermon was marked by crescendo, not diminuendo! The small-in-stature, newly ordained prophet called for Latter-day Saints to "lengthen our stride."

Among the General Authorities in attendance that day was Elder W. Grant Bangerter, who recalled being spiritually stimulated by President Kimball's remarks. "He had not spoken very long when a new awareness seemed to fall on the congregation. We became alert to an astonishing spiritual presence, and we realized that we were listening to something unusual, powerful, different from any of our previous meetings. It was as if, spiritually speaking, our hair began to stand on end," he later described. "Our minds were suddenly vibrant and marveling at the transcendent message that was coming to our ears. With a new perceptiveness we realized President Kimball was opening spiritual windows and beckoning to us to come and gaze with him on the plans of eternity."[2] Another Latter-day Saint analyzing the apostolic rhetoric of President Kimball noted that his 1974 sermon "outlined in detail how the Savior's command to take the gospel to all the world could be literally obeyed—and soon. The speech was not flamboyant in style nor did it announce any dramatic new program. It merely reviewed the clear commands of Christ to his former- and latter-day disciples."[3]

The Church that President Kimball began to lead at the turn of 1974, which was still largely focused on the American Intermountain West, looked very different from the Church in 2015, a mere four decades later. At that time, the geopolitical world was still frozen by the Cold War. There were no Mormon missionaries proselyting behind the Iron Curtain in post-war Germany or in the nations of the Soviet Union, comprising a sixth of the world's land surface. Similarly, the Church did not have congregations in mainland China, another communist nation covering much of Asia. Moreover, our religious representatives had barely penetrated the continent of sub-Saharan Africa. Four years later, in 1978, President Kimball would announce a revelation that opened the priesthood door to all worthy men regardless of race or color. "The long-promised day has come when every faithful, worthy man in the Church may receive the holy priesthood, with power to exercise its divine authority, and enjoy with his loved ones every blessing that flows therefrom, including the blessings of the temple," the First Presidency announced that September.[4] Keeping his own counsel, President Kimball continually oiled the hinges of spiritual history and, in some cases, kicked down the temporal doors with prophetic authority.

The complexion and geographical distribution of the Church have spread and evolved since President Kimball's clarion call for change in 1974. "That sermon helped transform the Church, releasing energies that almost doubled the missionary force in the next eight years, with similar increases in converts, new stakes organized, and total members. But the new energies were felt in a variety of other ways consistent with the humility and directness as well as sublimity of Spencer W. Kimball," one scholar documented.[5] A cursory review of the Church's numerical growth alone is illustrative. By the end of 1974, there were 3,385,909 members, 17,109 full-time missionaries, 675 stakes, 5,951 wards and branches, 113 missions, and just 16 temples around the world.[6] By year-end 1989 (the founding year of the LDS International Society), all of those numbers had more than doubled: 7,300,000 members, 39,739 full-time missionaries, 1,739 stakes, 17,305 wards and branches, 228 missions, and 43 temples.[7] By the end of 2015 (the last year represented by the society's essays in this volume), those numbers had again nearly doubled in many cases: 15,634,199 members, 74,079 full-time missionaries, 3,174 stakes, 30,016 wards and branches, 418 missions, and 149 temples.[8]

Ongoing global growth continues to be one of the Church's greatest opportunities (and challenges), just as President Kimball anticipated. Each year, hundreds of thousands of Latter-day Saints visit the reconstructed log cabin in Fayette, New York, where Joseph Smith organized the Church on 6 April 1830. Most are struck by its small size, given the magnitude of the twenty-first-century Church. "It took 117 years—until 1947—for the Church to grow from the initial six members to one million. Missionaries were a feature of the Church from its earliest days, fanning out to Native American lands, to Canada and, in 1837, beyond the North American continent to England," an official Church resource notes. "The two-million-member mark was reached just 16 years later, in 1963, and the three-million mark in eight years more. This accelerating growth pattern has continued with about a million new members now being added every three years or less."[9] Through convert baptisms and member births, there are now over fifteen million Latter-day Saints on the membership rolls of the Church.

Back in 1974, a modern-day prophet encouraged all Latter-day Saints to think in ways bigger, broader, and bolder about the ongoing globalization of the Church. In addition to the outreach of the leading quorums and the initiatives of official Church departments, many rank-and-file members have gathered on occasion to likewise share their best thinking about the past, present, and future of the global Church. The LDS International Society, founded in 1989, is one such group dedicated to thinking deeply about the kingdom of God in these latter days. The society is a collaboration between a number of entities at Brigham Young University, including the David M. Kennedy Center for International Studies, the J. Reuben Clark Law School, the Marriott School of Management, and the Alumni Association. Its stated mission is to foster "communication and contact among experts involved in international business, law, education, humanitarian service, and other professional activities; promotes shared interest and concerns of the society members; and provides support where possible for international programs of The Church of Jesus Christ of Latter-day Saints and Brigham Young University."[10] The women and men of the society include many of the most internationally minded Latter-day Saints who are anxious to help fulfill President Kimball's earlier call to help all of Heavenly Father's children enjoy the blessings of the plan of salvation. Most have lived many times in different places around the globe and are eyewitnesses to the growth of the Church.

Since 1990, the society's primary vehicle and gathering place has been their annual conference held at Brigham Young University each spring. Hundreds of thoughtful Latter-day Saints and their friends meet for a full day of meetings on a global theme and a luncheon to honor one of their members who has made a significant difference on the international scene. Between 2006 and 2015, featured topics have included "International Challenges Facing the Church," "Meet the Mormons: Public Perception and the Global Church," "Challenges in Establishing the International Church," "The Erosion of Religious Liberties—Impact on the International Church," "The Church and International Diplomacy," and "The Church and Humanitarian Assistance: In the Lord's Way."[11]

As regular attendees ourselves, we believe that some of the best thinking on the Mormon experience beyond North America occurs at the society's annual gathering, which has resulted in our desire to make some of the best of these conference papers more available to the larger community of Saints and scholars. In a previously published volume for the International Society,

Reid has advocated, "international LDS history *is* Church history. Church members need to realize that much of our most interesting history occurred abroad. We must remember that the 'restoration' of the gospel continues to occur every time a new country is dedicated by apostolic authority for proselyting." He called for a "recommissioning" of Mormon scholars who need to "refocus their scholarly gaze from Palmyra, Kirtland, Nauvoo, and Salt Lake City to Tokyo, Santiago, Warsaw, Johannesburg, and Nairobi. In the coming years, these international cities and their histories will become increasingly important to our sacred history. We need to tell these non-North American stories with greater frequency and with better skill."[12] This second volume of society speeches follows this called-for trajectory.

We have organized this book into five thematic sections, in which the essays are arranged chronologically by date presented. Part 1, "Poverty and Humanitarian Work," focuses on the challenge poverty creates in many parts of the world and how the Church is responding to it. In the first essay, "Demographic and Gender-Related Trends: Their Effect on Nations, Regions, and the International System," Valerie Hudson lays out a case linking declining birth rates and gendercide (female infanticide and female fetus abortion) to misogyny. She argues that the gospel of Jesus Christ holds the key to stopping this downward spiral. In their essay, Tim B. Heaton and Mallory J. Meyer demonstrate the terrible impact poverty has on society. After demonstrating how a growing portion of Church membership is being impacted by poverty, they advocate for Church members to be more supportive towards antipoverty efforts, both national programs and grassroots efforts. Bishop Gérald J. Caussé outlines five principles for helping those in need in his article, "Caring for the Poor and Needy in the Growing International Church." He suggests the best and most lasting solution is found in living the gospel of Jesus Christ because this solution knows how to adapt to every horizon, every culture, and every political and economic system. In the final essay in this section, "Zion's Fountains—International and Local," Sharon Eubank explains that the power of our heritage and our love of God, together with the broad scope of the institutional Church and the individual acts of service performed by millions of members, combine to hasten the work of caring for the poor and the needy around the world today.

In part 2, "Public Perceptions and Relations," Church leaders and scholars explore how the Church is attempting to position itself and how it is understood by others. Elder Lance B. Wickman, in "The Church in the Twenty-First Century: Public Perceptions and the 'Man with the Stamp,'" shares examples from Slovakia, China, and Vietnam to illustrate how General Authorities, other Church representatives, and Latter-day Saint private citizens combine their respective efforts in cultivating a positive, public image of the Church with those that play a critical role in obtaining legal recognition. Warner P. Woodworth, in his essay "Private Humanitarian Initiatives and International Perceptions of the Church," describes the work of several organizations such as HELP International, Eagle Condor Humanitarian, Ouelessebougou-Utah Alliance, Enterprise Mentors International, and Unitus to illustrate the tremendous good individual acts of global consecration and stewardship can create. Elder Anthony D. Perkins poses the question, "Are we making any progress in Asia?" in his essay, "Out of Obscurity: Perspectives from Asia." He describes five institutional steps that are bringing the Church out of obscurity in Asia. He also gives a contemporary assessment of how the "Mormon Moment" in the US is transferring to Asia and compares how public perceptions have changed over the past sixty years in Taiwan. Lastly, in his article "In the Public Eye: How the Church Is Handling Increased Global Visibility," Michael Otterson suggests the "Mormon Moment" is not a transitory moment but the latest phase of successive moments spanning the past 182 years. He describes seven categories of contributors.

"Peacemaking and Diplomacy," part 3, describes efforts to establish the Church globally and to promote peace. In the first essay, "By Persuasion, Long-Suffering, Meekness, and Love: On Diplomacy," Cory W. Leonard explores the notion of persuasion. He argues that when we combine the virtues of long-suffering, meekness, and love to our persuasive efforts we become better citizens, diplomats, and professionals. Elder Robert S. Wood, in his article "International Diplomacy and the Church," addresses the challenge of establishing the kingdom of God on earth across various separate political boundaries, each having legal authority within their jurisdictions. He explains that the Church's intent is to fulfill the Lord's mandate to take the gospel to all nations while promoting harmony and understanding and not undermining the trust essential to civil society and public peace. In the next essay,

"Women's Weapons of Peace," Bonnie Ballif-Spanvill outlines five methods which women are using to build a more peaceful world. She asserts that if we can get women to tell stories and do the activities that will develop peace-loving attributes in their children, this will empower them to be peaceful, and it will have a rippling effect through families, villages, and even countries. In the final offering in this section, Robert A. Rees and Gordon C. Thomasson discuss the responsibility we all have to "renounce war and proclaim peace." In "Dialogue: Religion as Peacemaker," they admonish all to choose peace, to become peacemakers, and to reject the argument that war is necessary for attaining peace.

In part 4, "Religious Freedom and Oppression," four experienced professionals discuss the erosion of religious freedoms and how this impacts the Church. In the first essay, "Let Them Worship How, Where, or What They May," William F. Atkin states that the most serious challenges to the Church in the United States and internationally are the attacks on religious liberty. He urges members of the Church to use their time, talents, and resources to promote and defend religious liberty and freedom of belief for all, particularly for those who are weak, disenfranchised, or otherwise defenseless. Cole Durham outlines several threats to religious liberties around the world in "Protection of Religious Liberties: Current Initiatives." He then discusses how the International Center for Law and Religion Studies is attempting to promote religious freedoms. In the next essay, "Erosion of Religious Freedom: Impact on Churches," Michael K. Young discusses disturbing trends within the United States that are eroding religious liberty. In order to stem this tide, he invites us to be attentive, seek allies, act for the right reason, and be vigilant. Hannah Clayson Smith closes this section with "Religious Liberty Initiatives: Preserving the 'First Freedom' at Home and Abroad." She provides numerous examples, categorized under five themes—religious autonomy, conscientious objection, defamation of religion, religion in the public square, and religious discrimination—to describe attacks on religious liberty within the United States.

In our final section, part 5, "Growth and Globalization," stories demonstrate challenges and successes in growing the Church. Ted E. Lyon, in "Migration—It's in Our Blood: Implications for The Church of Jesus Christ of Latter-day Saints," details the worldwide phenomenon of migration and the way many displaced people are finding their way into The Church of Jesus Christ of Latter-day Saints. While this influx of refugees creates several challenges, Lyon maintains that we have always welcomed refugees and their inclusion enriches the culture of the Church. The next essay from Daniel C. Peterson, "Sources of Tension between the West and the Islamic World," provides numerous examples that are fueling conflict. He offers a pessimistic view of the future and states there is no recipe for curing an inter-civilizational crisis that rests, to a very large degree, on mutual incomprehension. Elder Cree-L Kofford, drawing on his experiences in Asia, describes in "The Church and the Global Community" various ways the Church has adapted its programs to meet local circumstances. He urges leaders and members of the Church to be cautious when deciding how to implement programs outside the Wasatch Front. Elder Adesina J. Olukanni shares several challenges and successes from Africa in "'Organize Yourselves According to the Laws of Man' (D&C 44:4): Ethical Challenges in Establishing the International Church." He outlines five fundamental principles which have been helpful in navigating the complex environment in Africa. Finally, in the last essay from Elder Dennis B. Neuenschwander, "Challenges, Opportunities, and the International Church," he outlines his own five fundamental principles that he has found central to the process of expanding and establishing the Church in Eastern Europe.

ACKNOWLEDGMENTS

To begin with, we are grateful to the leadership of the LDS International Society for their support of this publishing project of their created content. Many thanks are due to William M. "Mac" Epps, president; Thomas Edgar "Ted" Lyon, executive director; and Cory W. Leonard, assistant director. Board members William F. Atkin, Fred Axelgard, J. Michael Busenbark, John P. "Phil" Colton, Lew W. Cramer, Elizabeth Crook, Wayne D. Crosby, John Dinkelman, W. Cole Durham Jr., Derek Miller, Jeffrey R. Ringer, Robert Edward Snyder, and Jonathan Wood all favored the production of this volume. Both Reid and Wayne have served on the society's board and have developed meaningful associations with their fellow members. Bill Atkin is to be thanked for his foreword, essay, and cheerleading of this volume.

We also appreciate the following Church leaders, administrators, and scholars for allowing us to reprint their conference papers in this collection of essays. Many thanks to William F. Atkin, Bonnie Ballif-Spanvill, Bishop Gérald J. Caussé, Cole Durham, Sharon Eubank, Timothy B. Heaton, Valerie Hudson, Elder Cree-L Kofford, Cory W. Leonard, Ted E. Lyon, Mallory Meyer, Elder Dennis B. Neuenschwander, Elder Adesina J. Olukanni, Michael Otterson, Elder Anthony D. Perkins, Daniel C. Peterson, Robert A. Rees, Hannah Clayson Smith, Gordon C. Thomasson, Elder Lance B. Wickman, Elder Robert S. Wood, Warner P. Woodworth, and Michael K. Young.

The Religious Studies Center's leadership team and editorial staff continue to show their commitment to Mormon studies through their print publications and online offerings. In 2008, they published *Global Mormonism in the 21st Century*, a collection of choice presentations from the first fifteen years of the society's annual conferences, this volume's precursor.

We appreciate the competence and goodness of publications director Thomas A. Wayment, executive editor R. Devan Jensen, production supervisor Brent R. Nordgren, publications coordinator Joany Pinegar, designer Madison Swapp, and the timely and professional assistance of their talented team of student editors: Kimball Gardner, Allyson Jones, Mandi Diaz, Emily Strong, Shannon Taylor, and Leah Emal. The RSC team is committed to excellence in both scholarship and production values, and it shows in their many publications.

Furthermore, we are also continually obliged for the support of the executive leadership of the Church History Department of The Church of Jesus Christ of Latter-day Saints, including Elders Steven E. Snow and J. Devn Cornish. Our Church campus colleagues Katrina Cannon, Jo Lyn Curtis, Scott Marianno, R. Mark Melville, Melissa McQuarrie, Erin Steeblik Tanner, Tyler Thorsted, and Kelsi Walbeck each made important editorial contributions to the production of this volume. Moreover, the librarians and archivists of the Church History Library provided helpful guidance and access to needed sources along the way. Together with all of these named individuals, we have created a volume worth careful reading and thoughtful pondering on the global Church.

Finally, we are grateful to be both professional observers and personal participants in this latter-day work of salvation. "We thank thee, O God, for a prophet" like diminutive Spencer W. Kimball, who, as he assumed the presidency of the Church, humbly confided to a fellow Apostle: "I am such a little man for such a big responsibility!"[13] But as Alma taught his son Helaman, "By very small means the Lord doth confound the wise and bringeth about the salvation of many souls" (Alma 37:7). Just imagine what lies ahead for the global Church and President Kimball's prophetic successors in the next forty years.

Reid L. Neilson
Wayne D. Crosby

NOTES

1. Spencer W. Kimball, "When the World Will Be Converted," *Ensign*, October 1974, 3–11. His sermon was reprinted (and shortened) as the First Presidency Message in the spring of 1984: "When the World Will Be Converted," *Ensign*, April 1984, 3–6.
2. W. Grant Bangerter, "A Special Moment in Church History," *Ensign*, November 1977, 26.
3. Eugene England, "A Small and Piercing Voice: The Sermons of Spencer W. Kimball," *BYU Studies* 25, no. 4 (1985): 82.
4. Doctrine & Covenants, Official Declaration 2.
5. England, "A Small and Piercing Voice," 82–83.
6. In Conference Report, April 1975, 25; R. Lanier Britsch, "Mormon Missions: An Introduction to the Latter-day Saints Missionary System," *Occasional Bulletin of Missionary Research* 3, no. 1 (January 1979): 22.
7. In Conference Report, April 1990, 27.
8. In Conference Report, April 2015, 37.
9. "Growth of the Church," *Mormon Newsroom*, http://www.mormonnewsroom.org/topic/church-growth.
10. LDS International Society brochure.
11. For a complete list of the last twenty-five years of annual symposiums, see Appendix 2: Past LDS International Society Conferences, 1990–2015.
12. Reid L. Neilson, "Introduction: A Recommissioning of Latter-day Saint Historians," in *Global Mormonism in the 21st Century*, ed. Reid L. Neilson (Provo, UT: Religious Studies Center, 2008), xii–xv.
13. Edward L. Kimball, *Lengthen Your Stride: The Presidency of Spencer W. Kimball* (Salt Lake City: Deseret Book, 2005), 8.

Part 1

POVERTY AND HUMANITARIAN WORK

Relief efforts after the 2010 Chile earthquake. (Courtesy of Intellectual Reserve, Inc.)

1

DEMOGRAPHIC AND GENDER-RELATED TRENDS

Their Effect on Nations, Regions, and the International System

VALERIE HUDSON

Valerie Hudson, then a professor of political science at Brigham Young University, presented this essay at "International Challenges Facing the Church," the International Society's seventeenth annual conference, April 2006, Brigham Young University, Provo, Utah.

Members of the LDS Church believe that the restored gospel is the cure for the world's ills. But it is interesting to explore in a more substantive fashion how that proposition actually plays out on the world stage. Today we will do just that, focusing on two important, world-changing trends in demography and gender relations.

THE FIRST WORLD-CHANGING TREND: SUBREPLACEMENT BIRTH RATES

At least three major civilizations of the world—Western, Slavic, and Japanese—are no longer replacing themselves. China is no longer replacing itself either, though it must be placed in a separate category because this lack of replacement has largely been an artifact of the government's coercive one-child policy. Though this finding of subreplacement birth rates in many countries has been reported widely in the media, we need to step back and contemplate the meaning of this phenomenon, which should startle us. No plague, war, or famine has caused this. Outside of a few small and isolated tribes in history, no significant human collective, let alone a major civilization, has voluntarily stopped replacing itself unless it embraced female infanticide, which these three have not. Furthermore, the civilizations in question are the most advanced, the most prosperous, and those with the longest experience—or at least rhetorical tradition, in the case of the former Warsaw Pact nations—of expansive political freedoms. Comparatively speaking, these civilizations are "haves," not "have-nots," with representation in powerful international bodies such as the G8. Subreplacement birth rates among the "haves" and increasingly among even the "have-nots" of the world represent an important and unprecedented development in human history, which calls for investigation.

Furthermore, there are some interesting subnational distinctions we should be aware of. For example, in the United States, the total fertility rates of non-Hispanic whites, blacks, Asians, Pacific Islanders, and American Indians are subreplacement; it is the fertility rate of Hispanics that keeps the United States within spitting distance of the replacement level.[1] In Europe, the fertility rates of immigrants from primarily Muslim countries pull up the birthrates of most nations, though in Europe—with a few exceptions, such as France, Ireland, and Iceland—countries are nowhere near replacement levels.[2] For example, in Germany now, one-quarter of all births are to foreign women. Interestingly, overall, the number of births in Germany last year was less than the number of births in Germany in the final year of World War II.[3] The population of both the United States and Europe is growing overall, but that is due exclusively to immigration, not to fertility. Furthermore, it has been noted that the fertility rates of second- and third-generation immigrants decline almost to the level of the native population.

Note also that there are some interesting non-Western nations with subreplacement birth rates: Turkey, Tunisia, Sri Lanka, and others. And, counterintuitively, some of these nations have a predominately Muslim population.

Of interest to this audience is that the gap between the US state with the highest fertility rate (Utah) and the lowest fertility rate (Vermont) is considerably larger than the gap between the European states with the highest and lowest fertility.[4]

Now these subreplacement or near-subreplacement rates have some important demographic consequences. First, the proportion of the population that is elderly increases while the proportion of young people declines. The median age of the populations of Europe is now well over thirty-five. This certainly will have important ramifications for the welfare states of Europe. States will have to budget for an increasing burden of elder care because traditional social security systems are based on having several workers per elderly person. In some countries now, the ratio is one worker to one elderly person. And what happens to a wealthy economy when it begins to lose manpower? Issues of outsourcing, worker protections, and other contemporary controversies begin to emerge.

A second important consequence is cultural transition. Given the subnational differences in fertility, North America will become predominantly Hispanic by approximately midcentury, and in the United States almost 30 percent by 2060. Europe is poised to become almost one-third Muslim at about the same time. Some scholars feel that these two population groups are much less likely to assimilate than previous immigrant populations. This lack of assimilation signals a different vision than that of the traditional melting pot. It signals real cultural and linguistic shifts within the richest and most powerful nations of the international system.

What is also very important about these demographic transitions is that they have been highly resistant to policy manipulation. Large financial incentives to give birth have been offered for many years by European nations with low birthrates; even extremely generous packages simply do not result in replacement or above-replacement birth rates.

Vladimir Putin has recently declared the subreplacement birth rates of Russia a national security issue and has offered $9,200 for the birth of second babies, among other initiatives. But if the experiences of Europe with such incentives prove a guide, even these incentives will be insufficient to reverse Russia's decline.[5]

THE SECOND WORLD-CHANGING TREND: GENDERCIDE

There is something else going on that is worthy of our investigation, a trend of equally immense significance and importance. About a year ago, the first Human Security Report was unveiled, showing that deaths from interstate and intrastate conflict had significantly attenuated over the last four decades to some of the lowest levels seen since recording began. But then the Geneva Centre for the Democratic Control of the Armed Forces issued its own report several months later, showing that one class of deaths had not only not abated but had actually increased significantly over the last forty years: deaths of females in peacetime. In fact, they went so far as to term this a "hidden gendercide," an appalling loss of human life hidden precisely because we see its source as "natural," unlike war, and so what is thought of as natural becomes invisible to us.[6]

I urge you to read the full report, but in this chapter I will focus on one particular aspect of the gendercide that is increasing at an alarming rate in several of the most populous Asian countries: female infanticide and female-fetus abortion.[7]

That there is an abnormal deficit of females in Asia can be fairly readily confirmed through standard demographic analysis. There are established ranges for normal variation in overall population sex ratios as well as in early childhood and birth sex ratios. These ratios are adjusted for country-specific circumstances, such as, for example, maternal mortality rates and infant mortality rates. When we use official census data, it is then a relatively straightforward task to determine if there are fewer women than could reasonably be expected in a given population. Of course, there are perturbing variables: for example, many of the Arab states of the Persian Gulf have very abnormal sex ratios favoring males, but this is due to the high number of guest workers, predominantly male, that labor in the oil economies of these states. Once these types of factors have been taken into account, we find that a deficit of females in Asia is a real phenomenon.

To see the scale of the deficit, some comparisons are in order. If we examine overall population sex ratios, the ratio for Latin America, for example, is 98 males per 100 females (using 2000 US Census Bureau figures)—the corresponding figure for Asia is 104.4 males per 100 females. But one must also keep in mind the sheer size of the populations of Asia: India and China alone compose approximately 38 percent of the world's population. Thus, the overall sex ratio of the world is 101.3 males to 100 females, despite the fact that the ratios for the rest of the world (excluding Oceania) range from 93.1 (Europe) to 98.9 (Africa).

Birth sex ratios in several Asian countries are also outside of the established norm of 105–107 boys born for every 100 girls. The Indian government's estimate of its birth sex ratio is approximately 113 boys born for every 100 girls, with some locales noting ratios of 156 and higher. The Chinese government states that its birth sex ratio is approximately 119, though some Chinese scholars have gone on record as stating the birth sex ratio is at least 121. Again, in some locations, the ratio is higher: the island of Hainan's birth sex ratio is 135. Other countries of concern in 2006 include Pakistan, Bangladesh, Nepal, Bhutan, Taiwan, Afghanistan, and South Korea. No data is available for North Korea.

Another indicator of gender imbalance is early childhood mortality. Boys typically have a higher early childhood mortality rate, which virtually cancels out their birth sex ratio numerical advantage by age five. The reasons for this higher mortality include sex-linked genetic mutations, such as hemophilia, as well as higher death rates for boys from common childhood diseases, such as dysentery. However, in some of the Asian nations just mentioned, early childhood mortality rates for girls are actually higher than those for boys. Furthermore, orphanage populations are predominantly female in these nations.

Other statistics also factor into the observed gender imbalance. In the West, for example, male suicides far outnumber female suicides. But in countries with deficits of women, female suicides outnumber male suicides. In fact, approximately 55 percent of all female suicides in the world are Chinese women of childbearing age.

What forces drive the deficit of females in Asian nations such as India and China? How do we account for the disappearance of so many women from these populations (estimated conservatively at over ninety million missing women in seven Asian countries alone)?

Some scholars assert that there may be a physical cause at work preventing female births, such as the disease hepatitis B, antigens of which have been associated with higher birth sex ratios. This may well be a contributing factor, but is not the primary catalyst. For example, it is worth considering the following experience of the municipality of Shenzhen in southern China. Alarmed at the municipality's rising birth sex ratio, which reached 118 in 2002, local officials instituted a strict crackdown on black market ultrasound clinics. Offering two hundred yuan for tips as to where these clinics could be found, officials then vigorously prosecuted the owners of the machines and the technicians using them, with prison terms affixed. By 2004—that is, in just two years—the birth sex ratio had dropped to 108.

It is fair to say that accounts such as these provide support for the thesis that the modern gender imbalance in Asia, as with historical gender imbalances in Asia and elsewhere, is largely a man-made phenomenon. Girls are being culled from the population, whether through prenatal sex identification and selective abortions that target females; or through relative neglect (compared to male offspring) in early childhood, including abandonment; or through desperate life circumstances that might result in suicide. The gender imbalance in Asia is primarily the result of son preference and the profound devaluation of female life.

One could justifiably suggest that this value ordering is not confined to Asia; why, then, is the deficit of women found almost exclusively there? This question can be approached only through a multifactorial cultural analysis, which we will not detail in this short chapter. Suffice it to say that one must examine variables such as religious prohibition or sanction of the practice; traditions of patrilocality and old-age security obtained through male offspring; issues of dowry, hypergyny, and caste purity in India; and the effect of interventions such as the one-child policy in China. Other factors to consider include the web of incentives, disincentives, and capabilities surrounding the issue of prenatal sex-determination technology.

Both China and India have announced new initiatives intended to help correct the increasingly skewed nature of birth sex ratios. China is offering old-age pensions and waiving certain school fees for families with only daughters. India has begun sting operations to enforce laws against prenatal sex identification by physicians. It is too early to tell whether these measures will be effective, and in the meantime, the horse has left the barn for the next two decades or more. We anticipate there will be twenty-eight to thirty million young adult men in excess of young adult women in India in 2020 and thirty to thirty-three million in China. Other nations in the region, such as Pakistan, Nepal, Bhutan, Bangladesh, Taiwan, and South Korea, have abnormal gender ratios in 2006. It will be interesting to watch the consequences of this gendercide in Asia unfold and affect domestic stability as well as regional and international security. Will the prospects for peace and democracy in Asia diminish in lockstep with the value of daughters there?

THE LINK

I'd like to propose that these two world-changing trends, population decline and gendercide, are intrinsically linked. At first that might seem rather counterintuitive—after all, gendercide is not a defining feature of, for example, Sweden. In fact, on most measures of gender parity, a country like Sweden, with low birth rates (and also low marriage rates and high divorce rates), comes out looking quite good.

In fact, some less-than-insightful commentators have opined that it is this very elevated status for women in nations like Sweden that has led to these low birth rates, implying that it is women who are mostly responsible for population decline, since they have left the home for the workplace in droves. And then they imply that if only we could somehow reverse the status of women and return to a more patriarchal type of society (patriarchy meaning a fallen patriarchy when men rule over women), then we would have higher birth rates. A lead article in *Foreign Policy* magazine[8] called "The Return of Patriarchy" argued just that. Of course, the author was trying to be sensational because it sells magazines, but I have even heard this line of reasoning from Latter-day Saints who should know better.

I would like to suggest that population decline and gendercide are actually two faces of the very same problem: misogyny. I'd like to suggest that if we really scratch the surface of disparate countries such as Sweden and Pakistan, we will see them as benchmarks along a road from high fertility and high gendercide to low fertility and the absence of overt gendercide but the presence of a more insidious and more modern misogyny. Let me describe three phases of evolving misogyny as I see them.

In the first stage, we see traditional hierarchy of men over women. Yes, there is marriage in these cultures, but it is marriage between a superior and an inferior. The superior male dominates and represses the inferior female. Birth rates are high, but marriage is not the source of joy within society. Men find pleasure in the double standard of sexual fidelity. Men permit themselves abuse of women, for whom they have contempt. Women find themselves in a position of terrible vulnerability and come to view marriage and men with grave suspicion and even fear. But men aren't happy either—when your lover and the mother of your children is the equivalent of an animal in your eyes, how can you expect to find happiness? You can find pleasure, but happiness will forever elude you.

In the second phase, we see societies that have come to the conclusion that both men and women are people, and people should be treated equally. But given the structural inequality of power between men and women, this conclusion results in the idealized person being male in nature. Both men and women are now judged by standards of maleness—they can be equal as long as they are both just like men. We enter a period where the difference between men and women is being consciously erased in the hopes that that will elevate the situation of women. Women who emulate men may find a secure place in society; those who choose a more traditionally female role will find themselves again in a position of great vulnerability. Women begin to have contempt for their own biology, for that is the source of potential vulnerability. Women no longer trust marriage as a viable way to survive economically, especially while raising children.

Men begin to abandon marriage and tout a single standard of promiscuity for both men and women as the route to equality in sexual relations in society—now both sexes have the equal right to completely uncommitted sex. Men also begin to abandon their children, seeing them as unintended consequences of sexual relations for whom they hold no responsibility. No wonder women begin to believe that having children is akin to committing economic suicide. A woman may be given a stark choice: she can have children, or she can have a relationship with a man:

it will be increasingly difficult to find a man to be an equal and committed partner in raising children, and birth rates will decline precipitously.

The final stage has not yet come about, but in an era of amazing breakthroughs in advanced reproductive technology, it may come to pass sooner than we would like to believe. At some point, the sexes will go their separate ways. They will no longer need each other for anything, except, perhaps, recreational sex. There are already advances that promise men the ability to have children without women and promise women the chance to have children without men. This stage is the culmination of the sexes' inability to imagine how to live together in harmony: They have tried hierarchy, and it doesn't work. They have tried erasing the differences between men and women, and that doesn't work. Eventually, they will stop trying altogether and give the entire project up as hopeless.

THE LDS CONNECTION

Now, you've been waiting patiently to hear the LDS connection in all of this, and we are now to the point where we can speak of this intelligibly.

The restored gospel of Jesus Christ is the strongest and most progressive force for women in the world today. The most profound feminist act one can commit is to share that gospel. It is the restored gospel that tells us that equality in the context of difference is desirable and attainable, something the world completely disbelieves. Think about the revolutionary aspects of our gospel concerning men and women:

> "God" means an exalted man and an exalted woman united in eternal marriage.
>
> We have always been either male or female, and we always will be.
>
> Our male and female bodies are great gifts to us.
>
> The highest heaven involves being married forever and having children forever.
>
> Men and women, though different in some respects, stand as equals before the Lord and before each other.

> Eve did not sin in partaking of the fruit in Eden and is to be honored for her role in the Fall.
>
> In fact, the two trees in the garden can be said to represent the two equally important stewardships of men and women.

What is the cure for low birth rates? What is the cure for gendercide? The cure for both is the very same thing—the teachings of the gospel concerning men and women, which preach a full and equal partnership between men and women, symbolized by the covenant of eternal marriage. This is the only way of life that does not ultimately end in sterility.

Let me read you the letter to the editor I wrote to *Foreign Policy* in response to the article on patriarchy:

> To The Editor:
>
> Phillip Longman ("The Return of Patriarchy") has put forward a noteworthy and persuasive argument concerning the evolutionary advantage of human social systems that reward paternal investment in family and children. But he is too quick to suggest that such a system is inescapably patriarchal, in the sense of female submission to male head of household. There are alternative systems that provide for the first without the odious second, and it is only such systems that are able to prevent what Longman rightly and refreshingly points out as the ultimate sterility of patriarchy. I offer my own culture as such an alternative system: I consider myself a feminist and am a full professor of political science. My husband and I have six children and would be happy to have more. We have an equitable marriage: he does the cooking; I do the laundry; we share the childcare. We are completely faithful to each other and have a happy marriage without taint of domination or abuse. From my perspective as a woman, why wouldn't I want to have many children with a wonderful man who is committed to me, our children, and our marriage? No patriarchal hierarchy or female submission is required to produce our above-average birthrate. And what my husband and I are extending into the future is not some inanimate abstraction like the family name but a vibrant living culture of gender equity and love—a truly joint male-female project of world

> improvement. Now that is the type of family system that endures and does not decay and become sterile. Find yourself a belief system that rewards its men not only for paternal investment in family and children but also for sexual fidelity, equal partnership between men and women, and abhorrence of domination or abuse in marriage, as we did—and then see what happens to birthrates. All in all, a far better and more effective prescription than the advocacy of traditional patriarchy.

Yes, we must understand what the key question is in order to find the cure for these stubborn and tragic ills afflicting the human family. Where in the world can we find a group of men dedicated to

> advocating a single standard of sexual fidelity?
>
> getting and staying married?
>
> upholding the equality, safety, and flourishing of women?
>
> having children and actively taking part in raising them?
>
> valuing their daughters as much as they value their sons?
>
> abhorring abuse, pornography, and neglect?
>
> affirming parity in burden sharing, including housework and decision-making, within marriage?

Where can we find this group of men? Why, right here in this audience: the men who hold priesthood offices in our Church are described by the answers they would give to these questions.

One of the most important ways that The Church of Jesus Christ of Latter-day Saints can shine as a beacon in these latter days is to loudly and repeatedly proclaim the truths concerning how God wants gender relations to be conducted: a single standard of fidelity, commitment to marriage, equal partnership in marriage, no subordination or hierarchy in the relation between men and women, and no tolerance for the abuse of women or children. Our Church authorities have been strong in their depiction of the equality of women and men before the Lord and before each other. And this depiction has involved standing up to traditional practices that undermine this ideal. In fact, lately, I've been daydreaming about a billboard campaign for the Church. Imagine a set of billboards placed in prominent positions in the major metropoles of the world. Consider the following quotes from various authorities on the subject.

"There is not a president and vice president in a family. We have co-presidents working together eternally for the good of their family. . . . They are on equal footing. They plan and organize the affairs of the family jointly and unanimously as they move forward."[9]

"God our Eternal Father ordained that men and women should be companions. That implies equality. . . . There is no basis in the gospel for inferiority or superiority between the husband and wife. Do you think that God our Eternal Father loves his daughters less than he loves his sons? No man can demean or belittle his wife as a daughter of God without giving offense to her Father in Heaven."[10]

"Any man who abuses or demeans his wife physically or spiritually is guilty of grievous sin and in need of sincere and serious repentance. . . . A man should always speak to his wife lovingly and kindly, treating her with the utmost respect."[11]

"There is no task, however menial, connected with the care of babies, the nurturing of children, or with the maintenance of the home that is not the husband's equal obligation. The tasks which come with parenthood, which many consider to be below other tasks, are simply above them."[12]

"Some Christians condemn Eve for her act, concluding that she and her daughters are somehow flawed by it. Not the Latter-day Saints! Informed by revelation, we celebrate Eve's act and honor her wisdom and courage in the great episode called the Fall."[13]

"Is yours a culture where the husband exerts a domineering, authoritarian role, making all of the important decisions for the family? That pattern needs to be tempered so that both husband and wife act as equal partners, making decisions in unity for themselves and their family."[14]

"The Lord forbids and his Church condemns any and every intimate relationship outside of marriage. Infidelity on the part of a man breaks the heart of his wife and loses her confidence and the confidence of his children. Be faithful in your marriage covenants in thought, word, and deed."[15]

"The Church cannot bow down before any traditions that demean or devalue the daughters of God."[16]

Remember that the bottom line for God in judging a society is actually family relations—not the presence of the gospel. Think of the Nephites during Jacob's time. The Nephites have the gospel, they have a prophet, they have a temple and temple ordinances, they have the scriptures. They have an abundance of spiritual riches in their midst. And yet Jacob says they will be destroyed while the Lamanites, who have none of these things, will be preserved. Why is that so? Well, you know the answer (read Jacob 3:7). Because of their abominable treatment of women, they had lost the vision of the true nature of God. And once that vision is lost, it cannot be reclaimed. But in societies where men and women love each other, support each other, and are faithful to one another, and likewise parents to children, the vision of the true nature of God is retained—and where it is retained, the restored gospel can be reintroduced and eventually find a welcoming home.

As the Church rises in support of women and as priesthood holders begin to conceive of themselves as part of a covenant brotherhood that has sworn to uphold, among other things, the equality, safety, and flourishing of all the daughters of God, you will see the eyes of all women turn to this Church. And when the eyes of the women turn and they begin to assess their men according to the Lord's criteria, you will see men begin to turn as well. For men are clearly no victors in any of the forms of civilizational misogyny—they suffer profoundly as well. Misogyny breeds misery for men as well as women.

It is only this third way, the Lord's way, that brings joy to both men and women, safety to men and women, and a fountain of everlasting life for all. Elder Jeffrey R. Holland and his wife, Patricia, said the following:

> In times of difficulty and stress ahead, it will be the women of the Church, as well as the men, who will speak persuasively of God's plan, of His eternal government, and of His priesthood assignments. In the years ahead, some of the great defenders of priesthood roles for men will be women speaking to other women. A woman can speak to another woman in language men would not normally use and with a fervor men would not dare invoke. God has a view of women, who they are, what they do incomparably, and what eternally they

will be. Women must seize that vision and embrace it, or they—and the human family with it—will perish.[17]

NOTES

For more information, see Valerie M. Hudson and Andrea M. Den Boer, *Bare Branches: The Security Implications of Asia's Surplus Male Population* (Cambridge: MIT Press, 2004).

1. "Social Change Report," *Ball State University's Center for Middletown Studies* 14, no. 2 (2005–07).
2. "Social Change Report."
3. Richard Bernstein, "Letter from Europe; A Quiz for Would-Be Citizens Tests Germans' Attitudes," *New York Times*, 29 March 2006.
4. "Social Change Report."
5. Fred Weir, "A Second Baby? Russia's Mothers Aren't Persuaded," *Christian Science Monitor*, 19 May 2016, http://www.csmonitor.com/2006/0519/p01s04-woeu.html.
6. Marie Vlachov and Lea Biason, eds., *Women in an Insecure World—Violence against Women: Facts, Figures, and Analysis* (Geneva: DCAF, 2005), 7.
7. Andrea M. Den Boer, conversation with author, 2004.
8. Phillip Longman, "The Return of Patriarchy," *Foreign Policy Magazine*, March 2006, 56–60, 62–65.
9. L. Tom Perry, "Fathers' Role Is Anchoring Families," *Church News*, 10 April 2004, 15.
10. Gordon B. Hinckley, *Cornerstones of a Happy Home* (pamphlet, 1984), https://www.lds.org/manual/cornerstones-of-a-happy-home/cornerstones-of-a-happy-home?lang=eng.
11. Howard W. Hunter, "Being a Righteous Husband and Father," *Ensign*, November 1994, 51.
12. Boyd K. Packer, "A Tribute to Women," *Ensign*, July 1989, 75.
13. Dallin H. Oaks, "Repentance and Change," *Ensign*, November 1993, 73.
14. Richard G. Scott, "Removing Barriers to Happiness," *Ensign*, May 1998, 86.
15. Howard W. Hunter, "Being a Righteous Husband and Father," *Ensign*, November 1994, 50.
16. Alexander B. Morrison, comment in question and answer session, International Society meeting, 1994.
17. Jeffrey R. and Patricia T. Holland, "Considering Covenants: Women, Men, Perspective, Promises," in *To Rejoice as Women: Talks from the 1994 Women's Conference*, ed. S. F. Green and D. H. Anderson (Salt Lake City: Deseret Book, 1995), 107.

2

POVERTY

Challenges for The Church of Jesus Christ of Latter-day Saints

TIM B. HEATON AND MALLORY J. MEYER

Tim B. Heaton, then professor of sociology at Brigham Young University, and Mallory J. Meyer, then a student at Brigham Young University, presented this essay at "'The Perplexities of Nations': Current Trends and the International Church," the International Society's eighteenth annual conference, April 2007, Brigham Young University, Provo, Utah.

Despite many efforts to alleviate poverty, nearly one person in five lives on less than a dollar a day. The prevalence of poverty more than doubles when considering those who live on less than two dollars a day—the World Bank's standard of poverty. This equates to more than 2.6 billion people living in poverty around the world.[1] In addition, poor countries have the highest rates of growth. These high growth rates translate into an increasing number of the world's inhabitants experiencing poverty. While these numbers are useful in tracking poverty's prevalence, they do little to illustrate the daily experiences of these billions of poor people—experiences wrought with lack of opportunity, hardship, humiliation, and pain. Because this high prevalence of poverty around the world is undeniable, it is imperative that we come to understand what poverty is, what problems are associated with poverty, and how we might best go about solving problems associated with poverty.

About half of the world's population lives below the World Bank standard. Poverty is much higher in Africa, somewhat lower in Asia, and lower still in Latin America. To complicate matters, population growth is most rapid in the poorest countries. Growth is below 1 percent for countries with less than 10 percent below the poverty line but more than twice as high in countries with poverty rates above 60 percent. It is not clear whether economic growth will solve the problem, because growth is often associated with rising inequality. Many are left behind in the wake of economic development. Some claim that "a rising tide lifts all boats," but recent trends in inequality and poverty suggest that a rising tide sinks some boats.

Furthermore, we cannot view poverty simply as the world's problem. Many members of the Church are in poverty, and this poverty continually creates challenges for these members. While the Church may seek to avoid the trends of the world, it is unable to escape the world's high poverty rates. Rather, the Church appears to mirror this trend. Because of the incidence of poverty among Latter-day Saints, it is crucial that Church leaders and organizations involve themselves in antipoverty work that seeks to overcome these problems.

We will first demonstrate the many problems associated with poverty. While some illustrations are provided through quantifiable data articulated by researchers, many illustrations come from the poor themselves, who are best equipped to describe the poverty situation. Second, we will reveal the poverty trends within the Church and offer possible additional problems associated with this poverty. Finally, we will look at national and local level approaches used to combat poverty. These approaches must be critically evaluated if we are to make our efforts of poverty alleviation more successful.

PROBLEMS ASSOCIATED WITH POVERTY

Health

Health is a major concern for many poor people. World Bank researchers involved in poverty assessments among the poor found that when Togolese children were asked to draw a poor person, they often drew them as ill or disabled.[2] If a person does not have his or her health, it is very difficult to perform the daily responsibilities that life requires. Wagstaff et al. found that prenatal care and a doctor's assistance at the birth of children are both related to healthier newborns. Further, access to these services may help promote healthier feeding practices. Data from Bolivia illustrates important differences. Less than half of children born to the poorest mothers have access to a doctor, but about 90 percent of children in more wealthy families have access to a doctor.

Nutrition

Malnutrition is a contributing factor in at least one third of deaths of children under five years of age. And not surprisingly, malnutrition disproportionately affects the poor.[3] In addition, the poor tend to perform worse on maternal and child nutritional statuses both within and across countries. One common standard for nutrition status is a child's height for age relative to the World Health Organization (WHO) standard. Children in Bolivia, for example, are near that standard at birth as indicated by a score of zero (zero indicates no deviation from the WHO standard). However, these same children lag behind recommended growth rates. By their second birthday, a substantial number of Bolivian children show signs of malnutrition. *Stunting* is defined as falling two standard deviations below the WHO standard. The average height for age among children in the poorest households is lower than –200. In other words, at least half of the poor children are malnourished. Children in homes that are more economically viable also fail to grow fast enough to keep with the standard, but they do much better than children in the poorest households.

Hunger

Narayan and others reported that lack of food plays a fundamental role in poverty. Many poor people around the world speak of hunger when asked to define poverty. A poor ten-year-old child in Gabon explained, "When I leave for school in the mornings I don't have any breakfast. At noon, there is no lunch, in the evening I get a little supper, and that is not enough. So when I see another child eating, I watch him, and if he doesn't give me something I think that I am going to die of hunger."[4]

Access to Education

Education is important not only because it can play a major role in getting out of poverty but also because it is associated with many other benefits, such as health, stable family relationships, and a higher quality of life. Unfortunately, children in poor households receive less schooling. As the data from Bolivia illustrates, poor children are less likely to begin school and are more likely to drop out at an early age (before age twelve).

Environmental Degradation

As high focus and priority has been placed on sustainable development, it has become important to consider the relationship between the poor and the environment. Many development professionals want to blame environmental degradation on the poor, but doing so is only blaming the victim. A poor person in the Kenya Participatory Poverty Assessments remarked that "the poor live at the whim and mercy of nature."[5] The poor must use their land for survival, though research indicates that they have special knowledge about the environment and are often just as concerned (if not more concerned) with sustainability as more affluent people are.[6]

Access to Clean Water

Many of the rural poor are vulnerable because they rely on natural sources of water.[7] The lack of water further perpetuates the hunger problem, as food security is challenged when it does not rain. Also, it can further perpetuate the health problems of the poor as they are forced to use water that is unsanitary. When the World Bank asked children in Vietnam to define people in poverty, they frequently defined them as having no drinking water.[8]

The WHO and UNICEF report that in 2004, 170 million urban people and 899 million rural people were without adequate sources of drinking water.[9] This figure is only a slight improvement for the rural poor. In 1990, over a billion people in rural areas did not have access to water. However, the number of urban dwellers without access to clean water has increased since 1990—from 107 million to 170 million.

Access to Roads

The rural poor are the least likely to have access to usable roads. Inability to access usable roads contributes to economic isolation and increased transaction costs.[10] In Mexico, further returns to land are greater when the village has a paved road, and overall welfare is improved through decreased transaction costs.[11] Researchers studying poverty in Papua New Guinea demonstrated that improving the access to usable roads in rural areas will have a direct impact on reducing poverty.[12]

Unsafe Neighborhoods

Poverty is often associated with unsafe areas and high crime rates. While discussing poverty with the poor, Narayan et al. reported that many poor women throughout the world spoke of increased crime and the fear that comes along with it. Women in Ukraine say they "worry when their children return late from school or work." Women in Moldova are afraid to work the night shift for fear of being assaulted. "Rapes of teenage girls, unfiled claims of child support by mothers due to fears of being beaten by the fathers, and even the crippling of a woman following a drunken argument among the couple" are all documented in case studies from South Africa.[13] The occurrence of crime is quite prevalent in poor areas, and this is causing great fear among the people.

Social Exclusion

The poor are often excluded from the broader society and, therefore, feel humiliated and vulnerable when seeking the help of the state. A poor person in Latvia remarked that "poverty is humiliation, the sense of being dependent, and being forced to accept rudeness, insults, and indifference when we seek help."[14] This creates a poverty trap—the poor are excluded from society, and because of this exclusion, they are unable to access the resources that they need. This social exclusion, both real and perceived, keeps them from being able to escape the poverty situation. While this problem may not be easy to quantify or measure, it is an important associate of poverty that should be addressed.

Psychological Aspects

Poverty research and alleviation efforts have largely focused on the economic factors of poverty, along with other quantifiable measures. However, there is error in this thinking. Poverty has a strong psychological component that only the poor can articulate. While Narayan and others found that poverty is specific to a place and location, they also discovered that it is almost always associated with voicelessness and powerlessness. The poor feel unable to control their lives and have very few choices available to them. After reporting that the poor feel helpless, a poor, elderly man in Uganda stated, "It is this feeling of helplessness that is so painful, more painful than poverty itself."[15]

Multiple Dimensions

With the aforementioned evidence, it is easy to tell that poverty has many dimensions. Each of these dimensions interacts to create the reality of poverty. It is not enough to claim that poverty is entirely about monetary security. It has dimensions that transcend far deeper than that, and if we are to combat poverty most effectively, we would be wise to consider its many dimensions. By focusing on the multidimensionality of poverty, we have a much clearer picture of what it actually means to be poor.

LATTER-DAY SAINT POVERTY

Trends

It is important to consider Latter-day Saints' country-level membership growth by poverty level of the country. Growth rates are especially high in countries with poverty rates above 50 percent. However, the majority of Latter-day Saints are not concentrated in the poorest countries. Most Church members live in countries with poverty rates below 20 percent, such as the United States, Canada, Japan, and most of western Europe. But the distribution is changing. The main difference in the distribution of Latter-day Saints between 1983 and 2005 is that by 2005, fewer members lived in countries with poverty levels below 20 percent, and more members lived in countries with poverty levels between 20 percent and 50 percent. Very few members lived in countries with poverty levels above 50 percent.

It is impossible to directly calculate the changing poverty rate among Latter-day Saints because the Church does not have precise information about members' incomes. One way to estimate the impact of growth is to calculate what the Latter-day Saint poverty rate would be if Latter-day Saints had the same poverty rate as people in the country where the members reside. If we make this assumption using poverty rates after the year 2000, we come up with an estimate of 21.2 percent. If Latter-day Saints were distributed as they were in 1983 (i.e., if the proportion of Latter-day Saints living in each country had not changed since 1983), then the poverty rate would be 17.5 percent. These estimates are far lower than the world's poverty rate, and the difference between 17.5 and 21.2 is not large. Still, the implication is clear: the growth of the Church in developing countries is increasing the percentage of members exposed to the risk of poverty.

Challenges for Latter-day Saints

In addition to the many previously mentioned problems associated with poverty, Latter-day Saints who are in poverty experience additional problems related to their membership in the Church. Attendance, participation, tithing, and the ability to hold and perform a calling all pose potential problems for impoverished members. Those in poverty may live long distances from the meetinghouse and have no way of getting to church. They may have no time to participate in Church activities because they are too busy working for the survival of their family. The commandment to pay tithing is likely daunting to Church members in poverty. Furthermore, as impoverished Latter-day Saints may find it difficult to hold and perform a calling, they are unable to truly integrate themselves into the institution of the Church. In order to feel a part of the group and gain identities as Latter-day Saints, these members need to serve in these capacities.

SOLUTIONS

The challenge of dealing with poverty is compounded by the multidimensional nature of poverty described above. Poverty increases the risk of poor health, lack of education, lack of infrastructure, and so on. In turn, poor health, lack of education, lack of infrastructure, and associated problems make it more difficult to get out of poverty. The final issue we consider is whether national-level policies or locally based programs are more effective in dealing with poverty.

National Level

Many antipoverty programs have been developed at the national level. These typically focus on the economic dimensions of poverty, providing cash transfers and food subsidies to the poor. They also place a large focus on infrastructure investments, such as building schools or hospitals or roads in an attempt to improve the poor's access to these kinds of services. A major benefit of national programs is they have the resources needed for these kinds of programs that they generally get through taxes, other international institutions, and outside donations.

National programs have recently started to place much emphasis on human development as a means to help the poor escape poverty. Mexico's Progresa program provides a good example of this. This program transfers money to poor households on the condition that they participate in human development activities. Mothers are given money for their children's school enrollment for attending the health clinic and taking their children there and for participating in health and nutrition learning meetings. Children are also given nutritional supplements when they go to the clinics. This kind of program is concerned with investing in the human capital of the poor in order to pull them out of the intergenerational poverty cycle.

Progresa has been heavily evaluated, and it seems to be an effective way of increasing school attendance and improving the health and nutrition among the poor.[16] Also, the fact that rigorous evaluation is inherent in its design is innovative and useful. Many national-level programs are not heavily evaluated and become products of the ruling official and party, only to be exchanged for a new program when someone new comes into office. Evaluations of national programs are needed in order to make them as useful as possible.

While researchers' evaluations suggest strong benefits from participating in Progresa, the poor do not share this same view. A large drawback of national-level programs is that the poor do not view them as being effective in creating job opportunities. Interviews with poor people in northern Mexico confirm this notion. The poor are happy to have the cash from Progresa because they are always short on money to buy food and clothes for their children. But they report that these programs do not address their need for more stable, higher-paying jobs. Owing to their extreme circumstances, the poor are less concerned about the long-term benefits of better nutrition and schooling for their children. Because national programs are developed for an entire nation, they are unable to integrate elements of the local contexts into the design of the program. In addition, national-level programs are far removed from the people, and they only exacerbate the dependency and powerlessness that poor people feel. National-level programs do little to address the psychological aspects of poverty.

Local Level

One alternative solution for poverty alleviation occurs at the local, grassroots level. These programs assume that the poor know their situation best, and they know what they need to improve the community's livelihood. The poor are given the responsibility to design, implement, and evaluate programs based on their self-addressed needs. Grassroots programs are developed within the local context of the poverty situation, and they integrate the many dimensions of poverty into their design. The poor share their expertise on their location and situation, and as they come to own the project, they are better able to address the psychological hardships associated with poverty (i.e., despair, powerlessness, humiliation). This process of participation of the poor throughout all program dimensions is an integral aspect of these programs. This process is both a means and an end to poverty alleviation. It is a means, as the act of sharing local knowledge builds the confidence and power of the poor people, and an end, as the knowledge they share brings new perspectives on successful poverty alleviation techniques.

Our experience in northern Mexico has allowed us to see how local development occurs. Every year, a group of students travels to northern Mexico for three weeks to witness and participate in grassroots development projects. For one of these weeks, the students camp in the Sierra Madre Mountains among the Tarahumara, the indigenous people who live there. A Mexican man named Juan Daniel is very familiar with these people; he has lived among them and has gained their trust. He acts as a bridge for them in obtaining the outside resources they need, while also encouraging development through local efforts. While there, we participate in projects that community members have developed themselves. We are not there to give development consultation to the Tarahumara but simply for the labor that we can provide.

We have helped install water piping systems on the tin roofs of homes so the people could turn the rainwater from their roofs into sanitary, usable water that was accessible right at their home. We also have helped with replanting Soltol, a plant they are dependent on for their economic well-being as they sell drinks and baskets they produce from it. We have helped them build rock retention walls to create soil beds for future planting. While the Tarahumara may need our labor efforts, they do not need us to tell them how to improve the well-being of their society. They gather together as a community to decide what projects should be done in the community, and with the help of Juan Daniel, they obtain outside resources that help put these projects into action.

While grassroots development has much to offer in terms of poverty alleviation, it is not without its challenges.[17] First, communities are not homogenous and should not be seen as such. It is likely that not everyone agrees on the community's needs. In addition, local leaders and authorities may capture these programs and control them, making grassroots programs look no different than national programs. Also, some type of help is needed from the outside to instigate these processes and to bring necessary resources to the community. These outside individuals or organizations play a vital role in community development. They must remember that their role is to facilitate and not to tell the community how projects should be developed or implemented. Furthermore, if these individuals know the challenges of grassroots development, they may use caution to overcome them. For example, if an outside individual recognizes that capture by local elites may be possible, he or she should take proper caution to ensure that all the voices of the community are being heard.

CONCLUSION

It is clear that effective antipoverty efforts are greatly needed to overcome the poverty problem that faces so many individuals around the world. And as we recognize the growing problem of poverty within the Church, we should feel even more inclined to become involved in antipoverty work. In his evaluation of the world's progress toward the Millennium Development Goals, D. J. Shaw stated, "Overcoming poverty is not a gesture of charity. It is an act of justice. It is a fundamental human right, the right to dignity and a decent life. While poverty persists, there is no true freedom."[18] As members of The Church of Jesus Christ of Latter-day Saints, we need to support antipoverty efforts around the globe. We must support national programs that aim to reduce poverty and address some of the problems associated with it. In addition, we must support grassroots poverty efforts that seek to overcome poverty by addressing many of the poverty dimensions that are not addressed by national efforts.

NOTES

1. The World Bank, *World Development Indicators*, 2006, http://www-wds.worldbank.org/external/default/WDSContentServer/WDSP/IB/2010/04/21/000333037_20100421010319/Rendered/PDF/541650WDI0200610Box345641B01PUBLIC1.pdf.
2. Deepa Narayan, Raj Patel, Kai Schafft, Anne Rudemacher, and Sarah Koch-Schulte, *Voices of the Poor: Can Anyone Hear Us?* (New York: Oxford University Press, 2000), 53.
3. A. Wagstaff, F. Bustreo, J. Bryce, M. Claeson, and the WHO—World Bank Child Health and Poverty Working Group, "Child Health: Reaching the Poor," *Public Health Matters* 94, no. 5 (2004): 726–36.
4. Narayan et al., *Voices of the Poor*, 35.
5. Narayan et al., *Voices of the Poor*, 57.

6. S. LaRochelle and F. Berkes, "Traditional Ecological Knowledge and Practice for Edible Wild Plants: Biodiversity use by the Raramuri in the Sierra Tarahumara, Mexico," *International Journal of Sustainable Development and World Ecology* 10, no. 4 (2003): 361–75.
7. L. N. Fonjong, N. N. Emmanuel, and C. C. Fonchingong, "Rethinking the Contribution of Indigenous Management in Small-Scale Water Provision among Selected Rural Communities in Cameroon," *Environment, Development and Sustainability* 6, no. 4 (2004): 429–51.
8. Narayan et al., *Voices of the Poor*, 47.
9. The World Health Organization and UNICEF, *Meeting the MDG Drinking Water and Sanitation Target: The Urban and Rural Challenge of the Decade*, 2006, http://www.who.int/water_sanitation_health/monitoring/jmpfinal.pdf.
10. R. Renkow, D. G. Hallstrom, and D. D. Karanja, "Rural Infrastructure, Transaction Costs, and Market Participation in Kenya," *Journal of Development Economics* 73, no. 1 (2004): 349–67.
11. F. Finan, E. Sadoulet, and A. de Janvry, "Measuring the Poverty Reduction Potential of Land in Rural Mexico," *Journal of Development Economics* 77, no. 1 (2005): 27–51.
12. J. Gibson and S. Rozelle, "Poverty and Access to Roads in Papua New Guinea," *Economic Development and Cultural Change* (2004): 159–85.
13. Narayan et al., *Voices of the Poor*, 41.
14. Narayan et al., *Voices of the Poor*, 30.
15. Narayan et al., *Voices of the Poor*, 39.
16. J. R. Behrman and E. Skoufias, "Mitigating Myths about Policy Effectiveness: Evaluation of Mexico's Antipoverty and Human Resource Investment Program," *Annals of the American Academy of Political and Social Sciences* 606, no. 1 (2006): 244–75.
17. R. Eversole, "Managing the Pitfalls of Participatory Development: Some Insight from Australia," *World Development* 31, no. 5 (2003): 781–95.
18. D. J. Shaw, "Dimensions of Poverty: Status and Solutions Towards the Millennium Development Goals," *Development Policy Review* 23, no. 4 (2005): 500.

3

CARING FOR THE POOR AND NEEDY IN THE GROWING INTERNATIONAL CHURCH

BISHOP GÉRALD J. CAUSSÉ

Bishop Gérald J. Caussé, then first counselor in the Presiding Bishopric of The Church of Jesus Christ of Latter-day Saints, presented this essay at "The Church and Humanitarian Assistance: In the Lord's Way," the International Society's twenty-fifth annual conference, April 2014, Brigham Young University, Provo, Utah.

For several years now, I have closely followed the work of the LDS International Society. As a General Authority coming from outside the United States, I have a special and passionate interest in the worldwide growth of the Church. My responsibilities in the Europe Area Presidency and now in the Presiding Bishopric have led me to face the modern miracle of this growth and the immense challenges it represents. I thank you for the very useful perspective you bring on this essential aspect of the work of the Church in our day.

I would like to share some thoughts about one of these challenges: providing Church welfare services in the growing international Church. Although my remarks will primarily address helping Church members, it should be noted that the Church also devotes considerable and growing efforts to humanitarian aid across the world, intended to assist those not of our faith who face challenging situations.

I vividly remember my first visit to Welfare Square, which occurred almost six years ago, around the time I was called to the First Quorum of the Seventy. This visit filled me with enthusiasm! It expanded my vision for accomplishing the mandate of the Church to help the poor and needy. Welfare Square is such a unique and extraordinary place. With its bishops' storehouse, bakery, Deseret Industries, cannery, dairy, employment resource center, and gigantic grain silo, this facility supports bishops who assist needy members. The kinds of resources available in this one small area are mostly unknown to members living outside the United States. I began to dream that one day, similar resources would be available to members throughout the world—that welfare operations like those on Welfare Square would cover the entire earth. Today, as a member of the Presiding Bishopric, caring for the poor and needy throughout the world is part of my daily work and responsibility.

In contrast to past ages, the dispensation of the fullness of times in which we live is not limited by geography. It is taking place in a "global" world where countries, cultures, and peoples have become intermingled and interdependent. The worldwide growth of the Church in our lifetime is especially striking. For several years now, we have witnessed an acceleration of the work beyond what most older members of the Church would have imagined fifty years ago. I recently had the privilege of visiting some African nations. I expected to find an emerging and still fragile Church. Instead, I found dozens of well-organized stakes of Zion, leaders with remarkable spiritual maturity, and committed and faithful members. Great nations such as Nigeria and the Democratic Republic of Congo are experiencing astonishing growth in Church membership and are on the verge of becoming the new Brazil or Mexico of the Church.

The challenge for Church leaders is to establish this growth on a solid and durable foundation—to make sure all new members are welcomed and fellowshipped into the Church and may benefit from all the spiritual and temporal resources that will help them flourish in the gospel. A remarkable fact about our time is that the majority of Church growth is in poor and developing nations. In 1980, about 20 percent of the members of the Church lived in developing nations. Today, that figure is closer to 45 percent and will continue to increase in the future. Many among the hundreds of thousands of people who enter into the waters of baptism each year live in modest conditions, some even in dire poverty. A great number of them have been unable to receive the education they desire. Not having stable employment, they must plan for their survival on a daily basis. Studies recently showed that 62 percent of Church members living in Ghana or Nigeria are considered to have insufficient income. Even in Brazil, that number is 50 percent. Between 20 and 25 percent of the members living in the Philippines, Ghana, Nigeria, or Samoa do not know how to read a Church magazine.

Unfortunately, often these temporal difficulties are not temporary. Frequently, they are perpetuated from generation to generation because of a chronic lack of infrastructures to support education, transportation, and health. Political disorders and destructive natural calamities also take a toll. In these conditions, the responsibility the Church has to reach out and lift up the poor and needy is more crucial than ever.

This responsibility may seem overwhelming as the Church grows in regions with complex and varied circumstances. The welfare programs in the American West were developed in a context of a homogenous and dense Church membership. They cannot be transported identically to countries where Church members are spread out and supporting infrastructures do not exist or are insufficient. Even so, we still have a mandate to care for the poor and needy wherever they live. As President Thomas S. Monson very rightly said, "We are a global Church. . . . There are those throughout the world who are hungry, . . . destitute."[1] He also said, "I think we should not put an artificial border around need. The Lord didn't and we shouldn't."[2]

How, then, can the Church fully ensure that its welfare services operate effectively throughout the world? How do we bring relief to the poor and needy wherever the Church is being established? The goal of the Church goes well beyond simply making monetary and physical resources available. It contemplates the spiritual progress and eternal salvation of individuals and families. The immense plague of poverty should not turn us away from the true challenges, which always have a spiritual component. President Dieter F. Uchtdorf said, "The Lord's way of caring for the needy is different from the world's way. The Lord has said, 'It must needs be done in mine own way' (D&C 104:16). He is not only interested in our immediate needs; He is also concerned about our eternal progression."[3]

The Lord's way relies on strong doctrinal principles whose purpose is the spiritual as well as temporal progression of individuals and families. These principles are eternal and universal. These are the principles we must spread and establish throughout the world. However, the application of the principles—the means, resources, and programs developed by the Church—may need to vary from one country or region to another to adapt to each environment. President Dieter F. Uchtdorf continued: "Every family, every congregation, every area of the world is different. There is no one-size-fits-all answer in Church welfare. . . . You're going to have to chart a course that is consistent with the Lord's doctrine and matches the circumstances of your geographic area."[4]

What are these doctrinal principles upon which the worldwide expansion of Church welfare should be based?

FIRST PRINCIPLE: CARING FOR OUR NEIGHBORS IN NEED IS AN ESSENTIAL REQUISITE OF SALVATION

The primary mission of The Church of Jesus Christ of Latter-day Saints is to invite all of Heavenly Father's children to come unto Christ, meaning to become the beneficiaries of His atoning sacrifice. *Handbook 2: Administering the Church* describes helping the poor and needy as one of the four divinely appointed responsibilities through which the Church accomplishes this redeeming mission.[5]

Christ Himself taught that our personal efforts to help the poor and needy are an important condition of our eternal salvation.[6] Twice during His earthly ministry, Jesus was questioned in these terms: "Master, what shall I do to inherit eternal life?"[7] The first time, He responded to the doctor of the law by recounting the magnificent parable of the good Samaritan, and He concluded with this famous exhortation: "Go, and do thou likewise."[8] The second time, when the rich young man kneeled at His feet, Jesus answered him: "Go thy way, sell whatsoever thou hast, and give to the poor, and thou shalt have treasure in heaven: and come, take up the cross, and follow me."[9] In both cases, Jesus answered His questioners with loving but firm invitations to consecrate their lives to helping their neighbors in need.

Caring for the poor and needy is not optional, nor is it merely an accessory in the Church of Jesus Christ. This responsibility cannot be added to or taken away according to the whims of the situation or local conditions. It is an indispensable element of the mission of the Church. Church members throughout the world, whether they live in developed or developing countries, all have a need to participate in this great welfare work in ways appropriate to their circumstances.

A good place to start is with ourselves as individuals and as families. Providing for our own temporal needs will help us live the gospel of Jesus Christ. It is difficult to blossom in the gospel when our thoughts and efforts are consumed with the worries of providing for the basic needs of our families. Temporal concerns—particularly oppressive ones—can often preoccupy our minds to the point that they take precedence over spiritual goals and affect our ability to reach our potential as sons or daughters of God. Brigham Young offered this sage counsel: "Prayer is good, but when baked potatoes and pudding and milk are needed, prayer will not supply their place on this occasion; give every duty its proper time and place."[10]

SECOND PRINCIPLE: WELFARE IS BASED ON THE OBSERVANCE OF THE LAWS OF TITHING AND OF THE FAST

President Gordon B. Hinckley declared: "I know that the people are in difficult circumstances. I know that many of them are unemployed. I know that many of them work for very meager wages. I know that they live in simple and inadequate little houses; the only thing they can afford. I believe they will not walk out of poverty unless they pay their tithing, small and meager as that might be."[11]

The observance of the laws of tithing and of the fast brings incomparable blessings, such as "closeness to the Lord, increased spiritual strength, temporal well-being, greater compassion, and a stronger desire to serve."[12] These spiritual blessings have a profound impact on the lives and the temporal self-reliance of Church members.

President Harold B. Lee reported that on one occasion, someone presented statistics to President Heber J. Grant that showed a sustained growth in the payments of fast offerings to the Church. He responded that his main concern was not about the number of dollars or cents "but that the Church needs blessings, and the only way we can receive the blessings is by keeping the laws on which those blessings are predicated; and the fundamental law pertaining to the welfare of our people was fast offerings." He added, "If our people observe the fast and consecrate their fast by paying an offering, we don't need to worry about the amounts of money."[13]

One reason the laws of tithing and the fast have such an influence in the lives of Church members is that everyone can participate in them, regardless of their income. Tithing is not a specific sum, which some may not be able to afford, but a percentage of our increase. Everyone can fast. No one is too poor to give something as a fast offering. Our challenge is to teach the members of the Church, wherever they are and whatever their condition may be, the importance of observing the laws of tithing, of the fast, and of consecrating their fast by paying their fast offering. Those with the means to do so are invited to make a generous fast offering donation. In helping their neighbors in this way, they can draw upon the blessings of heaven for themselves and their families.

THIRD PRINCIPLE: THE BENEFICIARIES OF WELFARE PARTICIPATE THROUGH THEIR WORK AND SERVICE

In his well-known speech, King Benjamin addressed the poor among his people in these terms: "Ye who have not and yet have sufficient, . . . I mean all you who deny the beggar, because ye have not; I would that ye say in your hearts that: I give not because I have not, but if I had I would give."[14] Everyone, even the most destitute among us, should feel responsible to help their neighbor with what they have, even if it is very little. No one is too poor, too vulnerable, or too marginalized to contribute something of worth. As President Dieter F. Uchtdorf said, "The lesson we learn generation after generation is that rich and poor are *all* under the same sacred obligation to help their neighbor."[15]

Truth be told, everyone has need of the blessings attached to service, especially those who benefit from Church welfare. By diligently participating in welfare work, they show gratitude and gain a wonderful feeling of worthiness, responsibility, and self-reliance. In service, they find solutions to their own problems. A sanctifying power strengthens their faith and hope. They emerge with more certainty from financial difficulties by giving in addition to receiving.

President Spencer W. Kimball shared a story at the April 1974 general conference. When he served as stake president in Duncan Valley, Arizona, the stake members were struck by a devastating flood. He promptly sent a telegram to Church headquarters in Salt Lake City that simply said: "Please send us $10,000 by return mail." He never received the awaited sum. Instead, three men appeared at his doorstep. These three men were President Lee, President Romney, and President Moyle. These brethren took him aside and taught him a memorable lesson. Speaking of welfare in the Church, they said: "This isn't a program of 'give me.' This is a program of 'self-help.'" President Kimball recalled the resulting wave of service that followed; men and women came from all over the valley. They rolled up their sleeves, and they went to work helping their neighbors and fellow Saints. Of that time, President Kimball said, "Now it would have been an easy thing, I think, for the Brethren to have sent us that $10,000, and it wouldn't have been too hard to sit in my office and distribute it; but what a lot of good came to us as we had hundreds of men go to Duncan and build fences and haul the hay and level the ground and do all the things that needed doing. That is self-help."[16]

Today, the principle of serving through self-help is in force more than ever, especially as the Church is being established in nations afflicted by poverty and buffeted by natural or man-made catastrophes. In November 2013, super-typhoon Haiyan, one of the most violent typhoons ever recorded, struck the central region of the Philippines, with winds reaching two hundred miles per hour. The typhoon sowed destruction, leaving entire regions completely devastated. Around six thousand people were killed in the disaster, and eighteen hundred are still reported missing. As soon as news of the catastrophe became known, the Church began to mobilize. Under the direction of the Philippines Area Presidency, and with the support of the Welfare Services Department at Church headquarters, the resources of the welfare system were pressed into service.

I remember the first coordination meetings held over the telephone with the Area Presidency. It became clear that providing shelters for the affected families would be one of the major challenges of the rebuilding effort. A census of members revealed that at least twenty-nine hundred families no longer had a home. In the Philippines, like in Duncan Valley, Arizona, it would have been easy to provide a one-stop solution. The Church could have purchased and shipped thousands of shelter kits and mobilized hundreds of workers, many of whom would have come from America. But it was not just a matter of efficiency and speed. Our first objective was that the Filipino Saints be given the opportunity to take charge, serve each other, and build their self-reliance. In the end, each family was invited to participate in the reconstruction of their own homes. Additionally, a training program was put in place, leading to the certification of about five thousand Church members in the main skills of construction—carpentry, roofing, electricity, and plumbing. All trainees were equipped with a tool bag provided by the Church, and they went to work. First, they helped build their own houses, and then they were required to help build nine other houses in the neighborhood. Once they had completed their apprenticeship by building ten houses, they were given a certificate that allowed them to work in construction earning money for their families.

As of today, almost two thousand of the planned three thousand houses have been rebuilt. But what fills us with joy is to know that hundreds of heads of families have found employment and are now actively participating in the reconstruction efforts of their own country. We recently received the good news that Catholic Relief Services is planning to hire hundreds of our members thus certified to work on their reconstruction sites.

I believe this is one of the most remarkable successes in the history of Church welfare. In serving each other to rebuild their communities, these valiant Filipino members also increased their self-reliance and that of their families. Even more importantly, they strengthened their faith and personal conversion.

FOURTH PRINCIPLE: THE GOAL OF WELFARE IS TO HELP INDIVIDUALS AND THEIR FAMILIES BECOME SELF-RELIANT

As was the case in the Philippines, one of the greatest blessings that can result from Church welfare is to help people become self-reliant. Speaking on the principle of self-reliance, President Brigham Young said: "My experience has taught me, and it has become a principle with me, that it is never any benefit to give, out and out, to man or woman, money, food, clothing, or anything else, if they are able-bodied, and can work and earn what they need, when there is anything on the earth for them to do. This is my principle, and I try to act upon it. To pursue a contrary course would ruin any community in the world and make them idlers."[17]

An appropriate question to ask of any welfare program is "How much self-reliance is it going to generate?" A good project is one that allows people to increase their personal talents and abilities and to learn through action and experience. A few months ago, my wife and I were assigned to visit the Church in the Democratic Republic of Congo. It is a fast-growing country with Church membership doubling every five years. We were particularly touched by the beauty of the children and youth in that country. Their eyes sparkled with faith and enthusiasm.

Unfortunately for them, the future is often bleak and uncertain. More than 80 percent of the Congolese citizens do not have stable employment and must survive day-to-day by whatever means they can. For many youth, the prospects of establishing a family and fully living the gospel seem tied to the hope of receiving an education and finding a job.

One of the most memorable moments of our trip was a beautiful ceremony held in Lubumbashi. During the meeting, Elder Dale G. Renlund and I awarded professional diplomas, presented by the LDS Business College, to about fifty young adults of the Church. The faces of those wonderful young people radiated with joy. This wonderful occasion was the result of a training program in construction skills launched by the Church for young people just returning from their missions. The program includes three successive phases. The selected students first spend several months completing a theory course that is taught in a Church meetinghouse by local members and missionary couples. After successfully completing this first cycle, students move on to the practical phase by working as interns at chapel construction sites. At the end of a successful internship, they receive an official diploma delivered by LDS Business College and are ready to be hired by construction contractors. As of today, two years after the program started, the Church has signed training contracts with several construction businesses in the Democratic Republic of Congo. Two hundred seventy-five young adults have received their diplomas, of which one hundred have now found permanent employment. Twenty-five others are pursuing more training or setting up their own businesses. The promising results of this program remind me of these words from President Henry B. Eyring: "Students who think they have limited possibilities can find hope, . . . they can now dream of what they thought was impossible."[18]

With this same objective, the Church is currently accelerating its efforts to develop the Perpetual Education Fund. In the twelve years of its existence, this inspired program has provided loans and support to more than fifty-seven thousand young adults seeking professional training and better employment. The Church is currently expanding this initiative by developing a network of self-reliance centers throughout the world. Those centers are providing personal coaching and assistance to those seeking employment. Beyond the financial and professional aspects, the program emphasizes the eternal principles of education, integrity, work, and self-reliance.

FIFTH PRINCIPLE: LOCAL PRIESTHOOD LEADERS ACT WITH THEIR KEYS

The Lord gave to the bishops of the Church the sacred charge of taking care of the poor and needy. From the Doctrine and Covenants we read, "And the bishop . . . should travel round about . . . searching after the poor to administer to their wants by humbling the rich and the proud."[19] I remember the meeting when the Presiding Bishopric presented to the First Presidency the response plan for Typhoon Haiyan. At the conclusion of the presentation, President Henry B. Eyring commented, "The most important thing is to allow the bishops to exercise their keys!"

I often note this great truth during my travels. Everywhere I have been, I have met impressive bishops full of wisdom and inspiration. No one at

Church headquarters could ever conceive of the local welfare solutions they are implementing. As Elder Robert D. Hales explained, "How does a bishop decide who to help when it appears all are poor? Poverty is relative. The Lord, in his infinite wisdom, calls bishops from the people whom he will serve. The bishop knows the people of his ward and understands local culture and economic conditions. When a bishop is ordained, he receives the mantle which enables him to discern the difference between wants and needs." Elder Hales added, "The farther away from the local bishop you get, the less able you are to make intelligent judgments, let alone inspired ones, because it is to the bishop the mantle is given."[20]

As recent natural disasters have shown, such as the tsunami in Japan or the typhoon in the Philippines, it is always more efficient to administer relief at the local level. Local solutions allow for rapid delivery of resources, are less costly, allow the local members to participate, and are better adapted to the local culture to meet real needs.

CONCLUSION

To the lame man who implored him for alms, Peter responded, "Silver and gold have I none; but such as I have give I thee: In the name of Jesus Christ of Nazareth rise up and walk. And he took him by the right hand, and lifted him up: and immediately his feet and ankle bones received strength. And he leaping up stood, and walked, and entered with them into the temple, walking, and leaping, and praising God."[21]

In the face of the daunting worldwide challenges of poverty and underdevelopment, how do we give the poor and needy among us the ability to "rise up and walk"? The best and most lasting solution is found in living the gospel of Jesus Christ. This solution knows how to adapt to every horizon, every culture, and every political and economic system. The welfare resources of the Church are limitless because they rest on true and eternal principles, are administered through priesthood keys exercised by tens of thousands of local leaders, and are supported by the consecrated service of millions of Latter-day Saints.

I testify that miracles pertaining to helping those in need are as real today as they were in Peter's time. They take place every day, whenever the righteous approach the Lord and choose to follow Him.

NOTES

1. Thomas S. Monson, "Until We Meet Again," *Ensign*, November 2008, 106.
2. Thomas S. Monson, quoted in "'Helping Hand' Should Reach Out," *Church News*, 6 February 2010.
3. Dieter F. Uchtdorf, "Providing in the Lord's Way," *Ensign*, November 2011, 54.
4. Uchtdorf, "Providing in the Lord's Way," 55.
5. *Handbook 2: Administering the Church* (Salt Lake City: The Church of Jesus Christ of Latter-day Saints, 2010), 2.2.
6. See Matthew 25:31–46.
7. Luke 10:25; Mark 10:17.
8. Luke 10:37.
9. Mark 10:21.
10. Brigham Young, in *Deseret News*, 10 December 1856, 320.
11. Gordon B. Hinckley, General Authority Training, 2 October 2001.
12. *Handbook 2: Administering the Church* (2010), 6.1.2.
13. Harold B. Lee, "Listen and Obey" (address given at the Welfare Agricultural meeting, 3 April 1971), Church History Library, Salt Lake City.
14. Mosiah 4:24.
15. Uchtdorf, "Providing in the Lord's Way," 54; emphasis in original.
16. Spencer W. Kimball (address given at the Welfare Services meeting, 6 April 1974), Church History Library, Salt Lake City.
17. *Discourses of Brigham Young*, comp. John A. Widtsoe (1941), 274.
18. Henry B. Eyring (inaugural address, LDS Business College, 13 October 2009).
19. Doctrine and Covenants 84:112.
20. Robert D. Hales, "Providing in the Lord's Way" (address given at the regional representatives' seminar, 5 April 1991), 3–4, Church History Library, Salt Lake City.
21. Acts 3:6–8.

4

ZION'S FOUNTAINS

SHARON EUBANK

Sharon Eubank, then director of LDS Charities at The Church of Jesus Christ of Latter-day Saints, presented this essay at "The Church and Humanitarian Assistance: In the Lord's Way," the International Society's twenty-fifth annual conference, April 2014, Brigham Young University, Provo, Utah.

I want to start off by telling you about an experience I had. The Church sent me on assignment to the United Nations to present about LDS Charities as a faith-based organization. We were the sixth faith-based organization in the UN's history to have this opportunity to talk about our work. I gave my part, and then there were other pieces, and then it was open for questions and answers. A woman in the back raised her hand and said in essence: "Look, let's just call this spade a spade. You are a Christian-based organization; you are sending out tons of projects and tons of money, but you do not care about charity; you care about missionary work. This is all a front for missionary work." When she said that, there was scattered applause in the room. Ah! I thought to myself. People believe that. They have a misconception about that. And so I want to address that here.

Bishop Gérald Caussé earlier spoke very eloquently about the doctrinal underpinnings for how and why the Church cares for the poor and the needy. Robert Hokanson gave some great examples with Bishop Estrada and the pig project in the Philippines regarding what the Church does to care for the poor and the needy inside the Church. I completely agree with Robert that there is no better development project program in the world than being a member of this Church. You cannot be a member of this Church very long without learning the practical skills of leadership, effective cooperation in a council, organization, social networking, and public speaking.

Everything we do in the Church is designed to help us progress. The motivation and energy for us to develop and progress comes from our covenants. We accept volunteer callings in the Church, we complete assignments that stretch us, we teach our children formally and informally about what makes a happy life, and we witness to each other from our own experiences why these work. But how do we apply those principles that work so magnificently to people who may not have had the same experience with covenants?

For LDS Charities—the humanitarian nongovernmental organization (NGO) operated by The Church of Jesus Christ of Latter-day Saints—our primary audience is people who are not members of the Church. How do we successfully work with people who may not be motivated by covenants? How do we encourage work and participation among recipients? How do we foster volunteerism in cultures that may have little tradition of service? And what about the question the woman at the UN asked? How do we work as a Christian-based organization legitimately caring for the poor and the needy and not leverage it into an opportunity to have the missionaries preach? Is caring for the poor and needy a work that is valuable as an activity all on its own?

We just finished general conference. We heard a lot about hastening the work. What do you think about when you hear the phrase "hastening the work"? Almost all of us think about missionary work, but the four divinely appointed responsibilities of the Church are doing missionary work, helping the Saints make and keep covenants, performing ordinances for family who have died, and (do you remember the fourth one?) caring for the poor and the needy. What does it mean to hasten the work in caring for the poor and the needy? What would that look like?

In my mind, it looks like dirt. I will explain this thought a little bit: Up by my house there is a big field, and it has been a farmer's junkyard for a long time. There is rusted equipment there; it is full of rocks, weeds, and everything you can think of. One day he hauled away the equipment, brought in a rototiller, pulled out the garbage, dumped nutrients into the ground, and plowed it. I thought, "He is getting ready to do something." After a while, he planted seeds. Then he watered those seeds, put in a big sprinkling system, nurtured those seeds, and had kids out pulling weeds in between. At the end of the summer, he was harvesting. I did not see him do this, but we know you can bind that harvest into sheaves.

That story is a good example of the spectrum I am talking about—hastening the work of caring for the poor and the needy is preparing the ground, digging up the junk and moving it out, pouring in nutrients, and getting the ground ready for something. Do we know what will be grown there? No, but it is now clean and ready. Hastening missionary work and helping people increase their knowledge of the gospel is like planting the seeds, watering them, and nurturing them. Hastening the work of making and keeping covenants is like harvesting the seeds that were planted. And binding into sheaves is temple work. This is a much broader spectrum of hastening the work than simply missionary work alone. And each stage of the work is critical.

If I talk about it a different way, it would look like this: On the spectrum of human activity, you cannot progress in this world unless you know that God loves you and he knows who you are. How do you know that? How do you have an experience that tells you that? It is done through relationships and people that care about us. There is a great quote by Elder Holland, who said, "Prayers are answered most of the time, I think, by God using other people. Well, I pray that He'll use us. I pray that we'll be the answer to people's prayers."[1] Serving another person with no thought for personal reward is the first divine act of a culture or people.

Once we feel the love of God, we cooperate. We have a desire to help each other leverage our combined resources. People who feel the love of God have a sense of wanting to build on each other's work. Once you have started cooperating, that act builds an identity, a unity: "We are the kind of community that makes sure our kids are in school," or, "We are the kind of community that cares about health." Cooperation builds identification, unity, and brotherhood. People start to feel empowered in the community where they live because of the unifying spirit that lives there.

Once a group is worried about unity, it worries about the things that wreck unity: addictions, violence, family breakdown, and corruption. If you are worried about unity, you start to focus on discipline and families because those are the things that create lasting unity. When people are interested in discipline and families, what else are they interested in? What are they prepared for? People thinking about unity and family are in the frame of mind to hear the gospel message because it is relevant to them. It makes sense to them. Now they are prepared to make covenants. When they hear the gospel message it is something they want because it resonates with their own experiences. Once you have made promises to the Lord, such as the covenant of baptism—to mourn with those that mourn, to comfort those that stand in need of comfort—now you can contemplate the idea of sacrifice. You are no longer consumed with, "What will make my life work out?" You are worried about, "What will help this entire group progress?" The Lord gives us endless opportunities to sacrifice: in our congregations, in our families, in our neighborhoods and communities, and in the LDS International Society.

By sacrificing our own comfort and desires for the good of the group, we are creating Zion. Zion is the place where we are all of one heart and one mind, and there is no poor among us.[2] The whole spectrum I have just described is all part of the work of salvation. This is what the prophets mean when they talk about hastening the work. Caring for the poor and the needy has to do with the beginning part of the spectrum. It is about helping the people feel the love of God, cooperate, and develop unity and brotherhood. Although we do not use those activities to preach the gospel in words or to hold formal missionary discussions, we are still preaching the preparatory gospel that will help clear that field and prepare that dirt for people to move along the spectrum as they are prepared and made ready. We trust the Lord to bring experiences to people so they can move along. We are moving along that spectrum, too. It is not like we are at the end of that spectrum. All of us are moving along it. The scriptures call the spectrum "the more excellent way,"[3] and it is no accident that Paul prefaces his great treatise on charity with that verse. The Book of Mormon prophet Moroni also wrote, "In the gift of his Son hath God prepared a more excellent way."[4]

With that introduction, I want to talk a little more about hastening the work of caring for the poor and needy, both at the Church institutional level and also at a personal level, because each one of us is trying to keep our baptismal covenants to care for the poor. There is a tremendous scriptural and prophetic mandate to care for people who are not members of this Church. Alma talked about how his community cared for people: "They were liberal to all, both old and young, both bond and free, both male and female, whether out of the church or in the church, having no respect to persons as to those who stood in need."[5] Joseph Smith's very famous quote says, "To feed the hungry, to clothe the naked, to provide for the widow, to dry up the tear of the orphan, to comfort the afflicted, whether in this church, or in any other, or in no church at all, wherever he finds them."[6] President Hinckley, speaking to the National Press Club in 2000, said, "Human suffering anywhere and among any people is a matter of urgent concern for us."[7] And in the February 2014 *Ensign*, President Monson said, "We are the Lord's hands here upon the earth, with a mandate to serve and to lift his children. . . . Are we doing all we should?"[8] We have a very strong mandate to reach out to people, not just to those within the Church but to people outside the Church, also.

The Church has always had an outreach to help others suffering disaster, even when our own resources were very limited, but the modern, formal beginning of LDS Charities started in 1985. What happened in 1985 that precipitated it? There was a terrible famine in the Horn of Africa. President Spencer W. Kimball asked the Church to fast and to give generously for the Africans' relief. The Church members fasted. We collected—in the very unusual way of giving money equivalent to two meals—six million dollars. Elder M. Russell Ballard and Bishop Glenn L. Pace and others went to Ethiopia and presented a portion of the funds to Catholic Relief Services, which was doing great relief work there. They accepted it and over time cooperated with us further. They taught us a lot about how to properly distribute funding in the midst of a disaster. From that experience, LDS Charities was born—and it has evolved over time. LDS Charities is the Church's registered NGO, and its board of directors is the Presiding Bishopric—of which Bishop Caussé is a member—and the Relief Society General Presidency. I am its vice president, or its chief operating officer.

Recipients are primarily people not of our faith. Since 1985, LDS Charities has provided 1.89 billion dollars in assistance in 189 countries. It is a huge scope, and it is possible largely because of the members of the Church who continue to donate generously both their time and their money. It started off with emergency-response programs, because that was the first experience we gained. In an emergency, the goal is to relieve immediate suffering and fill gaps in service. For example, we recently worked with a national government to assist in one of the Syrian refugee camps. The gap they were trying to work through was laundry. Can you imagine trying to do all the laundry for the thousands of people living in a camp? We asked about the availability of electricity and water, the use of wastewater, and what would be most efficient and culturally acceptable. We cooperated with the local officials and filled that gap.

In addition to immediately relieving suffering and filling gaps—and Bishop Caussé addressed this—we want to assist with ongoing recovery long after the media has turned to the next disaster. LDS Charities has experience staying to help the infrastructure get back up so people get their businesses back, the schools and hospitals are functioning, and people build their homes again. Bishop Caussé shared very interesting stories about people in the Philippines rebuilding their homes, then building nine other people's homes, and becoming certified in construction skills at the same time.

In addition to emergencies, there are lots of ongoing problems in the world—big intractable problems I do not know the answers for, but here are a few of them:

> **Slavery**—There are thirty million slaves in the world, and sixty thousand of them are in the United States.[9] They are people who are forced into prostitution or migrant work. This is three times as many slaves as existed in the 1700s and 1800s, and yet it is largely invisible to us. It is a modern problem occurring right in our neighborhoods, but we do not necessarily notice it.

Gender violence—The following statistic came out of the *New York Times* in 2014; it says: "Women worldwide . . . are more likely to die or be maimed as a result of male violence than as a consequence of war, cancer, malaria, and traffic accidents combined."[10] You can imagine the effect that statistic would have on families and the next generation.

Refugees—Right now there are three, possibly four, gigantic, unprecedented refugee crises going on. Three years ago there were thirty-five million refugees and displaced people, and now there are forty-seven million because of the conflicts in Syria, the Central African Republic, South Sudan, and other places. And 75 percent of refugees are women and children living in places designed to be temporary—places nobody else wants—after having endured the most unimaginable circumstances.

The under-age-five mortality rate—This rate is the number of kids who die before they reach their fifth birthday: 6.6 million children every single year, but this is down from 12 million in 1990.

LDS Charities has six signature programs we call major initiatives. They are Clean Water and Sanitation, Neonatal Resuscitation Training, Vision Care, Wheelchairs and Assessment Training, Immunizations, and the Benson Family Food program. I am often asked why we picked these six. In 2002, there was a desire to focus on and target specific needs. Instead of trying to do everything, we tried to select some areas where we might have real global impact. We felt we should use national-level partners, instruct using world-class curricula, and transfer expertise. Whatever we chose needed to fit the volunteer model we rely heavily upon.

How do these programs relate to the global initiatives I mentioned earlier? Clean water, neonatal resuscitation, and immunizations have a strong impact on the number of children under five who survive. Those three initiatives, along with others, have heavily contributed to the number of deaths going down since 1990. There is currently a pilot program working with the UN High Commission for Refugees to serve refugees in underresourced camps. Some camps have existed for twenty, thirty, or forty years, and the people in them will unfortunately never go back home. They are raising a second or third generation in the camps. The funding is not always available to fix their latrines or their homes, which were meant to be temporary. LDS Charities is piloting work with the UN (who administers the camps) to repair the aging infrastructure.

Bishop Caussé mentioned the immigrant pilot program we are running in US inner cities. We are looking at what we can do and what interventions work. This is why it is so important to listen to the description during this conference of some of the work done by others in the LDS International Society. What social innovation would change the game in some of these places? Where are the gaps?

The theme for this conference mentions "In the Lord's Way." LDS Charities is structured as a nongovernmental organization, but we operate in some respects differently from other NGOs because of the principles we are founded upon. Doing things in the Lord's way is going to make us different in several respects. One of those different aspects is that the work will largely be accomplished by volunteers and unpaid staff. Volunteerism is an intersection where institutional tenets and personal ministry combine. LDS Charities has a paid staff of twenty-two. Other organizations of roughly the same size have thirty-five hundred to forty-seven hundred paid staff members. There is nothing inherently negative about that; we leverage those partners and their expert staff heavily. But there is no other organization using volunteers to the same scope and proficiency as LDS Charities. There are currently eighty-six humanitarian or welfare missionary couples around the world. They are assigned eighteen to twenty-three months around the world, and they are often the on-the-ground coordinators of humanitarian projects. The couples do magnificent work because they put their arms around people, invest in relationships, and simply share fellowship and the love of God. There is not anybody better at doing that.

In addition to the couples, there are 498 volunteer technical specialists working with LDS Charities. These volunteers are doctors, water engineers, and rehabilitation specialists who use their vacation time, leave their practices, and go out for two weeks to transfer expertise to their colleagues in the world. After they come home, they stay in touch with them on Skype in a collegial exchange that has great impact. As I mentioned before, with such a small staff, there is no way to accomplish all that needs to be done without partnering with other respected NGOs. And that means we reach out across these bridges and use their expertise and our expertise to address an identified need. Somebody asked during Bishop Caussé's presentation, "Is not interfaith [work] one of the most important things we can do?" And the answer is, "Yes, it is," because working together to reinforce values and not specific doctrine is very important community work. By selecting local partnerships—people on the ground who will stay—we invest in the community infrastructure.

A second aspect that is inherent in doing things in the Lord's way is that project outcomes are less about the product and more about what happens inside the people. Let me share an example: Keith Barney is a professor at BYU–Idaho, and Jeff Griffin is a full-time seminary teacher in West Jordan. Both use wheelchairs, and both were volunteer technical specialists who worked as wheelchair trainers in Nepal recently. They did what is called "peer group training," teaching a World Health Organization curriculum about new life skills to Nepalese people who had just been in an accident. Newly paralyzed individuals are trying to figure out, "How do I make my life work now that I am going to be in a wheelchair?" The curriculum they taught was composed of important life skills, but do you know what people wanted to ask Keith and Jeff? "How did you get here in the plane? Are you married? Do you have kids? What do you do for a job?" They wanted answers from someone who really understood their situation. You can get a feeling for the cooperation and brotherhood that Keith and Jeff brought into the group. All of them together experienced a change. These are some of the great hallmarks of the Lord's Church: cooperation, fellowship, unity, respect—no matter what the religion or faith of the other.

For anybody who volunteers—and it does not matter if you have come from West Jordan and go to Nepal, or if you are Bishop Estrada and stay right in your branch in the Philippines—the thing we call the Holy Ghost can be with you more, and the Lord will richly bless you. Bishop Caussé said, "It does not matter if you have money or not. The Lord asks you to un-intuitively sacrifice your time or your talent or your energy, and when you do, he blesses not only you but everybody around you."

You see this principle at work when members of the Church in Haiti go door-to-door to tell their friends and neighbors about an immunization campaign. It doesn't necessarily do anything to benefit the volunteers—in fact it may be a drain on their time and resources—but they understand that this charitable tide lifts all boats. They are perfectly suited for this assignment. They come from the communities, they know everybody, they are Haitian, and they speak the right dialects to answer questions. They are the perfect complement to that project because they are working in their home communities. Being local has great power.

The third aspect of providing in the Lord's way is global reach with individual impact—two ideas that seem at odds with each other. LDS Charities is big enough to have a global reach and has enough local presence (like in the Haiti example above) to reach people one-on-one. My assignment at the UN was exactly about expanding our representation in these global bodies. We are developing relationships and experiences with other credible multinational NGOs so that people will not be worried that this is just a ruse to bring in missionaries. Charitable service is a credible activity all on its own and one in which we have the chance to express our love of God and all his children through service. Organizations need to have experience with us to know our intentions, but we are confident in our approach. However, the example of Jesus Christ teaches that the impact comes one by one. And I will share some of these stories.

Every time I speak somewhere or pick up the phone in my office, there is somebody asking, "How can I help? I want to help!" And as we expand our understanding of how to help, we understand the truth of this statement: there is no significant change without a significant relationship. And you cannot have a significant relationship with somebody if you are there for just a week. Our service does not have the same impact when we work in places that are far away and we are there for only a certain amount of time. We are the most powerful where we live, like the Haitian members. They speak the language; they know everybody. They understand what is culturally appropriate.

Let me give a second example. We are a church of refugees. When I meet with officials in various countries and talk about some of the issues they face, I sometimes bring this up. We have a heart for refugees because we were refugees ourselves. When the pioneers came to Utah, they came to a place that other white settlers did not want. There was no USAID fund, and there was no Church humanitarian fund to assist them. Those early members of the Church had to create a new civilization out of nothing by counseling with each other, by negotiating with people who were already on the land, by using the spirit of revelation, and by working. And they did. We are their children. We are the products of their efforts. You know the stories of the pioneers who came across the plains, and now you see the Conference Center filled up with their descendants. I was just in the Conference Center for the general women's meeting—attended by twenty-one thousand women. What must that feel like for our forefathers and our foremothers when they look through the veil at us?

Joseph Booth was a mission president in the Middle East in the early 1900s. Persecution was driving Armenian Christians out of Turkey's borders, and they came down to Syria where President Booth was living. The Armenian Relief Society presidency—refugees themselves—opened up a soup kitchen to feed incoming refugees. President Booth bought a bolt of fabric, and the women made clothing for people as refugees crossed the border. That is what members of the Relief Society do anywhere you put them on the earth. They may be refugees themselves, but they are going to reach out to other people. This is our heritage.

Now I am well acquainted with the current Relief Society president in Beirut, Lebanon, and with her little granddaughter Grace. They have a heritage from those Armenian refugees. One hundred years later, they are still reaching out in service projects to the Armenian community in Lebanon. Grace will be part of the next generation to carry it on. That is the legacy of those Armenian women who came. They serve wherever they happen to be.

There is a refugee camp in Jordan specifically for Syrians with children under four months of age. Everybody in there has a little, tiny baby. And guess what they need? They need diapers and formula. They need all the things little babies need. LDS Charities helped the refugee camp with gravel, infant formula, and diapers, but they needed a large quantity of hygiene supplies.

This is an example of how global reach and individual impact combine. We are not going to have Relief Societies in Utah make hygiene kits, and we are not going to put them in a truck to the coast and then ship them across the ocean, clear them from customs, haul them up to the remote camp, and pass them out. Instead, we contacted the two Arab-speaking branches of the Church in Jordan and asked the Arab branch president to negotiate the price to buy the supplies locally. He knows the vendors well. He has grown up in that market. After he bought the supplies, we invited our Greek Orthodox friends and our friends from the University of Jordan to come to our courtyard, and the three congregations assembled ten thousand hygiene kits. It took six days. They worked ten hours a day in five-hour shifts. They built boxes and put soap and toothbrushes into bags. Imagine what it is like to stand next to someone from the Greek Orthodox parish or next to a good Muslim friend who is a student at the university. These are individuals who have never interacted with each other previously, but for five hours (they have got to have something to talk about) they chat. What happened in that yard was just as important as the hygiene kits that went to the camps.

I read in the *Deseret News* about a Thai refugee who had just been resettled to Utah from a camp where he lived for his entire life. He was born in the camp, and his children are now with him as he was resettled in Salt Lake City. How many refugees have been resettled in Utah? Almost thirty-six thousand. Salt Lake City is one of the refugee-resettlement areas for the United States. When people think about doing something to help refugees, they often think about going to Burkina Faso or Syria. We have refugees in our own neighborhoods. We do not have to go far away to help them. They are excited to be in their new home in Salt Lake City, but what are they going to need? They are going to need friends more than anything else. The greatest predictors for whether people will successfully integrate into a new country are whether they learn the host language and have sincere friends.

Institutionally, LDS Charities has a partnership with the resettlement agencies in Utah. We assist each refugee family with beds and mattresses from Deseret Manufacturing and with bedding and quilts from the humanitarian center. The furniture and beds and mattresses are made as part of a workshop training program for whom? Refugees. We have a partnership so they learn work skills in a nonthreatening environment as they

We are all poor, and we are all needy. We need each other to move along. (Refugee camp in France. Courtesy of Intellectual Reserve, Inc.)

go through the workshop. They make those items, and then we turn that donation back to the refugee community.

We also operate a program that enables one hundred refugees at a time to learn work skills and English at the humanitarian center. They get paid to sort clothes, make mattresses, and develop warehousing skills. The other four hours a day they spend learning English. They get paid their salary to sit and learn in a classroom, because that is one of the biggest predictors of whether they are going to succeed in the community or not.

On a personal basis, what might people do to help? Volunteers for these refugee programs are always needed. The three agencies and the humanitarian center all need volunteers who will mentor, teach skills, or sit down with individuals and just talk—have conversations or go over their vocabulary word list. In about every school, there are going to be children who are refugees. They need people to reach out to them and be a friend. I do not know how many refugees are here on BYU's campus, but I promise you there are some. We could learn much by interacting with each other.

Let me share a final example that I hope might braid together the three strands we have been talking about—the power of our heritage, the scope of the institutional Church's efforts, and the impact of personal ministry—under a single theme of trees. First is the power of our heritage: Mary Ann Angell Young was Brigham Young's second wife. His first wife died, leaving two children. Brigham and Mary Ann married in Kirtland and had additional children. We ought to know more about Mary Ann. Everybody got along with her—every other wife, every neighbor, everyone loved her. She was a healer, an herbologist, and she loved trees.

When Brigham Young came to the valley, he got the temple under construction and the crops in the ground. He then turned around in August and went back to Winter Quarters and came back to Utah with a group in the spring. Mary Ann was in that group. What do you think she brought with her? Bare roots of trees. She was going to plant trees here. People said, "Do not plant fruit trees—it is too salty." Some Saints thought they would be better off in California. Brigham Young said, "Plant your fruit trees." Mary Ann planted her trees. Do you know where? South Temple used to be called Brigham Street, and it was the main road that ran through the Young farm. She planted the trees along Brigham Street, and some of those trees still exist. If you drive up South Temple, you will see the trees in the fall, with big leaves like dinner plates coming down. That was one of her legacies. It is not just a legacy of the trees; it is her legacy of faith. She is a woman that you could not hold down.

There is an *Ensign* article about her called "Indomitable Mary Ann." She was riding in a wagon, holding her twins, when it hit a big bump and one of the twins fell out of her arms and was run over by the wagon. The wagon master said, "Oh, it is so sad. That poor baby is going to die." She told him, "Do not prophesy ill of my little baby." She picked that baby up, molded his head back into shape, and nursed him back to health.[10] She was just that kind of woman. When she planted trees in this desert, it was a statement—not of a love of trees, but of faith.

Second is the broad scope of the institutional Church. Haiti has severe deforestation. If you look at a photograph from a satellite, you can see clearly the marked border between Haiti and the Dominican Republic. All of the trees have been cut down. Haiti did not do that just out of ignorance.

When they got their independence from France, they had to pay for that independence with resources. So they cut down those hardwood trees, and they shipped them to France. When a hurricane comes, there is nothing to hold down the soil. Haiti suffers a lot more than the Dominican Republic because of deforestation.

A Church leader living in the Dominican Republic sat next to an official from Haiti on a plane. He asked the official, "What is your dream for Haiti? What do you think ought to happen?" The man said, "We need trees. We need trees not only for holding the soil but for what it does for us as a people." The Area Presidency submitted a project, and LDS Charities cooperated with other agencies in Haiti to plant four hundred thousand trees: shade trees and fruit trees. It occurred in stages, starting in April 2013. Members of the Church from all the branches around Port-au-Prince went to their neighbors and said, "If you want a tree, dig a hole." They purchased trees from local nurseries with humanitarian funds and planted them on successive Saturdays, with whole communities working together for this cause. Now, might someone cut down the new trees and burn them for charcoal? Of course, but hopefully, as the residents of Haitian neighborhoods do the work themselves, Haitians feel pride and ownership in their communities.

Finally, the third strand is about the impact of personal ministry. I had a superb Mia Maid teacher when I was fourteen. She encouraged a very shy young girl by giving me responsibilities and praise. I thought she was the best. I would go anywhere on the earth because of her. She made all of us feel we were the most important part of any activity. When she suddenly died, we all felt such grief, even though we were now adults. We thought, "What do we do as a ward to remember her and how she made us feel?" Plant a tree. We planted a tree in her honor at the chapel. As it grows and spreads out, I still think of it because of her legacy of faith and how she changed my faith. Alma 32 looks like Shirley Cutler in my mind.

There are things from our heritage that teach us the kinds of people we are. There are things the institutional Church does that augment that legacy. But the things we do in our personal lives connect us in very real relationships to each other and change us forever.

My plea today is for each of us to find those opportunities where we can make a difference with our personal ministry. Work where you have the power, where you have the connections, the relationships, and the language. You have a spark that comes out of you and makes a difference in the world. The Lord works with people one-on-one. Although his Church is doing institutional things, and we can all participate to some degree, our greatest impact is what we do for each other one-on-one.

I will conclude by saying we are all poor, and we are all needy. An individual does not belong to some special category because he or she lacks money or education. We are all somewhere along that spectrum I described in the beginning, and we need each other to move along it.

As Bishop Caussé says, "The *how* has to be local." The time for exporting resources and programs is drawing to a close. The Church is mature enough all over the world that we can take what happened in Utah with the pioneers and create that same kind of feeling in other locations by using the local resources to build up the local communities.

Bishop Caussé mentioned that when he was a stake president in France he thought, "When will we get Welfare Square all over the world? Let's just populate the world with that kind of a square." Is he advocating that now? No. Now we have got to have pigs and Bishop Estrada in the Philippines, we have to have Haitians planting trees in their neighbors' yards, and have Jordanians putting toothpaste into bags for the refugee families next door. We have to have Shirley Cutler building up the social skills of shy fourteen-year-old girls. That is what is going to make the difference. It will not be something we export out of Utah. It will be something that comes up out of the councils, out of the hearts of the members, and out of revelation. That is how we are drastically different from other organizations. When the Lord said the earth is full, and there is enough to spare,[12] it does not mean it all exists in one place and we are going to parcel it out. It means the members of the Church and their communities and their interfaith friends, wherever they live, have the power inside them to find the right answers. It takes experience and relationships to bring out the solutions, and they *will* come out.

After trying many things, the best success has proven to be creating experiences where people feel the love and the individual value that God, their Father, has for them. Cooperation, unity, and fellowship are manifest in the Christian and Abrahamic tradition of loving God. People come together and sacrifice their time to do something they will not be paid to do, but they want to learn because it will save a baby's life or help a young paralyzed woman go to school. It looks like Bishop Wester, the Catholic bishop at the Cathedral of the Madeleine in Salt Lake, standing next to a Catholic priest from Jordan, an LDS bishop next to him, demonstrating the fellowship and unity of helping each other's projects work out.

This is how we live the gospel without words. You do not need discussion for it. You do need a heart that is filled with the love of God and with the Holy Ghost. The choir sang in general conference yesterday "Guide Us, O Thou Great Jehovah," and I just looked up the words because they struck me forcefully. The second verse says, "Open, Jesus, Zion's fountains; Let her richest blessings come. Let the fiery, cloudy pillar guard us to this holy home. Great Redeemer, Great Redeemer, Bring, oh bring the welcome day."[13] I like that, because when Moses struck the rock and brought forth water in the desert,[14] there was no way anyone thought a fountain was there. And yet there was. To me, that is the great symbol of what the Lord will do in his own way to care for the poor and the needy. All of us are in the desert where everything is scarce, where no one thinks there is any water. The Lord takes his people and strikes the rock, and a fountain comes up. And Zion is born.

We have the great opportunity and privilege to be part of this time, this restoration, and this dispensation. It is my great privilege to be a member of a church that takes on as its mission caring for the poor and the needy all over the world. I give you my commitment to use the funding in the best ways we know how. I also give you my thanks for the great work that is being done in institutions such as the LDS International Society, Brigham Young University, and others. The innovation for the future lies in ways we can all better support and cooperate with each other.

NOTES

1. Jeffrey R. Holland, LDS Charities Humanitarian Center video, 2014.
2. See Moses 7:18.
3. 1 Corinthians 12:31.

4. Ether 12:11.
5. Alma 1:30.
6. Joseph Smith, *Times and Seasons*, 15 March 1842, 3:732.
7. Gordon B. Hinckley (speaking to the National Press Club, 8 March 2000).
8. Thomas S. Monson, "Serve the Lord with Love," *Ensign*, February 2014, 4.
9. Nicholas Kristof, "Is Delhi So Different from Steubenville?," *New York Times*, 8 March 2014.
10. Kristof, "Is Delhi So Different from Steubenville?"
11. Rex G. Jensen, "Indomitable Mary Ann," *Ensign*, July 1993, 40–43.
12. See Doctrine and Covenants 104:17.
13. "Guide Us, O Thou Great Jehovah," *Hymns*, no. 83.
14. See Numbers 2:7–11.

Part 2

PUBLIC PERCEPTIONS AND RELATIONS

For the Church to be "recognized"—to be fully established—the members need to be free to meet, real estate for meetinghouses and temples must be obtained, missionaries must be permitted to enter the country and to proclaim the gospel message, . . . and so forth. The Church office building in Salt Lake City, Utah. (Courtesy of Intellectual Reserve, Inc.)

5

THE CHURCH IN THE TWENTY-FIRST CENTURY

Public Perceptions and the "Man with the Stamp"

ELDER LANCE B. WICKMAN

Elder Lance B. Wickman, then a member of the First Quorum of the Seventy of The Church of Jesus Christ of Latter-day Saints, presented this essay at "Meet the Mormons: Public Perception and the Global Church," at the International Society's nineteenth annual conference, April 2008, Brigham Young University, Provo, Utah.

The story is told of the man who survived the Johnstown (Pennsylvania) Flood of 1889, which led to the death of more than twenty-two hundred people. All the remainder of his days, he never missed an opportunity to recount his experience. Eventually, he passed on. Upon his arrival at the pearly gates, Saint Peter asked him whether he had any special requests; the man responded that he did. "I would like to tell everyone about my experience in surviving the Johnstown flood," he said. "Well," said Peter, "that's a little unusual, but I think it can be arranged." After a few days, Saint Peter approached the man and said, "We have everyone assembled now to hear your account of surviving the Johnstown flood, but there is one thing that you should know." "What's that?" said the man. "Well," said Peter, "Noah is in the audience!"

I feel a little like the man who survived the Johnstown Flood as I look into the faces of this audience. I recognize numbers of you whose vocations or avocations have been in international affairs. Some of you have served in the diplomatic service. Others have worked or studied abroad as businesspeople, teachers, or students. Many of you have served in the Church in other lands. I have not done any of those things; so in one sense, those of you who have done these things seem much like "Noah" from my vantage point. However, I do have a perspective to offer in my capacity as Church general counsel and as one who has the opportunity to observe the First Presidency and their associates at close range as they address international issues confronting the Church. Perhaps from that vantage point, if from no other, I have some observations that may be of interest to you.

The topic for this year's conference of the International Society is "Meet the Mormons: Public Perception and the Global Church." In an effort to say something relevant to that topic, I have titled these remarks "The Church in the Twenty-First Century: Public Perceptions and the 'Man with the Stamp.'"

We are a Church that believes in law. Two of the Articles of Faith give expression to our belief. Doctrine and Covenants section 134 is a more expansive declaration of our belief in law and the obligations that a church and civil government owe to one another.[1] This is necessarily so because the establishment of the kingdom of God on the earth has much to do with the law of human kind.

TWO CHURCHES

Doctrine and Covenants section 1 is a dramatic pronouncement, dating from the earliest days of the Church, of the worldwide character of the gospel message. Among other things, it states, "That the fulness of [the] gospel might be proclaimed by the weak and the simple unto the ends of the world, and before kings and rulers."[2] Doctrine and Covenants section 44 is even more specific in stating the close connection that necessarily exists between secular law and the establishment of the Church: "And many shall be converted, insomuch that ye shall obtain power to organize yourselves according to the laws of man; That your enemies may not have power over you; that you may be preserved in all things; that you may be enabled to keep my laws; that every bond may be broken wherewith the enemy seeketh to destroy my people."[3] In other words, the Lord promises that the elders of the Church would be given power to organize the Church "according to the laws of man" so that the Lord's people would be able to live His laws. Coupled with the mandate to carry the gospel to every quarter of the earth, it is quite obvious that the Lord has contemplated since the beginning of this dispensation that the Church would need to establish itself legally in every nation, legal system, and jurisdiction.

Some fifteen years ago, Dr. Samuel P. Huntington of Harvard University opined that there was a coming "clash of civilizations" between the East and West.[4] Some, at the time, downplayed his statement or severely criticized it. However, 9/11 and events subsequent to it have validated the fact that there is indeed a "clash of civilizations" that is occurring, particularly between the Western industrialized nations and the less-economically advantaged peoples girding portions of the midsection of the planet in various countries, historically referred to as "the East."

Whatever merits Dr. Huntington's statement may have as it pertains to the nations, the phrase "clash of civilizations" has a profound meaning as it relates to the challenges confronting the kingdom of God as it seeks to establish itself. In the Book of Mormon, in response to his prayerful request to see the vision his father had seen, Nephi was actually permitted to see even more. As he gazed in vision down through the stream of time, he saw that in our day there would be two fundamental organizations, or sources of power. These he referred to as "churches."[5] The first, and the significantly smaller of the two, was the "Church of the Lamb," or the kingdom of God. The other he referred to as the "great and abominable church," referring to the influence of the world. These two would be in opposition to one another and would remain so until the Second Coming and the advent of the Millennium.[6]

There are many applications to be seen around us of this metaphor of the two churches. At one level, each of us experiences this "clash" in our individual lives and the lives of those closest to us. But at another level, a geopolitical level, we can see it manifest in the Church's efforts to establish itself among the nations. It is against this backdrop of the clash between the gospel "civilization" and the materialistic or worldly "civilization" that the dynamics of the Church's efforts to "organize [itself] according to the laws of man" occur.

LEGAL RECOGNITION AND THE MAN WITH THE STAMP

We use a more convenient phrase than "organize according to the laws of man" in our everyday parlance. We speak of obtaining "legal recognition" for the Church. Those of us who have grown up in the United States, or in one of a handful of other countries with a strong civil-liberties tradition, tend to take for granted the so-called rule of law. We believe in such concepts as "blind justice" and that "no individual is above the law." We may take for granted that everyone else in the world accepts those same concepts. While I believe it is true that good people everywhere, regardless of culture or legal system, naturally believe in the notion of fundamental fairness, it also must be said that not every legal system treats these basic ideals of American justice with the same honor and dignity. Indeed, in many parts of the world, despite what law may be written on the books, the "real law" or source of authority resides with the official whose duty it is to enforce it. Stated differently, the law is not so much what is written as it is what some official declares it to be. Thus, we have what could be referred to as the "rule of man" rather than the rule of law.

This is what I am referring to in using that phrase, "the man with the stamp." In many places, in order for the Church to establish itself, to obtain legal recognition, the Church must gain the approval of the public official who is the de facto voice of the law—the man with the stamp. But what is meant by that term "legal recognition"?

As a practical matter, being legally recognized in a country is not an either-or proposition; rather, *it is a spectrum of shadings*. Think of it in terms of the various functions and activities of the Church. For the Church to be "recognized"—to be fully established—the members need to be free to meet, real estate for meetinghouses and temples must be obtained, missionaries must be permitted to enter the country and to proclaim the gospel message, we must be free to print and distribute our literature, we must be free to open and maintain bank accounts, members must be free to pay their tithing, and so forth. To the extent that any of these is legally unavailable, the Church is not established. To that extent it is not "recognized." To that extent, in a very real sense, we don't have a Church. To restate the matter in a more positive way, to the extent that those various functions and manifestations of Church activity are available in a particular nation, we can say that the Church is, to that extent, legally recognized.

There's really an evolution in status leading to full legal recognition. Almost always, the first phase of recognition is *registration*. By that I mean that a legal entity constituting "the Church" in the eyes of the government has been organized and registered as required by law. In most cases, this is by far the easiest phase. Registration usually involves retaining a lawyer and then completing and filing the necessary forms. Though simple, it is also essential. We tend to think of "the Church" as this ecclesiastical association led by prophets and apostles and stake presidents and bishops. But virtually all governments look to the legal entity, the "secular church" organized under their laws, as the identifiable church. Respecting the secular Church while serving in the ecclesiastical Church is a principle that Church leaders and members in a country must always remember.

The next phase of legal recognition might be referred to as *credibility*. What do I mean by that? For one thing, I mean that the Church always must be defined on the right side of what could be called the "cult line." Concerning terrorism, much of it in the name of religion, many nations are classifying religious organizations. As a minimum, we must seek to befriend the rule makers and to persuade them that the Church is a responsible and pacific organization. Government officials must see that Church teachings are conducive to public order. Credibility is the gateway through which the Church must pass in order to preach the gospel with vigor in any nation. Without credibility, we can go nowhere.

The ultimate phase of legal recognition I refer to as *respectability*. This is shorthand for a broad array of factors measuring the extent to which the Church's bona fides have been recognized by the institutions and representatives of government. The extent of the Church's respectability in the eyes of government is usually manifest in the extent of the legal approvals it has received, such as the number of missionary visas authorized; the ease in obtaining visas; and the facility with which meetinghouse properties, including temple sites, are purchased and qualified for construction. Ultimately, the degree of the influence—or more to the point, the lack thereof—that a dominant religious faith in the particular country has on impeding Church growth or operations is a key bellwether of respectability.

The less there is of such adverse influence, the greater is the evidence of the respectability enjoyed by the Church.

Each of these phases, especially credibility and respectability, depend on the quality of our relationships with the "man with the stamp." Developing these friendships is not simply a matter for lawyers representing the Church. To the contrary, developing cordial relationships with government representatives is a "team sport" for the Church. It begins with the President of the Church himself, who, as President Hinckley so exemplified, is his own "Secretary of State." As the President of the Church, his counselors, and members of the Quorum of Twelve Apostles travel across the earth, they frequently meet with senior government officials, often the presidents of nations. Area presidencies and senior temporal-affairs staff members also play an important role in developing and nurturing cordial government relationships. And, of course, public affairs directors and area legal counsel perhaps are the most continually engaged in developing positive government relations with public officials.

Even Latter-day Saints traveling internationally in their private capacity play an important role. Some of these deserve to be singled out. I realize that in doing so I risk leaving out mention of others who have made important contributions to the legal recognition of the Church. To any such here present, I apologize in advance.

No address concerning the nurturing of a positive, public perception of the Church with government officials would be complete without making reference to our beloved friend, Professor Cole Durham. Perhaps more than any other "private citizen" of the Church, Cole has had a profound influence in advancing the principles of credibility and respectability for the Church and in helping to develop political institutions in a host of countries that are friendly and welcoming to new faiths. His annual symposium on international law and religion, held here at BYU each October, culminating in a luncheon at Church headquarters for the attendees, is certainly one of the most important diplomatic outreach efforts made by the Church or its representatives each year.

Also worthy of special mention is Judge J. Clifford Wallace, a senior judge on the US Ninth Circuit Court of Appeals. Cliff Wallace has traveled widely across the earth, mingling with jurists and ministers of justice in many lands. Cliff sees many opportunities to mention his Mormon faith, and like Cole, he has been instrumental in helping the Church develop friendships with men and women of consequence in various nations.

All of these—General Authorities, other Church representatives, and Latter-day Saint private citizens—combine their respective efforts in cultivating a positive, public image of the Church with government officials and other opinion leaders that play a critical role in helping the Church to optimize its legal recognition in many countries.

CHALLENGES

I return now, however, to the circumstance in which the Church is compelled to function in this telestial sphere. I refer again to the ongoing "clash" between the two "civilizations" of the Church and the world at large. We face a number of challenges that sometimes hamper the development of strong relationships with government officials. What follows is a brief catalog of just some of the more significant categories of such challenges.

The "Cult Line"

As mentioned, many governments are concerned about the potentially subversive influence of some religious movements. Accordingly, they attempt to identify and then classify those they deem to be "cults." Once a faith group is classified as a cult, its prospects of obtaining credibility, much less respectability, are nil. This is a phenomenon that is particularly prevalent in Western Europe. There are probably a number of factors, both historical and political, that explain the prevalence of this challenge in Western Europe. The increasing size and influence of Muslim populations among the native peoples of Western Europe is likely among them.

Opposition from Dominant Religious Traditions

This phenomenon is certainly not new. It existed anciently, to a profound degree, during the mortal life and public ministry of the Lord Jesus Christ and continued in opposition to the Church he established. It has been an influence since the earliest days of the Restoration. In the modern world, however, it is not necessarily focused against our Church alone. In countries as widely separated as Latin America, Asia, and Russia, dominant faith traditions have reacted reflexively to the perceived invasion of other faith groups, including our church. Often, these traditionally dominant sects have considerable influence in the corridors of government and can pose difficulties.

Communist or Former Communist Nations

Communism and faith traditions have never existed comfortably side by side. Indeed, in the Soviet Union and Communist China, some faiths survived only by significantly diluting their religious practices and dramatically lowering their public profile. While, thankfully, the world has moved on from the hostility of the Cold War days, there are still vestiges of this antipathy.

Other Leftist Governments

Particularly in Latin America, the fairly recent emergence of some leftist governments has created relationship difficulties for the Church. Sometimes these relationship difficulties stem from a misperception on the part of government officials that the Church is an "American" institution and that somehow our missionaries and other representatives are "double agents," representatives of the US government as well as the Church.

Government Religious Regulatory Schemes

Sometimes the challenge comes in the form of awkward government regulations that are difficult for the Church to comply with. For example, in Spain some years ago, the government adopted laws requiring the Religious Affairs Office of the Ministry of Justice to enter into concordats—"treaties"—with broad classes of religious traditions. Accordingly, the government entered into concordats with the Roman Catholic Church, Judaism, Islam, and the Protestant sects. Obviously, none of these categories apply to the Church. Initially, the government urged the Church to simply affiliate with the Protestants to take advantage of their concordat. But that was not a good fit from our standpoint, and the Protestants didn't want us anyway! Finally, the government concluded that the Church was entitled to *notario arraigo* status, meaning that the government had determined that the Church was "well established" and thus entitled to its own concordat. Negotiations for such an agreement were progressing well when the infamous Madrid train bombings occurred in March 2004, which resulted in a Socialist government elected to power in Spain. This new government, although friendly, decided to revisit all of the concordats, and our efforts to obtain a concordat of our own have been stymied.

SUCCESSES

Fortunately, however, notwithstanding the challenges, we continue to make progress. Time allows us to refer to only four experiences. Even in these cases, when measured against the registration/credibility/respectability scale, the extent of legal recognition enjoyed by the Church in these respective countries is in its infancy. In three of the four, as will be apparent, the "credibility" phase of legal recognition has necessarily preceded the registration phase; and in two of the four, registration is still not complete. But each case represents significant progress in what would otherwise be seen as potentially adverse circumstances. Each of these may be seen as resulting from the development over time of a positive perception among government officials through the efforts of many Church representatives.

Slovakia

I begin with Slovakia. Most here will remember the *Church News* article in fall 2006 announcing the miraculous petition drive over the course of less than a week wherein some sixty missionaries from the Czech Prague Mission collected more than thirty thousand signatures of Slovakian citizens willing to endorse the registration application for the Church to establish itself in Slovakia. Only twenty thousand signatures were necessary to satisfy the registration requirement. A short time later, Elder David A. Bednar of the Quorum of the Twelve was on hand to actually receive the certificate of registration on behalf of the Church. These circumstances were indeed miraculous; but I like to think of them as the "second miracle" associated with the Slovakian registration.

The "first miracle"—and in some respects the more significant miracle—had its roots years earlier in some friendships made by none other than Cole Durham. In 1990–91, in the course of his seemingly numberless trips to Eastern Europe, Cole had met two Czechoslovakian officials. He invited them to his symposium, which in those days was a small, informal "bag lunch" affair. Cole introduced them to Elders Dallin H. Oaks and Dennis B. Neuenschwander. These officials introduced Cole to some of their associates. And one of these introduced Cole to Dr. Jan Juran, who in due course became the director of Church Affairs in the Ministry of Culture in Slovakia. The relationship with Dr. Juran was materially enhanced by Elizabeth Sewell, a BYU law student and later assistant to Cole, who speaks fluent Czech and had significant opportunities as a legal extern to discuss the Church and its registration problem with Dr. Juran. He then attended the symposium, visited Church headquarters, and was favorably impressed by what he saw.

Now comes the miracle: The Church has had a small presence of a few hundred members in Slovakia. The Slovakian Parliament had enacted a statute providing the path to legal registration for religious associations. In part, it provides that churches seeking registration must submit "a registration proposal . . . presenting proof that the number of its adult *followers* having their permanent residence in the territory of the Slovak Republic is at least twenty thousand persons" (emphasis added). But what was meant by that word "followers"? Did it mean "adherents" or "members," or did it simply mean "endorsers" or "supporters"?

The interpretive decision was within the jurisdiction of Dr. Juran. And he decided that the more liberal interpretation of mere endorsement or acknowledgment by any Slovakian citizens would satisfy the registration requirement. This set the stage for the collection of signatures by the missionaries. That they garnered more than 150 percent of what was required over the course of just a few days was, indeed, miraculous. But the quieter, even more fundamental, miracle had occurred in the nurturing of a genuine friendship with a good man, who became the "man with the stamp."

China

Next, I turn to China. The history of the Church in the People's Republic of China has yet to be written; it is very much in its infancy. That we have come as far as we have there is a tribute to the positive contributions of many Latter-day Saints, whose goodness, decency, and integrity have, over a significant period of time, persuaded Chinese officials that the Church may be trusted to keep its word and to honor, obey, and sustain the law.[7] I know that numbers of you here present have been among those who have made a contribution. It is impossible to give adequate "screen credits" to all, but I will list just a few: BYU folk dancers and English teachers; the Polynesian Cultural Center in Laie, Hawaii; Apostles Neal A. Maxwell, Russell M. Nelson, and Dallin H. Oaks; Elder Donald L. Staheli, the former CEO of Continental Grain Company; Area Seventy Chu-Jen Chia; expatriate "China hands"; and numerous Chinese citizens who have found and embraced the gospel of Jesus Christ while studying abroad and then returned home. The positive influence of these prompted a delegation of the PRC's State Administration of Religious Affairs (or SARA) several years ago to visit Church headquarters and Latter-day Saint congregations in various parts of the United States. The net effect of all this has been the development of a positive perception of the Church in key circles of the government. China is very much a country where credibility must precede registration.

And we are not yet registered, but we do have tacit government approval to conduct limited Church operations. Expatriate branches have held services and activities in the PRC for years with the approval of the government. However, it has been more difficult to obtain permission for Chinese nationals who are Church members to meet. But within the past few years a number of branches of native Chinese have been established. These "native" branches must remain separate in all respects from the expat branches. There can be no joint activities or meetings, no commingling of funds, etc. There is no proselyting. Only relatives of native members can be baptized in China. But we are meeting! And the Church is growing! Indeed, it is possible that when the history of the Church in China is eventually written, it will be shown that it grew from the inside out!

"Andalasia"

I turn now to a country that, due to the sensitivity of the situation, I shall not identify by name. I shall simply refer to it as "Andalasia"—a name that some here may recognize from the recent Disney film *Enchanted*. The Church is legally registered in Andalasia. We have numbers of congregations. Our members enjoy relative freedom to conduct meetings and activities. Within limits, proselyting is permitted, and we do have full-time missionaries, including foreign missionaries, serving there.

The problem in Andalasia has been in obtaining sufficient visas for foreign missionaries. The government previously has permitted only a small handful, which has significantly hampered efforts to grow the Church there. Then, a newly appointed ambassador to the United States from that country happened to visit Salt Lake City. It was just one of numerous visits the ambassador was making to various cities and regions in the United States on behalf of his government. While in Salt Lake, he met with the First Presidency and with a member of the Quorum of the Twelve. When he returned to Washington, DC, he became acquainted with Elder Ralph Hardy (an Area Seventy), the chairman of the Church Public Affairs Advisory Council there, and an LDS senator. He was very impressed by those whom he met and what he observed about the Church.

So, when he was advised of the difficulty the Church was having in obtaining missionary visas, he offered to personally issue whatever visas we needed. And that is what he has done and is doing. Now, that said, we at Church headquarters have tried to be modest in what we request so as not to take advantage of the generosity of this good man. But I can tell you that the number of visas for our missionaries has substantially increased as a result.

Vietnam

Finally, I come to a country that has deep personal significance to me. I speak of Vietnam. In past general conference remarks, I have made reference to my return to Vietnam after an absence of some forty years.[8] With my wife, Pat, I revisited the top floor of the Caravelle Hotel, among other places, in Saigon. It was there, on 31 October 1966, that then-Elder Gordon B. Hinckley of the Quorum of the Twelve dedicated Vietnam to the preaching of the gospel. I was present on that occasion. The circumstances of my being in attendance at that meeting were themselves extraordinary. I was an infantry officer. Our battalion was in the jungles and rice paddies in combat operations. Somehow I had learned of this upcoming meeting. There were three of us in our battalion who were Church members, and I was the senior in rank. So I went to the battalion commander and asked if we could be excused from combat operations for twenty-four hours to attend that meeting. I was actually surprised when he gave his consent.

We arrived as the meeting was about to begin. It was a wonderful meeting! There were about two hundred present, mostly servicemen, Army nurses, and Red Cross workers. But there were a few Vietnamese members present. Elder Hinckley was the final speaker. He gave a marvelous address. When he finished, he told us that before he left Salt Lake City he had visited with President David O. McKay. President McKay authorized him to dedicate that country to the preaching of the gospel if he felt so inclined. "I feel so inclined," he said. While we in our khaki and olive drab uniforms bowed our heads, this servant of the Lord offered a profoundly beautiful prayer of dedication. It was a Pentecostal experience! The Spirit of the Lord filled the room. It was truly one of the great spiritual experiences of my life.

In the intervening years, as I have visited in small congregations of Vietnamese members in the United States, I have remembered that prayer and looked forward to the fulfillment of the promises in it. And we are beginning to see them!

Some Vietnamese members have returned to Vietnam. General Authorities and Church legal counsel have visited the country. With the aid of counsel retained in Ho Chi Minh City, some members baptized decades ago have been found. As the country has opened to commerce, Latter-day Saint expatriates have come there to live. Small gatherings of Church members have begun to meet. Contact has been established with key government officials affiliated with the state Committee on Religious Affairs. Some of these government officials have accepted the invitation to attend the annual International Law and Religion Symposium at the J. Reuben Clark Law School and have attended a session of general conference. Some have sat at lunch with President Gordon B. Hinckley.

The result? The Church is now registered to hold meetings at specific locations in Ho Chi Minh City and Hanoi. There are about one thousand members in Vietnam, most of them Vietnamese, and the larger portion of them in Ho Chi Minh City. Although we do not have missionaries serving there yet and do no active proselyting, we are permitted to teach and baptize investigators who come to our approved meeting locations. And the Church is growing in Vietnam! We have missionaries from Vietnam serving in other countries, including the United States.

Our current effort is to obtain national registration. And our members are not yet allowed to pay tithing, so government approval is needed for that vital activity. But my point today is that the government officials with whom we are dealing are friendly to us as a result of the efforts of Church members and officers—Vietnamese as well as from elsewhere. Vietnam is another country where our credibility is leading the way to registration instead of the more traditional pattern of achieving registration first. It is just a matter of time until registration is accomplished. Then, I believe respectability will clearly be on the horizon, and the Church will be on its way toward full legal recognition.

I do not suggest that all this will happen tomorrow, or even next year. Patience is a virtue that is absolutely essential in every country as we move through the phases of registration, credibility, and respectability toward the ultimate goal of legal recognition. Particularly among the lands and nations of Asia is this the case. Kipling's famous line about the folly of trying to "hustle the East" certainly comes to mind.[9] But echoing in our ears are the Lord's own words in that very first section of the Doctrine and Covenants, "That the fulness of [the] gospel [will] be proclaimed . . . unto the ends of the world, and before kings and rulers."[10] And warming my heart are the recollections of an October day forty-two years ago when an Apostle of the Lord prophesied as much with respect to the land and the peoples of Vietnam.

THE NIGHT THE LIGHTS WENT OUT

There are literally countless evidences that the Lord's hand is in this matter of obtaining legal recognition for the Church in every country. We need only turn around and see where we have come from to see this illustrated. The Church now has an active presence in more than 165 countries and a presence of some kind in more than 180 countries. Simple arithmetic reveals that there really are not that many nations remaining where we do not have at least some presence. And, as I have attempted to briefly outline today, the process is a dynamic one.

But for evidences that the Lord's hand is in this work—that He is very much involved in helping to develop a positive perception in the mind of the "man with the stamp"—we need not rely only on numbers. A myriad of anecdotes and personal experiences likewise so testify. One in particular comes in mind.

A few years ago, the Washington Public Affairs Advisory Council had arranged a meet-and-greet event at the home of Senator Gordon and Sister Sharon Smith for key members of the diplomatic corps based in Washington—ambassadors from a number of countries, especially countries where we had been seeking to improve the quality of our legal recognition. All of our Latter-day Saint members of the US Senate, several LDS congressmen, and other government officials had been invited with their spouses. Sister Ann Santini of the Washington, DC, public affairs office and several other members of her staff had planned this event in great detail. I was assigned by the chairman of the Public Affairs Committee at Church headquarters to be the General Authority representative at this event.

I arrived at the Smiths' home in suburban Washington, DC. It is beautiful, and it was manicured to a gnat's eyebrow. A tent had been erected in the yard to host our guests, since it was September and warm in Washington. All was in readiness as the guests began to arrive.

But then seeming disaster struck! The sky clouded over with thunderclouds. The rain began to pour in buckets. Lightning flashed. Thunder rolled. Clearly the event could not be held outside. Even the tent was risky, since it was held up by metal poles, and the static electricity in the air was thick. Sister Santini, with her cadre of veteran Relief Society members, moved the entire thing indoors.

Then, real disaster struck! A bolt of lightning struck an electrical transformer a few blocks away, and the lights went out! In that moment, it seemed like this beautifully planned event was about to become a debacle of the first order!

And that is when Divine Providence entered in. Sister Santini, Sister Smith, and their associates swung into full Relief Society mode. Candles came out, platters of food were rearranged, and the event proceeded.

Now, it is important to understand that for ambassadors based in Washington, each of their evenings is normally consumed with more than one social event. The usual practice is to visit one, stay for a few moments, and then move on to the next. Doubtless, that is what many of these diplomats had planned this particular evening. But there was something about the combination of circumstances that September night in the Smiths' home, not the least of which was the improvisation of these Relief Society sisters, that was captivating. Although a few stayed but a short time and then left, the great majority of them—ambassadors from some of the most influential nations on the planet—just stayed. The intimacy of the candlelit circumstances, the warmth of the hospitality, and, I believe, the promptings of the Spirit kept most of them for an hour or even two. The conversations were informal, and family experiences were exchanged. And what would have otherwise been a semiformal diplomatic event became an informal social event among friends.

I have since told Ann that she could not possibly have planned such an outstanding event. Many of those diplomats who attended have since stated that that improvised event at the Smith home remains one of the most delightfully memorable highlights of their life in Washington. I will say again: the Lord's hand is in this work!

THOMAS KANE

Now, finally, some years ago, I wrote an article for the *Ensign* entitled "Thomas L. Kane: Outrider for Zion."[11] It was an article about Colonel Kane, a nonmember and great friend of President Brigham Young and the Latter-day Saints. Colonel Kane, whose influence with President James K. Polk led to the march of the Mormon Battalion, whose lectures and articles in eastern periodicals helped to deflect some of the extreme prejudice that was directed toward the Saints as the mob violence in Illinois intensified, and whose indomitable spirit and negotiating skills played a pivotal role in resolving the so-called Utah War of 1857–58. After Colonel Kane died in 1883, his wife wrote President George Q. Cannon, telling him that the last words spoken by her husband were his wish that his affections be transmitted to, as he put it, his "dear Mormon friends."[12] President Brigham Young had once said of Colonel Thomas L. Kane that his "name would be had in honorable remembrance among the Latter-day Saints to all generations."[13]

There are many Thomas Kanes in today's world. They are good men and women who are fair-minded and decent. Many of these are the "men with the stamps" who need only to be exposed to the goodness and decency of the Latter-day Saints. I believe that when the history of this dispensation is finally written in its entirety, many of their names will likewise be held in honorable remembrance by the Saints in all generations.

NOTES

1. Doctrine and Covenants 134.
2. Doctrine and Covenants 1:23.
3. Doctrine and Covenants 44:4–5; emphasis added.
4. Samuel P. Huntington, "The Clash of Civilizations?," *Foreign Affairs* 72, no. 3 (1993): 22–49.
5. See, for example, 1 Nephi 13:10.
6. 1 Nephi 11–14.
7. See Articles of Faith 1:12.
8. Lance B. Wickman, "Today," *Ensign*, May 2008, 103–7.
9. From Rudyard Kipling, "The Naulahka" (New York: MacMillan, 1892), lines 21–24.

   Now it is not good for the Christian's health to hustle the Aryan brown,
   For the Christian riles, and the Aryan smiles and he weareth the Christian down;
   And the end of the fight is a tombstone white with the name of the late deceased,
   And the epitaph drear: "A Fool lies here who tried to hustle the East."
10. Doctrine and Covenants 1:23; emphasis added.
11. Lance B. Wickman, "Thomas L. Kane: Outrider for Zion," *Ensign*, September 2003, 56–63.
12. As quoted in Albert L. Zobell Jr., *Sentinel in the East* (Salt Lake City: Nicholas G. Morgan, 1965), 228–29.
13. John Smith's Patriarchal Blessings, 1846–49, 211, Church History Library; emphasis added; capitalization and punctuation standardized.

These individuals are self-starters, people who do not wait to be commanded, those who act when they see a problem, and their service comes from pure and authentic motives. (Courtesy of Intellectual Reserve, Inc.)

6

PRIVATE HUMANITARIAN INITIATIVES AND INTERNATIONAL PERCEPTIONS OF THE CHURCH

WARNER P. WOODWORTH

Warner P. Woodworth, then professor of organizational behavior at Brigham Young University, presented this essay at "Meet the Mormons: Public Perception and the Global Church," at the International Society's nineteenth annual conference, April 2008, Brigham Young University, Provo, Utah.

My focus is on private humanitarian initiatives by Latter-day Saints that enhance the international perceptions of the Church as we reach out to others, alleviate human suffering, and fight poverty. Basically, as I see it, there are three ways Latter-day Saints may provide humanitarian service.

First, there are the traditional Church programs for the Saints, such as paying our tithing, making fast offerings, funding LDS welfare efforts for our members, contributing to the Perpetual Education Fund, and so forth. I've always believed that this should be our top priority—those offerings, those tithes that we give to build the kingdom of God on earth.

A second area is outreach and humanitarian assistance provided through other Church programs for our non-Latter-day Saint neighbors. These include the Church's Humanitarian Fund, Latter-day Saint Charities, and the many efforts of the Church to partner with other institutions such as Catholic Relief, governments in times of crises, the tsunami disaster in Indonesia, and other NGOs beyond our own, such as the Muslim Relief Society.

The third category, the one I'm going to describe, is that of our engaging in individual acts of global consecration and stewardship. These are what we might refer to as personal initiatives, not the Church's programs as an organization. These derive from the inspiration that comes when we pray about how we might help those around us, or when we see devastations that impact a community or a region or a country or our own neighbors next door—those who suffer and struggle in our own community. I might add that I believe it is critically important that we engage in these kinds of activities locally, not just globally, because those suffering in circumstances around us typically affect our lives. We can affect them much easier, much more rapidly, and with smaller costs than those globally.

These are the kinds of acts that President Gordon B. Hinckley referred to when he emphasized his concern that we not simply depend on large organizations or the institutional services of the Church. Rather, he advocated that we also engage in noninstitutionalized acts of service to the poor.

I'm going to be talking about the third type, individual acts of international humanitarian service. Let me reference President Cecil Samuelson's speech in January 2008 to the students and faculty of BYU, where he discussed the "unsung heroes" of BYU and mentioned several types of individuals he saw on this campus doing wonderful work to bless the lives of others, yet not being recognized for their efforts. He described these individuals as self-starters, people who do not wait to be commanded, and those who act when they see a problem. They tend to be what President Samuelson described as authentic individuals. They are real. They are true to themselves. They are not motivated by external rewards or pressure or recognition. Rather, their service comes from pure and authentic motives.[1]

I want to build off this theme and talk about a few LDS global humanitarian heroes who I have had the great blessing of working with. It seems best to discuss from one's own experience, one's personal witness about how we can impact the world for good. Telling others' stories may be interesting but not necessarily validating.

These groups include founders and leaders of such organizations as HELP International, Eagle Condor Humanitarian, Ouelessebougou-Utah Alliance, Enterprise Mentors International, MicroBusiness Mentors, Unitus, Empowering Nations, as well as others. In most cases, these are NGOs that I have cofounded and know well, having served on their boards, and so forth. So I know them best and will be talking from my own experience. We may not be trained PR or communication experts. We do not have professional contacts or staff who focus on getting our story to the public. Rather, we operate in the spirit of the great Mahatma Gandhi, who declared, "My life is my message."

I will mention various sources about our work that have led to positive views regarding the Church. As I describe some of these individuals, cases, and strategies, I want to acknowledge my colleague, Dr. Muhammad Yunus, who has been a mentor and partner with me in a number of these efforts. He has been an advisor to us in the projects we have launched out of the university, as well as among private groups of citizens and Latter-day Saints off campus. Yunus was the Nobel Peace Prize winner in 2006 for the work he has done with microcredit and the formation of the Grameen Bank of Bangladesh.

He once made an interesting comment after seeing my students and me doing humanitarian work among the world's poor in various parts of the world. Regarding the impact Latter-day Saints were having, he said, "Warner, you Mormons are incredible!" Furthermore, a number of times he has said, "Among your BYU students, it looks to me like you are establishing a kind of Mormon Peace Corps which is having a huge impact around the globe." That comes from a Nobel Laureate, who also happens to be Muslim! To me this is a great illustration of the way in which our good works can strengthen and improve public perceptions about the Church worldwide, as they see us actually practice our religion, our faith, and our beliefs in our lives.

This impact is growing exponentially. My students, alumni, and I have worked together since the mid-eighties. We now have some forty-three international projects. Twenty-two have become NGOs that now operate in thirty-one nations. In 2007 alone, we trained more than 200,000 microcredit clients. We grew our microentrepreneur base to 3.2 million families, meaning we now have over three million clients to whom we have given loans with our partners from the funds that we have raised. The fundraising itself is becoming tremendously significant. From just a few hundred thousand dollars ten years ago, last year these projects and NGOs we operate together raised over twenty-eight million dollars. In 2006, it was some ten million dollars, so that amount nearly tripled to twenty-eight million dollars a year later. This suggests there is no limit to what we can do above and beyond the programs of the Church, beyond the funds of the Church or institutions like USAID or the United Nations. There is so much possibility, and so many great LDS individuals out there who want to make a difference, from the most humble of circumstances to the wealthiest and most successful. Among these many cases, one is that of HELP International.

HELP INTERNATIONAL

This organization emerged after Hurricane Mitch decimated Central America at the end of 1998. There were twenty thousand dead, twenty thousand missing, and a million people homeless. In Honduras, 90 percent of the country's crops were lost, and 70 percent of its infrastructure was damaged. Huge bridges and highways like the Pan-American Highway were destroyed. The experts declared that the country of Honduras was set back fifty years.

The question that occurred to me as I saw that devastation on the nightly news day after day was this: Can business schools address a socio-economic disaster like this? Do we have anything to offer? Are we even relevant to the problems of global suffering?

I started to think about my challenge as a professor to find answers, to determine whether or not we could design some innovative strategies that would transform the Marriott School into a pro-poor institution.

I began to recruit a few students, and we launched an elective course on social entrepreneurship. We decided to prepare a game plan to go to Honduras at the end of the semester because it was the hardest hit country. I call this type of education we developed "action-based learning." It requires students and faculty to collaborate as colleagues in designing new social innovations, which we carry out during and following that semester.

We called the project HELP for Help ELiminate Poverty. The results of our venture were fairly incredible. We ended up with forty-six volunteers in Honduras that summer. They came from BYU, the University of Utah, and Stanford. We raised $116,000. With those monies, we started forty-seven communal banks consisting of groups of women. We gathered them together and trained them in how to become self-reliant, how to be social entrepreneurs, and how to be microentrepreneurs. Many of them had lost husbands and jobs. Roughly speaking, we helped to create about eight hundred new microenterprises. Those eight hundred jobs benefited an average of five people per family. This means that about four thousand family members were blessed through the loans we provided as we started these communal banks.

In addition to microcredit, our volunteers throughout the summer of 1999 provided about twenty thousand hours of on-the-ground community service. They delivered babies out in rural medical facilities. They shoveled mud out of schools, rebuilt the schools, plastered the walls, disinfected the damaged structures, and sanded and painted the walls. Others rebuilt houses or mentored street children. Still others started small gardens and trained families on how to become square-foot garden experts so they could grow enough produce to feed themselves nutritious vegetables throughout the year. Some BYU volunteers taught in schools after we got them reopened. Others provided computer training skills. We took supplies from LDS members in six states, who gave materials for newborn kits for babies and their mothers, hygiene kits for refugee families who had lost everything, school kit supplies, and basic materials for children's education. These were the days before the Church developed its big program to provide hygiene or humanitarian kits in formal ways. Each volunteer took supplies in his or her second suitcase. The kits were assembled in-country. We bought extra supplies with cash we took to the country, which also benefited the Honduran economy.

As time has progressed, this little organization that we started out as HELP Honduras has become HELP International. It has expanded since 1999 to include Honduras, Guatemala, Peru, Bolivia, El Salvador, Brazil, Uganda, and many others. We have had over seven hundred students from BYU and other universities engage in the work of HELP International:

serving the poor, training microentrepreneurs, aiding farmers, volunteering in orphanages, doing health care in rural and medical clinics, teaching square-foot gardening, building homes, and so forth. These outreach efforts have become a major strategy for doing good and for lifting the have-nots. HELP, as an LDS-related and BYU-initiated program, has served to build the reputation of the Church through individual acts of consecration.

Public perceptions of the Church have been strengthened by the work of HELP International. In Honduras, the UN, the Red Cross, and US government officials were all amazed by the initiative of these young students from BYU, or "The Mormon school," as they called it. Among the seven countries listed that HELP has labored in, there have been probably fifty news articles in the press, as well as at home in the United States. After the devastating destruction of two huge earthquakes in El Salvador, HELP began to work there with Habitat for Humanity. One of those leaders told me in Spanish something to the effect of, "Dr. Woodworth, I have never seen such dedicated volunteers as these HELP students from BYU. What is it about Mormonism that produces such hardworking, highly committed individuals?" The founder of FINCA International, our microfinance partner in Honduras, told me, "Your church must be amazing to give its young adults such high motivation to help the poor." In 2003, our volunteers and I were invited to a banquet with prominent government officials of El Salvador, along with the business community, the arts, and other citizens of the so-called upper class. The US ambassador said after meeting our group and hearing why we were present: "You know, I have the title of US ambassador to this country, but you young college students from BYU, you are the real ambassadors of America. It's wonderful, even amazing, to see the good you are doing, to see how you are building a positive perception of our country among these people." Similar recognition and appreciation about HELP was given by Guatemalan business and government leaders regarding the good we were doing over the years that followed in that country as well.

EAGLE CONDOR HUMANITARIAN

Another organization is called Eagle Condor Humanitarian (ECH). The mission of ECH is to enrich family life, to empower people, and to build self-reliance. Its purposes include providing employment opportunities, finding ways of raising the standard of living, offering humanitarian charity, and building an ongoing, perpetuating organization that would improve the lives of the meek and the humble in Peru. Eagle Condor organizes expeditions of LDS North Americans as humanitarian tour groups. Each person pays their own way, taking donated goods such as tools, books, clothing, medicine, and computers to spend ten to fourteen days laboring among the poor. They use their skills in building houses and schools, offering teaching, doing microenterprise training, and stocking libraries. In some cases, US specialists with professional skills such as medical or dental services provide their expertise in free clinics. This organization is an impressive example of Latter-day Saints reaching out to others and building them up. They built a Moroni Community Center in the highest village of the Peruvian Andes, Patacancha, where they taught the descendants of ancient Nephites and Lamanites who their ancestors were, and from where the name "Moroni" is derived.

The support the Church has enjoyed from these kinds of efforts includes the public perceptions, recognition, and gratitude expressed by the mayor of Chiclayo, a large Peruvian city with one million inhabitants. Also, in the Sacred Valley of the Inca near Cusco, local government leaders of small towns and villages have been greatly impressed by the work of Eagle Condor as they saw this LDS-connected NGO providing education to poor children, healthcare to families, literacy training to parents, and US medical equipment to the area. The police chief and the education minister of the state expressed gratitude to the LDS people of Utah for the work of ECH. It has opened doors to missionary work and raised the reputation of the Church as a caring organization. There have been news stories in papers and magazines, both in Peru and the United States, about the *Mormones*, as we are called in Spanish.

OUELESSEBOUGOU-UTAH ALLIANCE

Another case is Ouelessebougou-Utah Alliance (OUA). It may be one of the best-known examples of Latter-day Saints engaging in private initiatives, pursuing their own ways to impact the world for good. OUA is a Utah-based nonprofit that works cooperatively with villagers in southern Mali. It was founded in 1985 by a group of Christian believers, political leaders, local LDS Church leaders in Salt Lake City, housewives, students, and humanitarians concerned about the devastating drought in North Africa that was occurring during the 1980s. Ouelessebougou is a region of some seventy-two villages and about thirty-five thousand people.

Some years ago, I was asked by the OUA to launch a microenterprise economic development strategy. We created what we called a *caisse villageois*, or village bank, and began giving tiny loans out to the poorest of the poor in that region. Ouelessebougou was a place where government officials and the Peace Corps had told us that people were too poor for microcredit. Allegedly, they did not even possess money because it was a barter economy. They could never start a business. They could never receive a loan or pay it back. But we have been working there for over a decade now. The village became so successful so quickly that even the president of Mali, Alpha Konare, joined the bank and put in one hundred dollars of his own money to invest in providing loans to the villagers of OUA. With a convoy of SUVs, troops, and bodyguards, he attended our microcredit start-up event and delivered a great speech about how the white Mormons from far away in the United States had committed to help his country because of our love for his people.

For us as Latter-day Saints to go to that Islamic country and spend our own time and money during the vacation period of the Christmas season or New Year's or the week of Thanksgiving was always a spiritual experience. Some gave medical service as volunteers while others were professionals who provided dental care. Utah midwives trained pregnant women while public schoolteachers traveled at their own expense to teach literacy.

Elder Marion D. Hanks of the Seventy went to Mali on an expedition with several Utah business leaders and visited with the president of Mali. The president said, "You Mormon people of Utah are like a rope coming down from heaven to help my country, to help my people climb out of poverty." Since then, OUA has thrived tremendously, and it has been accompanied by positive coverage about the Church. Its reputation has been enhanced by television stories and print media for over two decades.

ENTERPRISE MENTORS INTERNATIONAL

Enterprise Mentors International is a microcredit NGO that was launched by Latter-day Saints in 1990. I had the privilege of being a cofounder as we started it in the Philippines. A small group of students and I spent most of the summer of 1989 in metro Manila assessing the temporal challenges and difficulties of Church members. We have been working in the Philippines since we incorporated that organization in 1990—eighteen years of providing microenterprise, providing training, offering development services, providing free consulting, and having an impact in the lives of some 336,000 people. From the Philippines, we then spread it to Mexico, Guatemala, El Salvador, and Peru. Today, we have twenty offices in these countries, providing training in microenterprise development and consulting services and loans. So far we have channeled a total of twenty-three million dollars to the poor. Annually, EMI and its partners help tens of thousands of families move toward self-reliance with training, loans, and business services.

The perception of this type of work by EMI has helped the Church's reputation and recognition both in the Philippines as well as in Latin America. We were honored by the president of the Philippines, Fidel Ramos, some years back. I have met with several government ministers who said they had never seen an NGO in the Philippines doing the kind of work this group of Mormons was doing. The same expressions were shared by various ministries in Guatemala, where I met with bankers and government officials. In San Salvador and in the country of El Salvador and in Mexico, we have had considerable news coverage in US national magazines and newspapers as well as stories about this group of Mormons. We have had wonderful opportunities to collaborate with business leaders in some of these countries who have joined our boards and been so impressed with the work of Latter-day Saints. The same is true of their national universities where a number of studies have been done on the work of the Enterprise Mentors model for economic development. The results have been quite outstanding.

UNITUS

An impressive case that has resulted in perhaps more PR for the Church than any other is called Unitus, meaning "unite us." This organization was established by a group of LDS academics, students, and entrepreneurs from coast to coast who had read my book *Working Toward Zion*, coauthored with Jim Lucas, and began to talk to me by phone and by email. Soon they started flying to Utah to meet and discuss how they could make a difference. Ultimately, after a year of debate, strategy-formation, and planning, we incorporated as an NGO.

We decided that rather than just being another NGO, we would do something unique—help small microfinance organizations grow solidly and rapidly. The work of Unitus as an accelerator has had a huge impact. As the first chairman of the board, I proposed we begin in Mexico, so we set up a new organization in Tula called ProMujer. Since then, we have established 489 Mexican communal banks and dispersed 8 million dollars. From there we went to India and found a wonderful little NGO called SKS whose potential for growth looked promising. We provided capital, training, expertise, and new technologies to the NGO, and it has now grown to be a huge success. Later, we expanded to Kenya, where we now have 140,000 borrowers; Argentina, where we have 20,000 or so; Indonesia; and other parts of the globe.

Unitus has now become a global MFI. The perceptions have been logged by the media in *Fortune*, *Forbes*, *Business Week*, *Wall Street Journal*, and the *Financial Times* of London about this group of Mormons and their friends. Accumulating capital and making major loans to small NGOs so they grow rapidly has been a marvelous story and great reflection on the Church. Some thirty news articles in seven different countries have appeared about this group of Mormons who are movers and shakers, fighting poverty around the globe.

At Unitus we have received three awards from *Fast Company* magazine, what is called an annual social capital award. We have also been honored by President Bill Clinton's Clinton Global Initiative. Our partners have enjoyed a great deal of international recognition and received awards for management excellence. Some of our staff and board members have been honored in their own right by everybody from Pierre Omidyar, the founder of eBay, to Microsoft's Bill Gates. Even former President Jimmy Carter recognized us several years ago. I was impressed to see this great, even extraordinary, humanitarian express interest in what we were doing and explore potential collaboration with his Carter Center.

MISCELLANEOUS LDS OUTREACH

So we have this expanding reputation as Latter-day Saints, all of which reflects on and strengthens positive perceptions of the Church. We are building these projects both locally in Utah as well as in Latin America, Asia, and Africa. Mormons are changing the world one family at a time, building self-reliance, building sustainability, setting up education systems, establishing economic and microenterprise programs, launching agricultural initiatives, and specifying in some cases how Church donations should be used for humanitarian services, for Latter-day Saint Charities, or for a particular global crisis such as the devastating earthquake in Pakistan in 2006 or the floods from the cyclone in Myanmar. These LDS individuals want to do more than just write checks to the Church. They want to act, to be involved personally. They are designing innovative projects. They are seeking to build awareness. They are creating new projects, new NGOs, and they are partnering with other NGOs around the globe. What follows are several brief synopses.

Cecile Pelous of France used to work in the Paris fashion industry, designing dresses for models from around the world—upscale fashionistas. But she began to feel her life as a Latter-day Saint and as a stake Relief Society president in Paris had a more eternal purpose and a more spiritual reason to exist. Out of that, she organized a little orphanage she called First Hope, and for twelve years she has been building that orphanage, expanding its services, and increasing the number of orphans served in Nepal. Cecile has enjoyed wonderful press attention and media recognition for the Church, not only in the United States but in Europe as well as Asia, appearing on multiple television shows, newscasts, documentaries, and so on. Cecile has essentially become recognized as a kind of Mormon

Mother Teresa, serving one of the world's most impoverished countries. She helps some of the world's poorest children have access to education, medicine, health care, security, and safety in an environment of a wonderful orphanage, preparing those children so when they turn eighteen and leave, they will maintain themselves.

Care for Life (CFL) is a small nonprofit organization laboring in southern Africa that was established in 1999. I have been so impressed with the family preservation program in Mozambique that they established, an approach that partners with the poor themselves. One of my former students from Brazil, Joao Bueno, designed the strategy and has been running it since 2005. Most of its members, donors, and board are from the Phoenix area. They are Latter-day Saints who, in addition to many commitments in their families, careers, and Church callings, have sought to reach out. They have raised millions of dollars for the poor country of Mozambique, a nation that emerged in 1992 from fifteen years of civil war.

In the process, CFL has helped them develop an impressive program to strengthen the families. They work with eight villages and about ten thousand people in rural Mozambique to build better lives. The NGO operates an intensive program to improve their lives by setting family goals to build stronger, better constructed homes, obtain loans with which to start small businesses, attend adult literacy classes to learn how to read and write, drink only clean water to avoid diarrhea, send their children to school instead of doing field work, and build and use family latrines for better health.

Care for Life has enjoyed tremendous recognition from the government of Mozambique, where both national and regional government officials have toured these villages and been so impressed to see what these Mormons are doing. A year ago they received a $750,000 grant to provide AIDS training and other health training services, not only to CFL villages but also throughout the nation. The government concluded this was the best program they had seen in all of Africa to help prevent the spread of AIDS. CFL has had numerous articles in the press in Africa, Arizona, and Utah. Most impressively, a year ago, there was a huge article in the *Christian Science Monitor* that went around the world. It generated enormous interest in the fact that this group of Latter-day Saints from Arizona would go to the far corners of the world to help one of the poorest countries in Africa.

There are many other LDS-related humanitarian organizations that we do not have time to cover. But I will mention them because, collectively, they have significantly improved the Church's reputation and image in a number of countries: Cause for Hope in Honduras that has established several small factories and a school to train young people; World Joy and Families for Children in Ghana; Ascend Alliance that is working in Latin America and Africa; Nova Geracao in southern Brazil, which helps teenage girls; Human Security in Thailand that focuses on peace-building, working with leading Buddhist monks in that country; Academy for Creating Enterprise that trains Filipino returned missionaries in business skills; Reach the Children, founded by New York LDS members that serves the poor in seven countries, mostly in Africa; Families Helping Families serving poor Church members in Honduras and Mexico; Choice Humanitarian, one of the oldest Mormon-related NGOs in Salt Lake City, which has been working for the past twenty years in a dozen countries in Africa, Asia, and Latin America; Yehu Microfinance in Kenya; and Rising Star Outreach, working with lepers in India. A number of these private LDS initiatives have led to recognition by senators in Brazil; John Kufuor, who is the president of Ghana; the vice president of El Salvador; dozens of village elders and chiefs in rural regions; local mayors; and other government officials in urban communities. My many student outreach efforts over the years have led to recognition of the Church by UN Secretary General Kofi Annan, Mother Teresa, Nelson Mandela, and other world leaders. The collective impact of these programs on the Church's reputation is truly incalculable.

EMPOWERING NATIONS

I want to end this session with one last case, a little more in-depth exploration of what we call Wave of Hope, or Empowering Nations. It was launched in 2005, which was the two hundredth anniversary of the Prophet Joseph Smith's birth. As that year began, many efforts were made by Latter-day Saints and the Church as a whole to honor the Prophet Joseph through conferences, speeches, symposia, musicals, and dramatic productions. A group of students and I decided that maybe one of the best ways we could really honor the Prophet Joseph was to practice his teaching in a pioneering way. The genesis of this began with the terrible devastation on 26 December 2004, as an underground earthquake launched the Asian tsunami, hitting eleven countries and devastating hundreds of thousands of people.

My first class for the new semester, January 2005, was a course called Social Entrepreneurship. I asked students if what we do at the Marriott School was relevant to global suffering. Did anything we teach at BYU have any relevance to major crises like this in the world? I watched the tragic story on TV each night: twenty thousand dead; the next night, forty thousand dead. The next day, one hundred thousand were dead. Men, women, and children of whole villages were destroyed. Millions became homeless. Hundreds of thousands more were missing. We were seeing the horrific consequences of that tsunami's destruction twenty-four hours a day. I proposed to the class that in addition to our readings, papers, and regular assignments, we launch a project together for tsunami victims. We could not do everything, but we could at least do something.

So we organized teams of students. Team members proposed that we should go to Thailand where about ten thousand had died. Students came up with the idea to call our project Wave of Hope, a direct contrast to Thailand's deadly experience with a wave of destruction.

What were the outcomes? We recruited a hundred Latter-day Saint volunteers from coast-to-coast, we raised some two hundred thousand dollars, and teams spent a month or longer laboring in the coastal area of Khao Lak. We had teams of hardworking young people from BYU helping to build houses in Thap Twan, Bang Sak, and Laem Pom villages. By the end of the summer, we had helped to build 120 new homes. We painted those homes. We plastered those homes. We cemented. We shoveled out the dirt so we could lay pipes and put in sewer and plumbing systems.

Together with other volunteers, we established a furniture-making wood shop with power tools. We taught villagers how to build their own furniture for the new houses we were constructing. We designed tables, chairs, benches, and shelves for these homes. They were simple pine wood furniture that the tsunami survivors, mostly women, learned how to make.

They not only furnished their homes. They gained dignity, rather than dependency. They also developed skills that would enable them to move toward self-sufficiency.

We also engaged in Khao Lak education programs. We refurbished schools and reopened them. Many volunteers from Wave of Hope, including returned missionaries who spoke Thai, taught in those schools. They taught English, computer skills, simple business principles, and world history.

The perceptions of the Church in Thailand and elsewhere were greatly enhanced through Wave of Hope. We had hundreds of volunteers from throughout the world express how impressed they were with this BYU group. One told me: "So many outsiders have come here from Europe and the US to help. But much of their time is spent snorkeling in the beautiful islands away from the tsunami areas, laying on the beach, drinking, having sex, and partying. We have never seen young people like your Mormons who have such a great work ethic. They seldom even rest, to say nothing of partying."

In July 2005, US Secretary of State Condoleezza Rice went to see Thailand's recovery. She toured one of the schools we worked to clean up and reopen. Upon seeing our BYU volunteers, she remarked that she was so impressed with these young BYU Mormons who were dedicating their summer to serve the tsunami victims of Asia. As founder of Wave of Hope, I and several other LDS volunteers were invited to a luncheon with General Lertrat Ratanavanich, the nation's no. 3 military official who headed up Thailand's entire rebuilding efforts. He told me he had two degrees from US universities, but in all his college years in America, he had never seen students like ours—laboring nonstop to give relief and support to his people. He expressed deep appreciation for our work and admiration for our Church, a religion he had never heard of previously. When I told him we had missionaries in Bangkok, he and local community leaders assured me that whenever the Mormons would want to begin working along the western coast of Thailand where we were, they would gratefully open the way.

Upon completing that first successful year, Wave of Hope formally became part of Empowering Nations, an NGO growing out of my course two years earlier. The next summer, we mobilized forty-six volunteers to work in poor communities in northern Ghana, and we have also sent teams back to Thailand, as well as to Brazil, Panama, Kenya, Peru, and Paraguay.

CONCLUSION

From all the above private initiatives begun by Latter-day Saints as individual acts of stewardship and consecration, much good has accrued to the international reputation of the Church. It will open doors in the future and speed up the expansion of the Lord's kingdom around the globe. Equally important, such dedicated labor among the world's poor facilitates our personal spiritual growth as we seek to, indeed, become the Saints of God on earth. In the words of Joseph Smith, "A man filled with the love of God is not content with blessing his family alone, but ranges through the whole world, anxious to bless the whole human race."[2]

NOTES

1. Cecil O. Samuelson, "BYU's Unsung Heroes," in *Brigham Young University 2007–2008 Speeches* (Provo, UT: Brigham Young University, 2008), 1–6.
2. *Teachings of Presidents of the Church: Joseph Smith* (Salt Lake City: The Church of Jesus Christ of Latter-day Saints), 423–34.

7

OUT OF OBSCURITY

Perspectives from Asia

ELDER ANTHONY D. PERKINS

Elder Anthony D. Perkins, then a member of the First Quorum of the Seventy of The Church of Jesus Christ of Latter-day Saints, presented this essay at "In the Public Eye: How the Church Is Handling Increased Global Visibility," the International Society's twenty-third annual conference, April 2012, Brigham Young University, Provo, Utah.

In this chapter, "Asia" will refer to the region designated by the Church as the Asia Area. This area ranges from Mongolia on the north to Indonesia on the south and from Taiwan on the east to Pakistan on the west. It excludes Japan and Korea, which are in the Asia North Area, and the Philippines, which is its own area.

The Asia Area is comprised of twenty-five countries and territories, with a combined population of more than 3.5 billion people, or one-half the world total. Yet Church membership in Asia is only 161,000, which is just a minuscule 1 in every 22,000 persons. Thus, to the vast majority of Asian people who have never met a Mormon, the Church is probably just one more obscure Western religion.

In 1834, Joseph Smith prophesied, "Brethren, . . . you know no more concerning the destinies of this Church and kingdom than a babe upon its mother's lap. You don't comprehend it. . . . It is only a little handful of

Priesthood you see here tonight, but this Church will fill North and South America—it will fill the world."[1]

If you visit the Church Newsroom website and look at the map of our meetinghouses across the world, you will see the ongoing fulfillment of this prophecy. North America is covered with red dots representing meetinghouses, as is South America, Western Europe, the Pacific, and North Asia. Red dots are beginning to cover Southern Africa. The last frontiers are Northern Africa, the Middle East, and Asia.

You might ask, "Are we making any progress in Asia?" I will respond, "Yes!" My remarks today examine this question and answer it from three perspectives:

1. a prophetic overview for the Church coming forth out of obscurity and darkness and how ancient prophecies are being fulfilled in Asia today

2. a contemporary assessment of how the "Mormon Moment" in the United States is transferring to Asia

3. a historical comparison of improving public perceptions about the Church and its members in Asia, drawing on lessons from Taiwan

PROPHETIC PERSPECTIVE

The English word "obscurity" is recorded only seven times in scripture and by four prophets: Isaiah, Lehi, Nephi, and Joseph Smith. These seers saw our day, and their inspired usage of the word "obscurity" informs us of what the restored Church of Jesus Christ should be doing, and I testify is doing, in the latter days.

In Isaiah 59, Isaiah—whose great writings Jesus invites us to search[2]—warned that personal and institutional apostasy would cause the house of Israel to wander and become lost along darkened paths. Isaiah declared to the house of Israel, "[But] your iniquities have separated between you and your God. . . . Their feet run to evil. . . . Their thoughts are thoughts of iniquity. . . . Therefore . . . we wait for light, but behold obscurity; for brightness, but we walk in darkness."[3]

That prophecy of apostasy was fulfilled several times, first by the northern kingdom of Israel, followed by the southern kingdom of Judah, then by the Church organized by Jesus Christ during His mortal ministry, and finally by the civilization of the Nephites. When Joseph Smith walked into the Sacred Grove in 1820, the house of Israel and the Church of Jesus Christ were mired in obscurity and darkness.

I will suggest five signs prophesied by these great seers indicating how the restored latter-day Church would one day emerge out of obscurity. Each sign will be illustrated with examples from the Asia Area.

SIGN 1: BOOK OF MORMON PUBLICATION

In Isaiah 29, which Nephi quotes and expounds upon in 2 Nephi 27, Isaiah foretells in great detail the coming forth of the Book of Mormon. Isaiah and Nephi see the people are in the "deep sleep" of apostasy until a book comes forth with words "out of the dust." They prophesy of Joseph Smith, through whom the Lord will do a "marvelous work and a wonder." Then Isaiah writes, "And in that day shall the deaf hear the words of the book, and the eyes of the blind shall see out of obscurity, and out of darkness."[4]

Spiritually deaf and spiritually blind people in Asia are hearing and seeing the Book of Mormon at an increasing rate. In the 1960s, the Book of Mormon was translated for the first time into Chinese. In the 1970s, the Thai and Indonesian translations were published. In the 1980s, a full Book of Mormon was printed in Hindi (India) and Vietnamese, with selections in several other languages.

In the 1990s, work was initiated on a number of translations, but none were completed during that decade. Then in the 2000s, the first translations were published in Cambodian, Mongolian, Sinhala (Sri Lanka), Tamil (India), Telugu (India), and Urdu (Pakistan). Vietnamese was updated in 2003. In 2007–08, an updated translation of the Chinese scriptures was printed in both traditional and simplified characters.

After only two years into the 2010s, updated Book of Mormon translations were issued in Indonesian and Thai. In the next few years, the first Lao, Malay, and Nepali translations will appear, and an update in Hindi is underway. Who knows?—by 2020 we may have completed translations into Bengali (Bangladesh and India), Burmese (Myanmar), and Marathi (India), each of which have over forty million native speakers.

Looking forward, technology may be the key for populous Asian nations to access the Book of Mormon. Today, because of various legal restrictions, only 5 percent of the people in Asia can possibly find a full-time missionary in their city who can give them a Book of Mormon to "heft."[5] Yet almost everyone in Asia owns a mobile device, if not a computer or tablet. Book of Mormon text is now available on the Internet in most Asian languages, with mobile versions now available in Cambodian, Chinese, Indonesian, and Mongolian, with additional languages forthcoming. Efforts are underway for text and audio scriptures on mobile devices.

The first and most crucial step to bring the Church out of obscurity in Asia remains publication and distribution of the Book of Mormon in any format. We cannot invite all to come unto Jesus Christ without this sacred volume of scripture.

SIGN 2: WELFARE SERVICE

In Isaiah 58, this ancient prophet beautifully describes an acceptable fast to the Lord, which includes dealing bread to the hungry, bringing the poor to our house, and covering the naked. Then Isaiah promises, "If thou draw out thy soul to the hungry, and satisfy the afflicted soul; then shall thy light rise in obscurity, and thy darkness be as the noonday."[6]

The hungry, poor, and naked in Asia are increasingly assisted by fast offerings and humanitarian donations. Many thousands of Church members are blessed in the Lord's way[7] as fast offerings in wealthier Asian locations like Singapore, Hong Kong, and Taiwan are sufficient to meet the needs of members in poorer nations like Cambodia and Mongolia.

Humanitarian projects bless the lives of millions. Currently, a volunteer force of thirty-one senior couples located in thirteen Asian nations is providing welfare training, assisting in employment and the Perpetual Education Fund, and coordinating millions of dollars in humanitarian projects. We carry out three types of humanitarian projects proximate to centers of strength where Church members can serve:

major initiatives with worldwide expertise are clean water and sanitation, wheelchairs and walkers, neonatal resuscitation, vision care, immunizations, asthma treatment, and food production

area initiatives bless the communities where our members live through assistance to institutions such as orphanages, handicapped training centers, and disadvantaged schools

emergency-response efforts include earthquakes and fires in China and Malaysia as well as devastating flooding in Thailand, Cambodia, Laos, and Vietnam in 2011

Our efforts do not go unnoticed by the general public or government officials. In China, recent wheelchair donations and childhood-asthma education projects were reported in local media. In a recent visit to Nepal, Church leaders received sincere gratitude from government officials for the Church and for our support of wheelchair donations, major water projects, and skills training to those who are blind or have Hansen's disease (leprosy).

Sometimes, many years of humanitarian service precede the Church being granted legal privileges such as national registration or missionary visas. As we demonstrate our willingness to help communities and live harmoniously with neighbors regardless of religious affiliation, governments have greater trust in the Church and its members.[8] Sincere efforts to follow the example of Jesus Christ in blessing the unfortunate and afflicted help the Church's light to rise from obscurity.

SIGN 3: THE CHURCH FOUNDATION

In section 1 of the Doctrine and Covenants, the Lord declares to Joseph Smith that The Church of Jesus Christ of Latter-day Saints is "the only true and living Church upon the face of the whole earth" with which he is "well pleased." He also reveals that priesthood leaders who receive the commandments in the Book of Mormon and Doctrine and Covenants "might have power to lay the foundation of this Church, and to bring it forth out of obscurity and out of darkness."[9]

Of course, the Church is "built upon the foundation of the apostles and prophets, Jesus Christ himself being the chief corner stone."[10] Upon this foundation, we must establish in each country a base of legal entities, organizational units, and priesthood leaders. This base is being set up at a quickening pace across Asia.

Currently, at least one congregation of the Church meets in nineteen of the Asia Area's twenty-five countries and territories. In twelve regions, the Church is registered or recognized with legal entities that enable both religious and humanitarian work. In four nations—Laos, Myanmar, Nepal, and Vietnam—Latter-day Saint Charities exists as a legal entity, exclusively for humanitarian work. And in three countries—Bangladesh, Brunei, and China—the Church has no religious or humanitarian legal entity. Church officers continue to meet regularly with government officials in all of these nations to ensure we maintain or obtain an appropriate legal base.[11]

The organizational foundation of the Church is also expanding. Upon my assignment to the Area Presidency in July 2007, the Asia Area had sixteen stakes and twenty-two districts. By July 2012, the Asia Area had twenty-one stakes and forty-seven districts, with the first stakes recently created in the countries of Mongolia, Indonesia, and India. Taiwan's eleventh stake was formed in 2010.

More importantly, these stakes and districts are led by dedicated local priesthood holders. Taiwan's first stake was organized by Elder Gordon B. Hinckley in 1976 with Chang Yi Ching called as president. His son, Chang Ting Tsung, now serves as president of the Tainan Taiwan Stake—two generations of devoted stake presidents and now three generations of faithful Latter-day Saints.

President Nadeem Khokar serves as president of the Lahore Pakistan District. He and his parents were converted from Methodism in 1991. He later served a mission to Preston, England, and his four children are now the third generation of Pakistani Church members. Asia is blessed with many such leaders who faithfully follow the teachings and example of Jesus Christ.

SIGN 4: RIGHTEOUS MEMBERS

In 2 Nephi 1, the aged prophet Lehi begins providing his final instruction and edification to his children. He prophesies of their posterity and pleads with his family to "be a choice and favored people of the Lord."[12] He counsels, "Awake, my sons; put on the armor of righteousness. Shake off the chains with which ye are bound, and come forth out of obscurity, and arise from the dust."[13]

Each year across Asia, thousands of people shake off incorrect traditions that lack a fullness of gospel truth and put on the armor that comes from righteously keeping God's commandments. Asia is the center of the non-Christian world. Estimates are that 34 percent of Asia's 3.5 billion people have no religious belief, with most of those living in China and Vietnam. Asia has one billion Hindus, primarily in India and Nepal. More than 700 million Muslims, or one-half of the global total, reside in Asia—concentrated in Indonesia, Pakistan, India, Bangladesh, China, and Malaysia. Over 400 million Buddhists live in China, Thailand, Myanmar, Taiwan, Sri Lanka, and Cambodia. Only 140 million people in Asia, or 4 percent of the total population, are Christian.

And yet the clarion call of the restored gospel of Jesus Christ is gathering the elect in Asian nations from every religious and socioeconomic background. The Nyugen family lives in a home built of discarded lumber and tin that sits on stilts along the flood-prone Mekong River near Phnom Penh, Cambodia. Signs of faith in Jesus Christ and love for his prophets are evident throughout this formerly Buddhist family's humble home.

Sumit Aurora converted from Hinduism while living in New Delhi, India, during college, and he now resides in Lucknow, India, where there is no Church branch. Each weekend he travels seven hours by train to New Delhi and has not missed a sacrament meeting in a year. Such modern pioneers push heavy spiritual handcarts to live the gospel, and when they do so, the Church comes out of obscurity one by one as their family, friends, and associates see powerful examples of the abundant life.

SIGN 5: TEMPLE COVENANTS

In 1 Nephi 22, Nephi expounds upon the words of Isaiah and records remarkable prophecies about our day. Nephi emphasizes the "great worth" of the marvelous latter-day work is "making known of the covenants of the Father in heaven unto Abraham."[14] We understand this to mean the priesthood and temple ordinances and covenants by which "shall all the kindreds of the earth be blessed."[15] After God's children are "gathered together" to know the Father's covenants, Nephi concludes by promising "they shall be brought out of obscurity and out of darkness; and they shall know that the Lord is their Savior and Redeemer."[16]

A growing number of Asian Saints are qualifying themselves to receive temple ordinances and keep the associated covenants. We are grateful for the two temples that currently provide light to Asia—one in Taipei and one in Hong Kong. Because of personal sacrifice and generous allocations from the general Temple Patron Assistance Fund, many more members from every Asian nation can go to the temple.

In each of the past few years, about 250 newly married couples and long-married converts from across Asia were sealed as husband and wife for time and all eternity. Some couples travel to the temple alone, like Roshan and Sheron Antony from Sri Lanka, who both served missions in the Philippines and returned to be sealed in the Manila Temple. Some couples coming to be sealed travel with large groups, like most members from Mongolia, whose trip to the Hong Kong Temple is a two-week event requiring a minimum of three days each way by train. And some couples are like Lawrence and Saritha William from India, who were sealed in the Hong Kong Temple in 2002 and then saved for eight years to return.

In February 2012, a milestone was crossed, with ten thousand Latter-day Saints in the Asia Area holding a current temple recommend. To me, this is astounding! Such faithful members have truly come to know Jesus is their Savior and Redeemer.

These five signs of the Church coming out of obscurity and darkness—Book of Mormon publication, welfare service, Church foundation, righteous members, and temple covenants—are increasingly evident in the Asia Area. With this prophetic perspective in place, I now turn to an assessment of current events.

CONTEMPORARY PERSPECTIVE

The cover of *Newsweek* magazine (13–20 June 2011) showed presidential candidate Mitt Romney in mid-leap, wearing missionary attire, with the text "The Mormon Moment" emblazoned across his torso. The mocked-up photo was a takeoff of a poster for the popular Broadway musical *The Book of Mormon*, which opened in March 2011. That cover story is just one example of US media that has been awash in Mormon-related content for the past year. It has been eye-opening for me to consider the question, "Is the US 'Mormon Moment' transferring to Asia?" The simple answer is, "Yes," but the more accurate answer is, "It depends."

"Yes"—The Mormon Moment in Asia

On the surface, Asia is experiencing an "in-the-public-eye" Mormon Moment as illustrated in Indonesia and India.

In late January 2012, *Kompas*, the largest newspaper in the world's largest Muslim-majority nation, Indonesia, printed a short cover article using the term "Mormon Moment." Adapted from a Reuters story, the article mentioned Mitt Romney and Jon Huntsman, *The Book of Mormon* musical, HBO's *Big Love*, *Twilight*, and findings from the just-released Pew Research Center's survey of US Mormons.

In early March 2012, print and electronic media in India were saturated in two Mormon-related stories—the presidential campaign of Mitt Romney and the proxy baptism of national founding father Mahatma Gandhi. Of the latter story, the *Hindustan Times* declared, "Hindus Shocked." But such interest quickly led to two newspaper articles that favorably profiled local members in India.

Several years ago, articles of any kind about the Church or its members rarely appeared in Indonesian and Indian media.

"It Depends"—Public-Perception Influences

To more deeply understand the communication of events coming out of the United States, in February 2012, I conducted a simple survey and follow-up interview with about fifty Chinese senior priesthood leaders living across mainland China, Hong Kong, and Taiwan. Each man was asked to review a list of potential "public-perception influences" that can be grouped into several categories:

> Well-known politicians: Governor Mitt Romney, Ambassador Jon Huntsman, Senator Harry Reid
>
> Church policies: Polygamy (Warren Jeffs), proxy baptism (Holocaust victims), same-gender marriage (Proposition 8), Priesthood ordination (race and gender)
>
> Church initiatives: "I'm a Mormon" advertising campaign, Mormon.org website, Church Newsroom
>
> Popular culture: *The Book of Mormon* musical, *Big Love* TV program, *Twilight* books and movies
>
> Prominent members: singers (David Archuleta), actors (Jon Heder), athletes (Jimmer Fredette), commentators (Glenn Beck)

For each of these potential influences, the priesthood leader was asked to rate how often Chinese-language media mentioned the Church and, when mentioned, rate whether the effect on public perception toward the Church was positive or negative. Three conclusions emerge from this simple survey and indicate that not all public-perception influences are created equally, at least when transferring from the United States to Greater China.

First, presidential politics matter a lot. Almost 80 percent of Chinese priesthood leaders have read or viewed something about the religion of US presidential candidates. Of these informed men, 40 percent judge that Chinese media mention the Church "almost always" or "frequently" when reporting on Governor Mitt Romney and Ambassador Jon Huntsman. Also, 70 percent of our leaders think the effect of stories about Governor Romney and Ambassador Huntsman are "very favorable" or "favorable" toward the Church, with few "unfavorable" scores. In contrast to presidential politics, the importance of the US senate majority leader and his Church membership is known by few Chinese priesthood leaders (and probably most Americans).

Second, Church policies matter but are misunderstood. About 65 percent of Chinese priesthood leaders have read or viewed Chinese media content referring to the Church's historical or current policies, like polygamy, proxy baptism, same-gender marriage, and priesthood ordination. Of these informed leaders, 75 percent think the effect of such stories is "very unfavorable" or "unfavorable" toward the Church, with few "favorable" scores. Reports about the Fundamentalist Church of Jesus Christ of Latter-Day Saints (FLDS) and their leader, Warren Jeffs, were particularly corrosive.

Third, nothing else matters much. Less than 45 percent of our priesthood leaders in Greater China are aware of Church initiatives like the "I'm a Mormon" advertising campaign and the Mormon.org or Church Newsroom websites. Only 30 percent of these leaders know anything about a Latter-day Saint (LDS) connection to US popular culture, like *Big Love*, *Twilight*, and *The Book of Mormon* musical. Those who do know rated the effect as neutral, except in Taiwan, where *Big Love* has been actively promoted and leads nonmembers to think the Church still allows polygamy. Only 10 percent of our leaders in Greater China recognize prominent US Church members who are singers, actors, athletes, or commentators, the exception being David Archuleta, because the TV program *American Idol* is broadcast in many Asian cities.

If the conclusions from this small sample survey of Chinese priesthood leaders apply across Asia, and I think they do, then we should not be surprised when Asian media is blanketed with stories of presidential campaigns and posthumous baptism.

IMPLICATIONS FOR PUBLIC AFFAIRS

Clearly, visibility from the US "Mormon Moment" is accelerating the Church's rise out of obscurity in Asia, in both positive and negative ways. Credibility and respectability for the Church to come out of darkness requires both institutional and individual action.

The Church must reach out to assist content sources. Most stories about the Church in Asian media are direct translations from or adaptations of English-language content from sources such as Reuters, the

Associated Press, Pew Research, and academia. If the original writers get the facts or context wrong, then readers in Asia will be misled.

We need to watch for and correct mistranslations. Even if the English story is accurate, Asian readers may misunderstand the Church's position through faulty translation. For example, when many articles were written about Warren Jeffs and the FLDS Church, various Chinese translations for "fundamentalist" caused great confusion, which we took action to correct.

Until recently, we lacked an institutional Church voice in any Asian language where the media and interested observers might quickly access the Church's official position on doctrines and practices. The Chinese-language Church Newsroom should be launched in April 2012, and efforts are under way on Mormon.org in Chinese. We hope search-engine optimization in Chinese will soon follow.

We increasingly need individual Asian members to heed Elder Ballard's invitation to "join the conversation."[17] They can clarify and correct very outdated falsehoods that populate the comments section of many online stories about the Church on Asian-language websites and that circulate in social media outlets like Facebook.

Thus, the US Mormon Moment has had an impact on the Church in Asia; a few public-perception influences are helping bring the Church out of obscurity; implications include that Church members need to "join the conversation."

HISTORICAL PERSPECTIVE

I now revert to a historical comparison of the Church's image in Asia, drawing on personal experiences in Taiwan and Asia over the past thirty years. My thesis is the Church's image has evolved during its sixty-year presence in Taiwan, and that evolution pattern can be applied to other Asian lands.

A SHIFT IN PERCEPTION

As mentioned earlier, I conducted a simple survey and follow-up interview with about fifty Chinese priesthood leaders living in Greater China. One part of my questionnaire asked them to list words that would describe public perception about the Church in Greater China fifteen to twenty-five years ago. I was not surprised when the most common words listed were "cult," "false beliefs," "polygamy," and "foreign."

These Chinese leaders were then asked to list words expressing public perception today. While some of the old words have not entirely gone away, the more common terms are now "family values," "wealthy," "community service," and "kind members."

Each man was asked to list the key factors that led to a positive shift in public perception over the past fifteen to twenty-five years. Equally mentioned responses were humanitarian and service projects, Church public affairs efforts, favorable media coverage, and prominent members. But the factor mentioned three times more than any other was the example of Church members' actions.

Finally, our Chinese leaders were asked to choose the most common response when a friend or stranger first learns they are a Mormon. As one might expect, a somewhat positive distribution can be seen. About 5 percent mock, 17 percent giggle, 38 percent are neutral, 32 percent respect, and 8 percent praise. This positive shift in perception over the past twenty years described in this simple survey confirmed my personal observations from living in Taiwan and working with LDS colleagues whose Taiwanese experiences predate my own.

CHURCH IMAGE EVOLUTION IN TAIWAN

The first four missionaries arrived in Taiwan on 4 June 1956, and since that day, young men in white shirts and ties have remained the most powerful image of The Church of Jesus Christ of Latter-day Saints on this island. Yet I will contend that perceptions of the Church have evolved through three stages, each lasting about twenty years.

Stage 1: Nice Neglect

In the late 1950s and 1960s, Taiwan's population was very poor, mostly uneducated, and wary of renewed civil war. "Mormon missionaries who came from abroad were often the first foreigners that some Taiwanese people met. The young, nonthreatening missionaries gave the Taiwanese the opportunity to meet, talk with, ask questions of, and get to know non-Chinese people coming to Taiwan willingly. The missionaries projected a positive image; they were volunteers, they lived modestly, and, most of all, they wanted to learn about the local people and their history, culture, and traditions, as well as to teach the gospel. As a result, the missionaries were received much more favorably than were US servicemen and women."[18]

During this first twenty-year period, many of Taiwan's pioneering leaders and their families joined the Church. Membership grew from zero in 1956 to about five thousand by 1970. By 1976, strength was sufficient for Elder Gordon B. Hinckley to organize Taiwan's first stake in the capital city of Taipei.

Stage 2: Strangely Suspect

When I arrived in Taiwan in late 1979, a third mission had just been created, and the significantly expanded missionary force was still the most obvious Church image. Taiwan's people assumed all LDS missionaries were Americans, and that was troubling to many, because the United States had recently shifted national recognition from Taipei to Beijing. Everyone knew we rode around on tall bikes, but few people knew what we taught, and falsehoods were pervasive. In response, our mission developed a simple tract entitled, "Who Are We?"

One challenge was the phrase "Devil's Gate Cult"—a twisted interpretation of the Chinese characters used for "Mormon Church." This phrase sheltered typical anti-Mormon ideas such as paying Buddhists and Taoists to convert ("rice-bowl Christians"), infiltrating Taiwan society as CIA operatives, recruiting Taiwanese girls for Utah harems, and even sacrificing children in our temples.

Fortunately for the Church's perception in Taiwan during the late 1970s and early 1980s, a pop culture Mormon Moment was underway. Donny and Marie Osmond captured hearts in Taiwan with their syndicated TV show and songs such as "Puppy Love." As I knocked on doors in those years, it seemed as if every household knew Donny and Marie were Mormons and liked their wholesome family image. This feeling was so enduring that in 2005, when Marie Osmond met her oldest son in

Kaohsiung at the end of his mission, Taiwanese newspapers allocated an entire page to the story.

Despite some opposition, Church membership in Taiwan grew to eight thousand by 1980 and more than doubled again to seventeen thousand by 1990. The Taipei Temple was dedicated during this period, in 1984.

Stage 3: Rising Respect

As time advanced into the 1990s and 2000s, the Church became increasingly respected for the good it represented and did in Taiwan. While good examples by members and missionaries were the most important factors for this shift in perception, institutional action also played a major role.

The Church has become recognized for community service. When a massive 7.6 magnitude earthquake killed 2,400 people in 1999, local media recounted stories of missionaries using flashlights and first aid supplies from their 72-hour kits to escort people out of damaged buildings and provide basic treatment. When the typhoon Morakot killed almost seven hundred people in 2009, a newly constructed LDS chapel housed relief operations. The media profiled members and missionaries from around the island who gathered for cleanup activities and worked together with a Buddhist relief organization.

The Church is respected for its family values. When Ma Ying-jeou was mayor of Taipei, the Church supported his administration's family initiative with a values-based family home evening manual. Later, after his election as Taiwan's president, we presented him with "The Family: A Proclamation to the World."

Amid such progress, the enduring icon of the Church in Taiwan is two missionaries, each straddling a bicycle while wearing a white shirt, a colored tie, a black tag, a shoulder bag, and a safety helmet. How ingrained is this image? I offer two examples.

About seven years ago, the government printed a basic reading book for third-grade children entitled *Society*. Its pages are filled with typical Taiwanese street scenes and people engaging in polite dialogue. On one page, two small figures on bikes are shown stopped at a crosswalk. A zoomed-in view of the scene shows a girl waving and saying, in English, "Hello!" to two perfectly attired and happily talkative missionaries. How interesting to contemplate that on an island with twenty-three million people, a snapshot of society would not be complete without representation of only a few hundred young men and women.

Just a few years ago, the makers of the "Home Style Noodles" brand launched a thirty-second ad with missionary look-alikes at its center. In the ad, a woman opens her door and two men ask if she has time to chat. She invites them inside and offers refreshments. They say "no" three times to foods that are fried, use preservatives, and contain MSG. The housewife is perplexed about how to host these young men (who have a strict interpretation of the Word of Wisdom). In a moment of inspiration, the housewife knows to prepare packaged noodles, which they joyfully consume while being too busy to chat. Again, how interesting to consider a company linking its brand to an image of a minority religion.

Undoubtedly, the Church in Taiwan is well into the "Rising Respect" stage of image evolution. Such respect accelerated Church membership in Taiwan to twenty-seven thousand by 2000 and fifty-three thousand by 2010.

As societies modernize, they often lose their traditional values and moorings. Earlier in Taiwan, the Church was seen as young and foreign, perhaps not an institution you would entrust with your children. Now, with rising respect, many parents in Taiwan see the Church as conservative and established—just the place you hope your youth might go to be socially safe.

What about the rest of Asia? Will Asian nations follow in Taiwan's path? I think so.

CHURCH IMAGE ACROSS ASIA

The Church is probably in the "Nice Neglect" stage in Asian nations like Bangladesh, Brunei, Laos, Myanmar, Nepal, and Vietnam. Our in-country presence is less than ten years, our membership is just in the hundreds, and our senior missionaries are viewed as friendly, nonthreatening people. We undertake humanitarian endeavors while working with government officials to obtain legal privileges. Our activities are "below the radar," and opposition is fairly limited.

In many Asian countries where the Church has been operating for about fifteen to twenty years, we are probably entering or well into the "Strangely Suspect" stage. Such nations might include Cambodia, China, India, Malaysia, Mongolia, Pakistan, and Sri Lanka. Interestingly, when membership in centers of strength has grown to the point where stakes are being considered or created, opposition seems to accelerate: false rumors circulate in the media and government; anti-Mormon websites proliferate; challenges arise to Church registration, meetinghouse licenses, or missionary visas; physical attacks on missionaries occur; and investigations of Church officers and members by the national security or intelligence agencies are common.

Perhaps our greatest protection during the "Strangely Suspect" stage is strict obedience to the eleventh and twelfth articles of faith. When we "allow all men the . . . privilege" to "worship how, where, or what they may,"[19] then leaders of an Asian country's predominant religion are less opposed to our presence. When we are "subject to . . . rulers . . . in obeying, honoring, and sustaining the law," then a nation's leaders do not see us as a threat to political stability.[20]

As Church members follow these two Articles of Faith, we begin to move past the "Strangely Suspect" stage. Many Asian nations have a ministry of religion—in China it is called the State Administration for Religious Affairs or SARA, which has departments for Buddhists, Catholics, Muslims, Protestants, and Taoists. For many years, the bureau that oversaw our activities carried the title "Cults." Recently, that bureau's name changed to "New Religions." I call that progress!

One element of Church image moving from suspect to respect is a country's economic development and outside exposure. Today, people from China and India are more likely to meet a Latter-day Saint during travel to North America, Europe, or Australia than in their home countries, and many do.

For Asian nations where the Church has had a presence for thirty to forty years—like Indonesia, Macau, Singapore, and Thailand—we are hopefully moving from "Strangely Suspect" to "Rising Respect." Persevering through restrictive government regulations or overcoming public affairs debacles can take many years of exemplary citizenship and community service.

In Taiwan and Hong Kong, where missionaries and stakes have been established over the course of nearly sixty years, the Church has surely moved into the "Rising Respect" stage. Media is generally positive toward the Church, as is much of the populace, but challenges still arise on occasion, just as in the United States. For example, our Hong Kong public affairs council recently faced a situation where several high school principals in school assemblies warned their students to avoid Christian cults disguised as English tutors. Our Church name was specifically mentioned on several occasions.

If "Neglect-Suspect-Respect" is a general pattern as Church membership grows, we should also recognize each stage can exist simultaneously within different parts of a populous Asian nation. The Church can be respected in a national capital like New Delhi or Beijing, suspected in a commercial center like Bangalore or Shanghai, and neglected in an outlying city like Rajahmundry or Shenzhen.

Looking forward across Asia, I predict this pattern will continue, but the twenty-year duration of each stage will compress. Compared to our entry into Taiwan in 1956 or even into Cambodia in 1994, transportation and communication advancements will shorten the "Nice Neglect" stage. Hopefully, the "Strangely Suspect" stage will also be brief so the Church can move quickly toward "Rising Respect."

We know the devil is speeding up his efforts against gospel truths,[21] but the Lord has promised, "Behold, I will hasten my work in its time."[22] By looking at Asia's past we learn perceptions are shifting, Church image is moving through stages, and the Lord's work is hastening.

PERSONAL MORMON MOMENTS

In summary:

1. From a prophetic perspective, priesthood leaders are directing institutional steps to fulfill the five signs foretold by ancient and modern seers that would bring the Church out of obscurity.

2. From a contemporary perspective, Church members are exerting individual efforts in realms such as presidential politics that increase "in-the-public-eye" Mormon Moments, for better and worse.

3. Yet from a historical perspective, I am convinced that "personal" Mormon Moments are what really mattered in changing perceptions toward the Church in Taiwan, and such one-to-one moments will still matter most as the gospel moves forth across the face of Asia.

To close, permit me to share a story that illustrates how "in-the-public-eye" Mormon Moments and "personal" Mormon Moments are combining to bring the Church out of obscurity in Asia.

In June 2011, our Singapore public affairs council was finishing open house preparations for a new meetinghouse in north Singapore. An invitation was extended to the second-highest person in Singapore's national government: Deputy Prime Minister Teo Chee Hean. He accepted the invitation, and plans were made to guide him through classrooms depicting various Church programs.

As we began the tour, Minister Teo's comments reinforced the importance and impact of "in-the-public-eye" Mormon Moments. He stated the Singapore government emphasizes a diverse yet harmonious religious environment, and his visit would underscore that emphasis. He remarked that the tipping point for his decision to attend our open house was the impending presidential campaigns of Governor Mitt Romney and Ambassador Jon Huntsman. Minister Teo wanted to know more about the faith of these two politicians, one whom he knew well but with whom he had never discussed doctrines of The Church of Jesus Christ of Latter-day Saints.

In the middle of our open house tour, Minister Teo experienced two personal Mormon Moments. In the room set up to display the Church's youth programs, a fifteen-year-old young man described Aaronic Priesthood offices while Minister Teo skimmed through a Duty to God booklet. Minister Teo asked, "Where did the titles deacon, teacher, and priest come from?" For me, eternity almost hung in the balance while I silently prayed this boy's answer would be inspired. After a brief pause, the young man replied, "These titles came by revelation from God through his prophet Joseph Smith." I could scarcely contain myself from hugging this worthy priesthood holder who stated a profound truth.

Calmly proceeding on, we moved to the display of the Young Women program. Similarly, a delightful young woman articulately described the program and answered Minister Teo's questions while he thumbed through a Personal Progress booklet. When her short presentation concluded, Minister Teo asked, "How old are you?" She replied, "Thirteen, sir." Minister Teo turned to me and said, "Your religion produces outstanding youth." He is right!

When each of Asia's 3.5 billion people has the opportunity to interact with even one faithful Church member and experience a personal Mormon Moment like Deputy Prime Minister Teo encountered in that Singapore open house, then the Church will truly come out of obscurity.

I witness Jesus Christ is able to do His own work,[23] and He is doing it today in the Asia Area, where more than one-half of our Heavenly Father's children reside. The Church's future in Asia will be glorious as the gospel light continues to break forth out of obscurity upon these ancient lands and among these noble people.

NOTES

1. *Teachings of Presidents of the Church: Joseph Smith* (Salt Lake City: The Church of Jesus Christ of Latter-day Saints, 2007), 135–47.
2. See 3 Nephi 23:1–3.
3. Isaiah 59:2, 7, 9; emphasis added.
4. Isaiah 29:18; 2 Nephi 27:29; emphasis added.
5. See "The Testimony of Eight Witnesses," Book of Mormon.
6. Isaiah 58:10; italics added.
7. See Doctrine and Covenants 104:14–17.
8. See Doctrine and Covenants 44:4, 6.
9. Doctrine and Covenants 1:30; emphasis added.
10. Ephesians 2:20.
11. See Doctrine and Covenants 44.
12. 2 Nephi 1:19.

13. 2 Nephi 1:23; emphasis added.
14. 1 Nephi 22:8–9.
15. 1 Nephi 22:9.
16. 1 Nephi 22:12; emphasis added.
17. See M. Russell Ballard, "Sharing the Gospel Using the Internet," *Ensign*, July 2008, 58–63.
18. Richard B. Stamps, "The Cultural Impact of Mormon Missionaries on Taiwan," *BYU Studies* 41, no. 4 (2002): 103–14.
19. Articles of Faith 1:11.
20. Articles of Faith 1:12.
21. See 2 Nephi 28:20; Moroni 7:12.
22. Doctrine and Covenants 88:73.
23. See 2 Nephi 27:20–21.

The 2002 Winter Olympics were coined as a "Mormon Moment" by many journalists. (Courtesy of Intellectual Reserve, Inc.)

8

IN THE PUBLIC EYE

How the Church Is Handling Increased Global Visibility

MICHAEL OTTERSON

Michael Otterson, then managing director of the Public Affairs Department, at The Church of Jesus Christ of Latter-day Saints, presented this essay at "In the Public Eye: How the Church Is Handling Increased Global Visibility," the International Society's twenty-third annual conference, April 2012, Brigham Young University, Provo, Utah.

Forty-plus years ago, when I started work as a junior reporter on my first newspaper, a hard-bitten, tough news editor spelled out my job for me in stark terms. "Otterson," she said, "if you can't break down the entire story into a single short paragraph in your head, then you won't be writing for newspapers."

She was right, and it was good advice at the time. Fleet Street in London was then the hub of the larger British journalistic world I was entering, and some London tabloids had specific and tight limits on the length of a first paragraph. If memory serves, it was sixteen words for the mass-circulation *Daily Mirror*. And I learned to do it.

Now, decades later, the specifics of journalism styles and approaches have changed; however, for many in the news media, the core mentality has not. Much of TV and radio news, many newspapers, and what passes for news on the Internet is still about superficiality, overreporting the irrelevant while simplifying to the point of banality, creating tension where there is none, meeting deadlines, beating the opposition by telling a story no one else has, and doing it all in ninety seconds or 350 words.

When we take this journalistic worldview and present it with as rich and complex a subject as The Church of Jesus Christ of Latter-day Saints, the media industry's instincts are to try to tell the story in sixteen words. That's pretty difficult when nine of those words are used up by the full name of the Church. Or to put it another way, a whole era of history is reduced to a single "Mormon Moment."

We all understand that the alliteration is irresistible, and the term "Mormon Moment" will continue to be used widely. I'd like to trace something of the history of this term and flesh it out with some additional dimension and perspective. Meanwhile, I congratulate the International Society for choosing the title it did—"In the Public Eye"—rather than the "Mormon Moment."

History has not recorded the name of the journalist who created the phrase "Mormon Moment," but the earliest reference I have found was a headline in *U.S. News and World Report* in November 2000. The story was about a new Mormon temple in Houston. The Church's growth, according to the story's author, was "a tangible sign of the rising fortunes of . . . the Salt Lake City–based Church."

Two years later, the media identified another "Mormon Moment" when the 2002 Winter Olympics arrived in Salt Lake City. That was an extraordinary period. Once again, label-prone journalists wanted to call them "The Mormon Games," but "Mormon Moment" was used again, too. In one three-week period in 2002, 1,300 journalists came through our public affairs facilities in the Joseph Smith Memorial Building.

Five more years and we entered the US presidential campaign season of 2007–8, with "Mormon Moment" rising in favor once again. And today, if you Google "Mormon Moment," you'll get some 175,000 hits.

Twelve years from the year 2000 to today is a long "moment." But since we are trying to get perspective, let's step back even further. Was the spring of 1820 in a secluded wood in upstate New York a "Mormon Moment"? Was the turbulent period of 1820 through 1844 a "moment," which saw the publication of the Book of Mormon, the restoration of the priesthood, the initial rapid growth of the Church, the first missionary successes overseas, the series of relocations from New York to Ohio to Missouri to Illinois? What about the epic journey under Brigham Young—the Mormon equivalent of the Jewish Exodus—and the difficult birth of Salt Lake City, including the tense period ten years later when federal troops arrived to quell the supposed Mormon rebellion? That surely was a "Mormon Moment."

Then of course, there was that momentous Manifesto of 1890, officially ending polygamy, followed ten years later by the refusal of the US Senate to seat the senator from Utah, Reed Smoot—a "Mormon Moment" if ever there was one.

Then we entered a period of relatively quiet consolidation, and the Church emerged fifty years later without the great burden of financial debt and, surprisingly, with newfound respectability—a very significant fifty-year transitional "moment," followed by an incredible growth surge that began in the sixties and has continued, essentially unabated.

In the 1970s, we saw the priesthood extended to men of all races, which set the stage for unprecedented growth in many parts of the world, not just Africa. The 1970s also saw the rise of organized opposition to the Church on a scale not seen since Joseph Smith's day, mostly coming from fundamentalist Christian pastors. Books, movies, and tracts—everything is thrown at the Church. And we are now into living memory, and I don't need to belabor the point.

Perhaps after 182 years of successive moments, it's time to change the paradigm. Of course the "Mormon Moment" is going to live on in the journalistic lexicon, but let's now try to examine where we are today, with the expectation that this is not a transitory moment that will end but simply the latest phase in the historic emergence of the Church to a higher level of public consciousness. I will do that by examining seven specific and enduring contributors to this higher Church profile, not necessarily in order of importance. The first is the emergence of Latter-day Saint celebrities.

CATEGORY 1: LDS CELEBRITIES

Of course, we all know a lot of the interest right now is being driven by the fact that one man is running for president of his country, and he's a Latter-day Saint. We all know that, right? We don't need to mention any names? Just to make sure we all know the person we are talking about, let me show a picture [shows a picture of Yeah Samake].

You were expecting someone else, perhaps. For those who may not know, this is Yeah Samake, a BYU alumnus and a candidate for president of the African nation of Mali, one of the poorest countries in the world. At least, he was running for president until a military coup removed the incumbent president. Now the situation is unclear.

I show his picture to make my first important point as to what is driving public attention. It is not all about American presidential politics. One contributing factor to the rising profile of the Church is the emergence of individual Latter-day Saints as celebrities in different parts of the world.

This is not a new phenomenon, but it is accelerating. I remember in England in the 1970s the huge popularity of the Osmonds (who are still fondly remembered there by that generation) and also of people like golfers Billy Casper and Johnny Miller.

Today, Latter-day Saint celebrities are almost too numerous to mention. Many come from the world of sports. Others are in arts and entertainment. Some have made names for themselves in business and industry, others are emerging in academia, and several have been very successful in politics.

I've put up a slide of several faces; you will recognize most of them, and you may have a different visceral reaction to one or two simply because you may not necessarily identify with their politics or with some other aspects of their very public life. This, of course, is only a small sample of prominent Latter-day Saints.

Not all of these individuals have a measurable impact on the Church's reputation—at least not on a macro level—but some do because they make no secret of their faith. Collectively, they have the net effect of raising the Church's profile and adding to the national and international conversation about Mormons.

Purely from the Church's point of view, the most helpful voices are those who, in a very natural way and without being preachy, let people know they are Latter-day Saints. One of the best examples is Clayton Christensen, a Harvard business professor who has a world reputation as a pioneer in business innovation.

On his professional website, right under his biography, is a link, "Why I Belong and Why I Believe," that eloquently explains his faith and membership in The Church of Jesus Christ of Latter-day Saints. When *Forbes* magazine recently wanted to do a cover story on Brother Christensen, he agreed only if he could talk about his religious faith, which is an integral part of who he is. The resultant article was extraordinary. In about six weeks, the *New Yorker* magazine will publish a major feature on Brother Christensen, including his faith, which will likely run up to ten pages. In May, he will publish a book based on an article already published, "How Will I Measure My Life."

While Brother Christensen is a ready example, there are thousands of Latter-day Saints who have achieved respect and prominence in their own fields of endeavor who are raising the profile of the Church. It's worth mentioning that none of these individuals is ever positioned by us as speaking for the Church. They speak for themselves, and they represent themselves as individual Latter-day Saints. Our membership is diverse. It has been described as a big tent—bigger than many people suppose. The Church does not, could not, and should not try to control those individual voices. All we can do is point out to the media that they speak as individuals and may or may not reflect official Church teachings or policy positions.

CATEGORY 2: LDS POLITICIANS

In some ways, this is a subcategory of the first, but because of its impact, it deserves to stand on its own. Latter-day Saints have been elected as senators, congressmen, and state governors for over a century, but none seemed to penetrate public consciousness in a major way until 2007, when a former governor announced his intention to run for president. In the current campaign of 2011–12, at one stage (until mid-January) two of the remaining five nominees were Latter-day Saints.

Unquestionably, this factor is driving much of the current media interest and has given rise to this sense that the "Mormon Moment" is temporary. Obviously, when the election is over—depending on the outcome—this element may fade rapidly. But it's my central premise today, as I'll show later, that the Church's profile will remain high beyond the US presidential election.

The presidential campaign presents significant challenges and opportunities for the Church. The most obvious challenge is keeping the institutional Church out of the political campaigning. This is wise for all kinds of reasons. The most compelling is simply that it is not part of the Church's mission to campaign for political candidates or influence.

The Lord states in the Doctrine and Covenants that the Church should stand independent. That suggests it must keep its distance from the mechanisms of party politics. "That through my providence, notwithstanding the tribulation which shall descend upon you, that the Church may stand independent above all other creatures beneath the celestial world" (D&C 78:14).

This does not prevent the Church from exercising its right to express its views to government on issues of the day that it feels have moral implications or that affect the Church and its members directly—Proposition 8 is an example—but that is very different from Church leaders engaging in party politics and election campaigns.

Moreover, Church leaders—the "Brethren" in our Latter-day Saint vernacular—are focused on preaching the gospel of Jesus Christ around the world and strengthening members. That is their mission and their great preoccupation. Like some other members of the Public Affairs staff, I am privileged to have significant interaction with the Brethren, and I can personally attest to the fact I have never once heard a suggestion from any one of them that the Church institutionally should support a party candidate or campaign. It does not happen.

Another reason for avoiding party politics is equally obvious. We have a diverse membership, and since good principles are found in different political parties, our people are free to choose for themselves which political candidates to support or not support. The Church will not alienate a substantial portion of its members by supporting a candidate from one party and excluding another. And, of course, this applies in any country of the world.

This, I think, is one principle we have successfully conveyed to political journalists to the point of convincing them. From the very start, we proactively contacted and met with political journalists and emphasized Church policy by staying out of the campaign. In 2007 and 2008, two members of the Quorum of Twelve—Elder Ballard and Elder Cook, who then both had responsibility for Public Affairs—in company with Public Affairs staff, visited a string of editorial boards to help educate journalists. We acknowledged the inevitability of the Church becoming a part of the conversation from time to time, and we invited them to contact us if they had questions about the Church. We told them we would not engage in conversations about individual candidates, discuss whether their positions on issues were in alignment with the Church, or comment on their individual Church activity. We have kept to that principle, and I think journalists have appreciated it.

It is not always easy to distance ourselves from politics when others are determined to drag us in. Some of you will have seen the following clip from CNN, but it's worth showing at least part of it because of the lessons it teaches. [Anderson Cooper video clip]

This came out of the blue at a rally for one of the nominees, and we had no way of avoiding it. Despite our neutrality, the name of the Church was dragged into a political rally by someone who has no such reservations about mixing his own faith with campaign politics. You can see how we dealt with it—we asserted our neutrality, we incorporated our key message about a Christ-centered church, and we had the anchor promote Mormon.org as a source for viewers. In addition, previous behind-the-scenes work with CNN helped inform Anderson Cooper's interview. If you have seen all of this interview, you'll know this wasn't a good day for the pastor. Over the next few days, many nationally prominent figures, including journalists, spoke out against the pastor for pulling religion into the campaign in such a crass way.

It will be very important for our members to understand this insistence on institutional neutrality. I am aware of occasional letters we receive at headquarters that contain "helpful suggestions" from members for particular candidates that the writers would like us to pass on. No doubt those will increase in volume as the season unfolds, but there will be no mail delivery via the Church. As a signal both to members and nonmembers, the Church has posted on its Newsroom website for several years its explicit political neutrality policies, and it is probably worth reading this section: "Elected officials who are Latter-day Saints make their own decisions and may not necessarily be in agreement with one another or even with a publicly stated Church position. While the Church may communicate its views to them, as it may to any other elected official, it recognizes that these officials still must make their own choices based on their best judgment and with consideration of the constituencies whom they were elected to represent."[1]

CATEGORY 3: ACADEMICS

A third factor that is driving attention is the growing list of academics who are researching or writing about The Church of Jesus Christ of Latter-day Saints. I'm not talking about scholars of Church history who have been prominent in their own circles for years and who have added substantially to the amount of serious literature on the Church but instead a new generation of scholars who are being more and more frequently quoted in mainstream media—scholars such as sociologist David Campbell, coauthor of *American Grace: How Religion Divides and Unites Us*, an award-winning and truly groundbreaking work. Another is Matthew Bowman, a Mormon with a doctorate in American religious history from Georgetown, whose book *The Mormon People* may become a commonly used reference for journalists. Another to be published in the next few months by author J. B. Haws will be a history of Church public affairs, published by the Oxford University Press, the first such study I am aware of on this topic. While it is not my place to endorse any of these authors and what they write, it is beyond dispute that the serious work in which they and others are engaged is raising the Church's public profile in significant ways with thoughtful observers.

We are also seeing significant attention paid to the Church by non–Latter-day Saint scholars who have access to mainstream media. The Pew Forum on Religion and Public Life has invested its own resources and significant research relative to Latter-day Saint life and practice. That research has received heavy attention in the news media, especially here in the United States.

For ten years, a twice-yearly Faith Angle Forum has convened in Florida for a select group of nationally respected journalists and distinguished scholars. This in-depth discussion of some of the most crucial issues facing Americans today, now sponsored by the Ethics and Public Policy Center, has included Mormon-related topics in the last two such gatherings.

This past month, a trio of sociologists from the University of Pennsylvania and Indiana University–Purdue released a new study that captured how deeply committed Latter-day Saints are, not only to their own faith but to their wider community. According to this robust study of churchgoing Latter-day Saints, Mormons are the most "pro-social" members of American society, giving far more in time and money to Church and secular causes than other Americans.

There are, of course, many other scholars, and this isn't intended as a complete list. These scholars are significant not only for the works they publish but also because they have become sources for journalists who are looking for comment. There is great value in independent, well-informed, and balanced commentary from respected scholars in such situations.

CATEGORY 4: LDS BLOGGERS

How much influence individual Latter-day Saint bloggers as a whole have on the public's perception of the Church is a matter of conjecture. The term "bloggers" covers a wide field. Frankly, the term "bloggernacle," which has been invented to describe the collection of blogs focused on Latter-day Saint themes, is an apt one. This is only a slice of the blogging world. For some members, these blogs provide an important and valued voice for discussion, but so far they operate under a kind of tabernacle-like dome under which contributions from bloggers echo to and from defined audiences. Only occasionally does something spill outside to non-Latter-day Saint mass media or even to the rank-and-file Church membership.

Other Latter-day Saint bloggers write outside the bloggernacle and don't limit their audiences to Church members. Recently, the Church's Research and Information Division, at our request, asked a sizeable sample of Latter-day Saint leaders and another sample of Latter-day Saint members in several parts of the United States about their familiarity with these bloggers who are sometimes quoted in mainstream media. From a sample of over four hundred bishops, no blogger in this category of what I might call "independent voices" registered awareness above 3 percent. Among members generally, it was even lower.

Some of these bloggers are obviously agenda driven. I do not say that disparagingly. They are what they are, and the Internet offers everyone a voice. I mention it only to note in passing, because some bloggers push themes that are very different from the official voice of the Church, and we sometimes have a challenge in explaining that to journalists.

Mormon blogger Jana Riess recently put it this way:

> I think that anyone who speaks to the press about Mormonism should be aware of having an agenda and knowing what that agenda is. A few weeks ago, I was contacted by a national network news producer who was pulling together a story about Mormonism. She wanted to get me on camera to share my experiences as a Mormon feminist. I said I would be happy to help, but that the list of people she had talked to did not yet include enough conservative or traditional Latter-day Saints. For balance it would be important to include those voices too.
>
> Everyone who has ever been involved in Mormonism . . . has some kind of Mormon story. In that sense they—we—can and should speak for Mormonism. We do not speak for the LDS Church, however, and we can't claim expert status merely on the basis of limited involvement and cursory knowledge of Mormonism. Reporters should try to achieve balance . . . and Mormon pundits should adopt measures of accountability.[2]

I congratulate Jana Riess on that kind of honesty and transparency, which takes some strength of character. She is absolutely right to remind a TV network that they have a responsibility to portray what she calls "traditional Latter-day Saints," or what I call "the Mormon worldview."

Some time ago, the website GetReligion.org, which specializes in monitoring media coverage of religion, cautioned readers of Mormon bloggers to look for official attribution and not just take the writer's word as "gospel."

The website noted that "if people make claims about evolving Mormon doctrines, look for names, titles and clear statements of attribution."[3]

All of these disparate voices have their right to expression, but as individuals, they do not speak for the Church and should be careful not to imply they do.

More significant collectively to the rising awareness of the Church may be the plethora of so-called "Mormon mommy bloggers" on the Internet. Mommy bloggers, for those who may not know, are the army of mostly stay-at-home mothers who also blog about their husbands, their kids, their lives, and their faith. In the interest of full disclosure here, I must admit to a bias—I have six daughters, all of whom blog, and a couple of them are outstanding writers and photographers. None of their blogs have large followings, but many Latter-day Saint blogs do, and they have raised the Church's profile among a segment of the public that we would not have expected.

A little over a year ago, a very fine writer named Emily Matchar from North Carolina wrote an article called "Why I Can't Stop Reading Mormon Housewife Blogs." Describing herself as a secular, childless woman who has never baked a cupcake, Matchar acknowledges she and a number of her friends are drawn to these LDS women's blogs with a strange fascination. She asks herself why, and she answers her own question:

> Well, to use a word that makes me cringe, these blogs are weirdly "uplifting." To read Mormon lifestyle blogs is to peer into a strange and fascinating world where the most fraught issues of modern living—marriage and child rearing—appear completely unproblematic. This seems practically subversive to someone like me, weaned on an endless media parade of fretful stories about "work-life balance" and soaring divorce rates and the perils of marrying too young/too old/too whatever. . . .

"It seems that a lot of popular culture wants to portray marriage and motherhood as demeaning, restrictive, or simple, but in the LDS Church, motherhood is a very important job, and it's treated with a lot of respect," says Natalie Holbrook, the New York–based author of the popular blog *Nat the Fat Rat*. "Most of my readers are non-LDS women in their late 20s and early 30s, college educated, many earning secondary degrees on the postgraduate level, and a comment I often get is, 'You are making me want kids, and I've never wanted kids!'"

Indeed, Mormon bloggers like Holbrook make marriage and motherhood seem, well, fun. Easy. Joyful. These women seem relaxed and untouched by cynicism. They throw elaborate astronaut-themed birthday parties for their kids and go on Sunday family drives to see the fall leaves change. . . . They often have close, large extended families; moms and sisters are always dropping in to watch the kids or help out with cake decorating. Their lives seem adorable and old-fashioned and comforting.

"I've gotten e-mails from readers thanking me for putting a positive spin on marriage and family," Holbrook says. "It's important to acknowledge the hard parts—and I think we all do—but why not focus more on the lovely and the beautiful? That positive attitude is a very common theme throughout all aspects of the Mormon faith."[4]

Maybe it's something to do with our tradition of journal keeping, but thousands of Latter-day Saint women who are writing about familiar themes of home and family seem to have created a new media niche that is raising the Church's profile in unexpected places.

CATEGORY 5: POPULAR CULTURE

Popular culture is an incredibly powerful force in conditioning public opinion and increasing awareness. It may be the factor over which we have the least influence, but it may be one of the most significant in terms of how many members of the general public see the Church.

As a defined community grows, its emergence into popular culture becomes inevitable. We should not underestimate the powerful, formative influence popular culture has in shaping and conditioning ordinary public opinion. Movies, plays, books, music lyrics, and even humor in conversation are all signs people are beginning to pay attention. As Catholics and Jews have known for centuries, popular culture includes parody and satire, and that can be uncomfortable for the target. By its nature, parody does not pretend to accurately portray the subject of its attention. How targeted communities respond to such portrayals is very important.

We don't have to look far to see examples of Mormon-themed cultural expression. The best example of the powerful influence of popular culture over the past year is the Broadway musical *The Book of Mormon*. This is an irreverent and at times blasphemous production most Church members would be too uncomfortable to sit through. Nevertheless, it has been widely portrayed as being implicitly kind and positive to the Church, and in the end, it portrays missionaries as heroes.

How to respond to such a situation is challenging, because an attitude of defensiveness is likely to further alienate an already cynical public. It was for this reason that we phrased our response to the musical this way: "The production may attempt to entertain people for an evening, but the Book of Mormon as a volume of scripture will change people's lives forever by bringing them closer to Christ."[5] Because it was not defensive, this statement was very widely reported, sucked the oxygen out of the potential for a story about conflict, and lifted us above the fray onto higher ground. One of the show's producers praised the statement as "a perfect First Amendment–loving reaction."[6]

Humor and parody is especially difficult to deal with. Many of you will have seen various Mormon-related clips from the comedy show *The Colbert Report*. Stephen Colbert can be biting in his sarcasm and parody, but in one piece he portrayed Mormons as "irresistibly cool." Humor, I suggest, if not mean spirited, is generally best met with good grace or humor of our own.

Maintaining an appropriate institutional relationship with popular culture is challenging. For example, television shows like *Big Love* and *Sister Wives* feed polygamy themes and negative stereotypes into the public domain. In the interest of simple truth, we cannot let some things go unchallenged. We have pushed back hard and consistently, but, hopefully, always in a dignified way, both on misrepresentation and on insisting that journalists make distinctions between The Church of Jesus Christ of Latter-day Saints and polygamous groups. We have made significant progress over the past ten years, and we continue to do so, but polygamy remains one of the persistent associations with the Church in the public mind.

We can find evidence that Mormons have penetrated popular culture in the most unexpected places. Over the past few months, in addition to a lot of attention on the musical, the *New York Times* has run two articles on Mormons in popular culture. One of these was an introduction to the latest and hottest trends in young Mormon fashion. (Did you know there was something called Mormon fashion? And no, it's not what we wear at the Church Office Building.) The headline on this story is "To Be Young, Hip, and Mormon."

As if that wasn't enough, the other was an article about the venerable tradition of Mormon cuisine, with the image of a casserole dish of potatoes au gratin. The caption reads: "Updated Funeral Potatoes."

And before we leave popular culture as a factor in our rising visibility, we should note that over the past few years we have seen reality TV shows and competitions go out of their way to include Latter-day Saints in their casts. It is these kinds of shows that launched David Archuleta, Ken Jennings, and others. We confess ourselves to be bewildered by this trend.

CATEGORY 6: CHURCH INITIATIVES

Over the past year or so, American media interest in the Church has become intense. Every day, the Public Affairs Department scans the Internet and other sources for articles or broadcasts that mention the Church. I usually look at that report when I arrive at the office each morning. Sometimes such stories require a response, sometimes not. Often they represent interactions we have already had with journalists, and we are interested in seeing how their stories turned out.

Through the course of a typical day, our media staff engages dozens of times with media inquiries—sometimes up to fifty a day. Often we are responding, but often we are pushing an idea for a story we think will help people better understand the Church.

The industry term for all of this is "earned" media—it is publicity we don't pay for, and it may be good or bad. In addition, the Church has its own way of elevating its public profile in positive ways that guarantees a more accurate portrayal. The Public Affairs Department is not responsible for paid advertising in the Church—that responsibility falls to the Missionary Department. I can't claim any credit for the highly successful "I'm a Mormon" campaign that has been airing in many localities in the United States and a little outside of it. In our view, it is a superbly orchestrated campaign, allowing members of the Church to tell their own stories honestly and in unscripted ways.

The campaign is deliberately designed to break stereotypes, which it does by portraying a diverse membership. Each person has his or her own story, but all of them are united in a belief in the restored gospel. The nonmember audience gets a chance to meet real members, up close and personal. Each closes with an affirmation: "And I'm a Mormon."

The spots invite viewers to Mormon.org, the primary Church website for curious nonmembers, where they will find thousands more members whom they can talk to if they wish.

Not unexpectedly, some news media outlets have tried to portray the stereotype-busting ads as a stealth campaign to support a presidential candidate—emphatically not true. You will know the Church has run TV, print, and radio ads for many years, and planning for this campaign began long before the political season. In fact, the advertising schedule deliberately excluded primary states to avoid all appearance of having a political agenda.

We did frankly take advantage of *The Book of Mormon* musical running in New York. Since print ads seemed to be everywhere and taxis were driving about with "Book of Mormon" on their roofs, it made sense to accept that free advertising graciously and add New York to our own advertising schedule as well.

Our initiatives are not confined to the news media. The core purpose of our department is defined as "building bridges with opinion leaders to foster mutual understanding," and that's true whether or not particular opinion leaders agree with us. They are found in various endeavors—certainly the news media but also interfaith leaders, leaders of ethnic or cultural minorities, members of Congress, state governors, ambassadors, academics, think tanks, and those who represent advocacy groups. All of these groups have members who, from time to time, have interests that overlap with the Church, hence our interest in helping people better understand who we are and the values we represent.

It is very common for members of the Quorum of the Twelve to include visits to opinion leaders on occasions when they have other assignments, and there have been many mutually helpful conversations that have flowed from these engagements. It is all about increasing mutual trust, respect, and understanding.

CATEGORY 7: CHURCH GROWTH

In my view, the rising public awareness of Latter-day Saints in almost all of the categories I have covered today is a subset of one major factor, and that is the continued growth of the Church.

Without a rising membership that is felt in every field of endeavor, many of these other factors would be far less significant. Ever since their arrival in these valleys, the Saints have sent some of their members on missions around the world. What has happened in the last half of the twentieth century and the first dozen years of the twenty-first is something profoundly significant.

A map of membership distribution in the United States shows that while we have members in every state, there are large groups of Latter-day

Saints in the Intermountain West and in a corridor in the northeast, especially in and around Washington, DC. In addition, we have significant membership in Florida, Texas, California, the Chicago area, and in the northwest around Seattle and Portland. This is reflective of what we sometimes call the "Mormon Diaspora." Families who move for work or BYU students who seek their careers away from Utah are helping fuel this.

In practical terms, although the center of gravity for Latter-day Saints is still clearly in the west of the country, our members everywhere are our best advertisement. They are schoolteachers and students, professional associates and fellow factory workers, bankers and businessmen, artists and musicians. All form a part of the rising tide of Church membership, with its potential for interaction with the nonmember public and for greater education as to our beliefs and practices.

Much of what we have discussed has been focused on the United States, but there are significant international implications for what is happening here that will be discussed by others. I might just mention that the profile of the Church in most countries of the world is greatly influenced by its reputation in the United States. In my three years in public affairs in England and twelve years in Australia, I found that to be overwhelmingly true, and every major story—especially controversies involving the Church in the US—spilled over to the local media, although usually abbreviated.

Nowhere has that been clearer than in the current presidential campaign. Who the president of the United States is matters to citizens of other countries, and so the media reports many of the aspects that are seen here.

As far as the Church is concerned, the French are calling it "the Mormon Wave." Swedes and the British say Mormons are coming into "the mainstream."

Some of the recent interest from media around the world includes magazines from Sweden, Finland, Russia, Brazil, and Slovenia, as well as a great deal of coverage in British media. In recent months, those we have engaged include the following:

Germany: *Frankfurter Allgemeine Zeitung*, *Der Spiegel*, *Rheinische Post*, *Die Welt*, and German Public Radio

UK: *Daily Mail*, *The Economist*, *The Guardian*, BBC, *The Times*, and Scottish newspapers

France: TV stations France 2, France 4, and France 24; *Le Monde* and other French papers (these frequently link to the Paris temple development)

Norway: newspapers

Denmark: TV

Switzerland: TV and public radio stations

Poland: TV

Korea: KBS television

Arabia: news agency Al Jazeera

Japan: broadcasting corporation NHK

Latin America: Brazilian newspapers and a national magazine; Telemundo, the Spanish-speaking TV network

International media: Reuters and the English-language *Voice of America*

To help cope with this international interest, we are in the process of launching some fifty international versions of our Newsroom website. A half dozen of these have been launched in the past few weeks, and more are going online every week. These sites will be helpful for local leaders and members to keep abreast of issues with which they may not be familiar.

It is much more than politics. It is much more than a moment. After 182 years, the Church may have reached the point that the Lord described in Doctrine and Covenants 1—finally, the Church has emerged "out of obscurity," at least in some parts of the world.

At times during the current season, it seems like our challenge is no longer to bring the Church out of "obscurity and darkness" but to ensure the illumination it gets is truthful and fair. There are two kinds of obscurity: there is the kind that relates to invisibility and the kind that relates to misunderstanding. Joseph Smith said in his history that he endeavored to "disabuse the public mind"[7] of false ideas about himself and his work, and we are still working on that project. If phase 1 had to do with the Church's visibility, then phase 2—which will be about achieving understanding—still mostly lies ahead.

The current period and the time ahead will be demanding of Church members. While there are opportunities for the general public to better understand the Church, it is obvious that dissenting voices and Church critics will seek to exploit this higher profile for their own objectives. Because we understand the principle of opposition in all things, and because we see precisely this kind of pushback whenever prophets have preached the gospel through the ages, we know there will be times when we will need thick skin. We may also need a sense of humor. Above all, we will need a spirit of kindness and forgiveness, remembering that our claim to be followers of the Lord Jesus Christ is most convincing when our actions are in harmony with our beliefs.

NOTES

1. "Political Neutrality," http://www.mormonnewsroom.org/official-statement/political-neutrality.
2. Jana Riess, "Who Speaks for Mormonism?," *Religion News Service*, 26 March 2012.
3. Terry Mattingly, "LDS 'Evolving' on Sexuality? Says Who?," *Get Religion* (blog), 2 September 2011.
4. Emily Matchar, "Why I Can't Stop Reading Mormon Housewife Blogs," *Salon*, 15 January 2011.
5. Lyman Kirkland, "*Book of Mormon* Musical: Church's Official Statement," 7 February 2011.
6. Andrew Goldman, "The Fogies of 'South Park,'" *New York Times Magazine*, 23 September 2011, http://www.nytimes.com/2011/09/25/magazine/talk-trey-parker-and-matt-stone-of-south-park.html.
7. Joseph Smith—History 1:1.

Part 3

PEACEMAKING AND DIPLOMACY

9

BY PERSUASION, LONG-SUFFERING, MEEKNESS, AND LOVE

On Diplomacy

CORY W. LEONARD

Cory W. Leonard, then assistant director of the David M. Kennedy Center for International Studies at Brigham Young University, presented this essay at "The Church and International Diplomacy," the International Society's twenty-fourth annual conference, April 2013, Brigham Young University, Provo, Utah.

In 2008, my awareness of "International Diplomacy and the Church" grew when the David M. Kennedy Center for International Studies at Brigham Young University commemorated its twenty-fifth anniversary. The center produced a short film titled *The Kennedy Way*, featuring never-before-seen footage from David Kennedy's life and exploring his attributes evidenced through his family and work as an international banker, as US secretary of the treasury and ambassador to NATO, and as special representative of the First Presidency of the Church. Learning more about Kennedy confirmed why he was the ideal namesake for BYU's flagship international core and a model of persuasion, skill, and leadership.

Efforts to address barriers to the Church's legal recognition, explained in the *Encyclopedia of Mormonism* by Martin Hickman, provide an example of diplomatic work:

> When President Kimball decided that legal recognition should be the first goal, he sent Kennedy to Greece, where recognition had long been withheld despite the vigorous efforts of Church leaders. Kennedy learned from his contacts in the Greek government and the U.S. embassy there that the key to recognition as "a house of prayer" required the approval of the Archbishop of Athens and All Greece, His Beatitude Seraphim. In a crucial interview, Kennedy pointed out that the Greek Orthodox Church enjoyed full freedom of religion in the United States, that the Greek government had honored President David O. McKay for the aid the Church had sent to Greece after the devastating earthquake of 1953, and that the Church was fully recognized by most of the other countries of Western Europe. Greece eventually gave legal recognition to the Church. Other countries where recognition would be sought and eventually granted included Yugoslavia, Portugal, and Poland.[1]

Indeed, like David Kennedy, effective diplomats and leaders must adeptly wield the soft power of persuasion. What do we know about persuasion that may be of interest to Latter-day Saint professionals?

PERSUADE AND BE PERSUADED

Life involves persuasion. Each day, we are persuaded, and frequently we persuade others. We encounter decisions that force our resolve and judgment. We may ask: What will I make of my life? How will I make a living? How will I make a difference in the world? Or on a more basic level, how can I solve this problem, deal with this difficult personality, or convince someone to my understanding? (Toddlers are particularly difficult, in my limited experience.)

Persuasion is the art of shaping beliefs and decisions and is an essential part of our lives as citizens, professionals, and Latter-day Saints. Persuasion is also a key part of diplomacy—as it involves consensus building, decision-making, and power. It is in that regard I would like to explore the notion of persuasion.

PERSUASION AND THE GOSPEL

We recognize that the greatest power on our planet, the power to act in the name of God—or priesthood—can be "handled only upon the principles of righteousness."[2] This concept is part of what President Dieter F. Uchtdorf recently referred to as the "owner's manual" of the priesthood[3] and what President Heber J. Grant noted to be one of his most oft-quoted verses in the Doctrine and Covenants:[4] "No power or influence can or ought to be maintained by virtue of the priesthood, only by persuasion, by long-suffering, by gentleness and meekness, and by love unfeigned; by kindness, and pure knowledge, which shall greatly enlarge the soul without hypocrisy, and without guile."[5]

Why are these principles of power and influence included together? What is it about persuasion, long-suffering, meekness, and love, among other virtues, that makes them essential? And how can they be applied in the myriad of social interactions we have as lifelong learners and disciples?

Early in the Book of Mormon, Lehi had a dream in which his family was commanded to obtain critical records on plates of brass. The only problem was that these records were located somewhere other than where the family was, and it meant doing something that several of the sons were not planning on, nor were they enthused about doing—namely, going back. Lacking agreement and after "consult[ing] one with another," the sons made the decision by chance on who would face Laban, casting lots. Laman was chosen to head back to Jerusalem. He subsequently failed to get the plates and returned to tell his brothers the bad news.[6]

At this point, the brothers were finished, but Nephi was not willing to give up just yet. He gave them a charge that "as the Lord liveth, and as we live, we will not go down unto our father in the wilderness until we have accomplished the thing which the Lord hath commanded us,"[7] followed by a series of reasons, including the need to be faithful, the context of Jerusalem's wickedness and its imminent destruction, and the key role of the records for linguistic and spiritual continuity. His plea worked. "And it came to pass that after this manner of language did I persuade my brethren, that they might be faithful in keeping the commandment of God."[8]

In this case, Nephi persuaded his brothers to do what they should have already understood was the right thing to do—to go and try again to get the plates. But just like us, they needed to be engaged in a conversation, to be reminded and persuaded. (It is interesting to note that for some reason, the brothers did not have a hard time returning to Jerusalem once more to persuade Ishmael and his daughters to join them in the wilderness.[9])

Later on we see how their attitude changed when they lost their commitment to their father's vision and escalated to violence, or hard power, against their younger brother. At that point, their choices were mitigated by an angel[10]—but Nephi's efforts throughout illustrate the process of persuasion and show how dialogue played an important part in Nephi's relationship to his family and his commitment to truth.

LEARNING AND PERSUASION

Today, we might associate persuasion with something different from Nephi's familial entreaties. Jay Conger, a professor of business at Claremont McKenna, addresses common misunderstandings about persuasion:

> Persuasion is widely perceived as a skill reserved for selling products and closing deals. It is also commonly seen as just another form of manipulation—devious and to be avoided. Certainly, persuasion can be used in selling and deal-clinching situations, and it can be misused to manipulate people. But exercised constructively and to its full potential, persuasion supersedes sales and is quite the opposite of deception. *Effective persuasion becomes a negotiating and learning process through which a persuader leads colleagues to a problem's shared solution.* Persuasion does indeed involve moving people to a position they don't currently hold, but not by begging or cajoling. Instead, it involves careful preparation, the proper framing of arguments, the presentation of vivid supporting evidence, and the effort to find the correct emotional match with your audience.[11]

Indeed, we know persuasion is a theme that cuts across many different academic and professional fields. And in an even larger sense, persuasion is at the core of the learning process because it changes the way we perceive and understand reality, influencing our attitudes and creating our vision of the world.

Learning involves active engagement in introducing, evaluating, and deciding which ideas have merit and which do not. As a proud graduate of this institution, I experienced one of my formative learning experiences in honors courses where Dean Hal Miller took us into a world of new "conversations" where we could engage in a discussion with some of the greatest minds and on important topics in the world of ideas. We wrestled with Plato, plumbed the Bhagavad Gita, pondered St. Augustine, and wrote alongside Montaigne. Our job as students was to read, to question, and to determine what was persuasive and what was not. More often than not, we missed the point—yet Dr. Miller carefully and patiently explained and answered questions as we stumbled along the path of learning.

As Latter-day Saints, our spiritual foundation influences all aspects of our learning, professions, and family life. Also, experiencing give-and-take and intellectual back-and-forth helps us to increase our understanding and ideally make better decisions, as Hugh Nibley explained in a talk given to Pi Sigma Alpha, the political science honor society:

> A discussion with God is not a case of agreeing or disagreeing with him—Who is in a position to do that?—but of understanding him. What Abraham and Ezra and Enoch asked was "Why?" Socrates showed that teaching is a dialogue, a discussion. As long as the learner is in the dark, he should protest and argue and question, for that is the best way to bring problems into focus, while the teacher patiently and cheerfully explains, delighted that his pupil has enough interest and understanding to raise questions—the more passionate, the more promising. There is a place for discussion and participation in the government of the kingdom.[12]

But persuasion is merely a tool, and instruments can be used for different moral purposes.[13] It seems essential that section 121 of the Doctrine and Covenants places persuasion in close quarters with at least three qualities previously introduced, namely meekness, long-suffering, and love. These virtues can modify and direct our persuasive efforts, especially as we interact in a world filled with conflict, strife, and disagreement. Let's consider each virtue separately as we try to understand how they relate to our persuasive efforts.

LONG-SUFFERING

Defined, "long-suffering" means "an enduring disposition" or "having endured mental or physical discomfort for a protracted period of time patiently or without complaint." It might seem a stretch to our modern world, but if we hope to persuade others, we must listen to their concerns and create a space for others to engage in conversation, just as Nephi did with his siblings.

Orson Scott Card, an LDS author and frequent columnist, recently observed the following:

> Even within our country, some Latter-day Saints will strongly disagree with others about the actions of our government. Because I have written extensively on political matters, I have received many letters from Saints who disagree with me, asking, "How can you hold that opinion and still be a faithful Latter-day Saint?" (Of course, some of the letters are not so politely worded.)
>
> I get such letters about equally from the left and the right, and about almost every topic I've covered. . . . But the point of freedom is that we should not assume that people who disagree with us are unworthy of full membership in our community, or that their voices should not be heard.
>
> On the contrary, it is essential that all voices be heard in order to reach wise decisions that take into account the needs and judgments of all people.[14]

Students are especially adept at and enjoy new opportunities in social media—where an incredibly wide range of viewpoints, ideas, and arguments reside. On occasion I have watched with horror as my Facebook page becomes the staging ground for a battle of opposing views that mirrors many newspaper discussion boards, sports websites, blogs, and anywhere that open (and especially anonymous) interaction is allowed. My students tell me it is appropriate to delete or censor my online "friends," but I secretly hope my students' inner angels will help these commenters regain a sense of decorum, if not a measure of kindness.

Henry David Thoreau wrote, "Thaw with his gentle persuasion is more powerful than Thor with his hammer. The one melts, the other but breaks into pieces."[15] And yet it seems that some online contributors would rather be Nordic superheroes than a force of nature. That is because the language and tone of many comments online preclude a conversation. Discussions can become less about respecting or enduring other views and more about making our point heard.

These discussion-enders may be insensitive responses, but as part of communities, and especially learning communities, they become deal breakers that replace dialogue with an awkward silence at best and "sharpness" at worst—usually without the "increase of love" we are advised to employ afterward.[16] More importantly, they demonstrate a lack of long-suffering in our demeanor because we do not want to have to listen to something that does not fit our thinking. We recognize not all ideas are equal or even correct—that is why we need to learn. But being long-suffering increases our chances of gaining understanding, and it keeps us connected to those in the discussion.

Clearly, this is a very small part of being long-suffering, as many with greater trials can attest. But this important virtue may give us resolve to find ways to stay connected, to be patient, and to try and better understand others.

MEEKNESS

Meekness is another virtue recommended to us and, like the others, is a subject matter unto itself. We know personal growth occurs best when we submit to God's will, but as President Ezra Taft Benson taught, "Either we can choose to be humble or we can be compelled."[17] One way we can immediately experience our limitations is through cross-cultural interactions in our smaller, more globalized world.

Cultural differences are rarely more apparent than when we experience another place firsthand. Several years ago, our family traveled across Europe on a study abroad, and while contending with different food, language, and environments—mostly in large, urban cities—our eight-year-old son, Jack, concluded, "In Turkey, they don't seem to understand our personal space or our family bubble." In fact, he and his younger brother were regularly pinched and patted, observed and provoked, and he was not prepared for all of that attention. Buses were crowded—unlike the one he is used to riding. City streets were filled with a myriad of smells, sights, and sounds that were unfamiliar and frightening at times. And many things seemed so very different—from electric plugs to the experience of worshipping with sixty members of the Church in a city of thirteen million people.

In these instances, we can withdraw, retreat, or become outright defensive. We can also fail to see what is happening before us. But when we approach these new cultural adventures with meekness and humility, we can begin to understand our limitations in new ways. In a letter to Edward Partridge, Joseph Smith wrote: "We ought always to be aware of those prejudices which some-times so strangely present themselves, and are so congenial to human nature, against our friends, neighbors, and brethren of the world, who choose to differ from us in opinion and in matters of faith. Our religion is between us and our God. Their religion is between them and their God."[18]

Elder Neal A. Maxwell, nearly thirty years ago, addressed this topic on BYU campus, noting that "in the ecology of the eternal attributes these cardinal characteristics are inextricably bound up together. Among them, meekness is often the initiator, the facilitator, and the consolidator." He further explains the link to persuasion this way:

> Since God desired to have us become like Himself, He first had to make us free, to learn, to choose, and to experience; hence our humility and teachability are premiere determinants of our progress and our happiness. Agency is essential to perfectibility, and meekness is essential to the wise use of agency—and to our recovery when we have misused our agency. . . .
>
> In contrast, we see in ourselves, brothers and sisters, the unnecessary multiplication of words—not only a lack of clarity, but vanity. Our verbosity is often a cover for insincerity or uncertainty. Meekness, the subtraction of self, reduces the multiplication of words.
>
> Without meekness, the conversational point we insist on making often takes the form of I, that spearlike, vertical pronoun. Meekness, however, is more than self-restraint; it is the presentation of self in a posture of kindness and gentleness. It reflects

> certitude, strength, serenity; it reflects a healthy self-esteem and a genuine self-control.[19]

LOVE

Finally, a virtue that guides our persuasion efforts is real love. This may well be the hardest part of a gospel approach, because it is so easy for us to become enamored with our own ideas, accomplishments, and interests. It is also quite difficult to love at close range when our family, friends, or colleagues do not appreciate our efforts. And it is harder still when we face down our real or perceived enemies.

Starting in 1999, I attended a number of UN conferences in New York, Nairobi, Geneva, and elsewhere, where I was involved in multipart negotiations with countries and groups that had opposing views on a number of policy issues. This competition of ideas—common to the sports arena, courtroom, marketplace, or among the electorate—often led to zero-sum outcomes through long negotiation. Try as we might to break through and find common ground, discussions were difficult, and both sides were regularly frustrated. Some of these differences were procedural, but I was struck by the degree to which our opposing sides displayed personal animosity and open hostility.

We occasionally had hard-won victories at the expense of the other side. The lack of empathy was readily apparent and in some ways understandable. Since then, I have often thought about these experiences and the possible lessons.

Recently, someone who has been involved in these issues was interviewed. In talking about how to address these types of intractable conflicts, she said that as a result of thinking about them over a long period of time, she recognized the need for and advocated a type of "sportsmanship" that seems to me to be an essential part of a Christian approach in such areas:

> The need to approach others with enthusiasm for difference is absolutely critical to any change. You know . . . I'm the toughest of fighters. And you know I love a good fight. And I love to win. But I think what I have learned is that you have got to approach differences with this notion that there is good in the other. And that if we can't

> figure out how to do that and if there isn't the crack in the middle where there are some people on both sides who absolutely refuse to see the other as evil, this is going to continue.[20]

How do we meekly, patiently, and lovingly engage with others, especially when the stakes are the highest? For me, this gospel ideal of love warrants our serious consideration. President Uchtdorf observed the following:

> We must realize that all of God's children wear the same jersey. Our team is the brotherhood of man. This mortal life is our playing field. Our goal is to learn to love God and to extend that same love toward our fellowman. We are here to live according to His law and establish the kingdom of God. We are here to build, uplift, treat fairly, and encourage all of Heavenly Father's children.[21]

There will always be times when we must take a stand for what is right. But I believe we can try to do so in a loving and genuine manner, avoiding ad hominem and mean-spirited attacks. I recognize that possessing love unfeigned is extremely challenging, but I have seen examples throughout my life from my parents, wife, colleagues, and students that give me hope.

CHANGING MINDS AND HEARTS

Recently, filmmaker Sidney Lumet passed away. He was known for a remarkable film titled *12 Angry Men*, which portrays the compelling transformation of divergent viewpoints over a short period of time. In the film, a young man of low social status has been accused of murdering his father. As the title suggests, twelve jurors are chosen to deliberate his fate, and they bring with them lifetimes of experience and pain, as well as their own idiosyncratic perspectives.

The entire 1957 film version takes place in one room and occurs in real time. Initially, it appears to be an open-and-shut trial. But one lone juror, juror number eight, played by Henry Fonda, quietly voices his dissenting opinion. He does so through the first part of the film by listening quietly, thoughtfully assessing each juror's view, and asking probing questions.

As the film progresses, it becomes clear he is beginning to persuade other jurors one by one, but the way in which he does it still surprises me. Through continued engagement with the others—including the last holdout juror—and a great deal of listening and discussion, juror number eight eventually persuades all eleven to the "not guilty" conclusion.[22]

Nationalism is just one obvious aspect of diplomacy. And yet we know of Latter-day Saint diplomats who proudly wear the flags of at least seven countries. Ultimately, as Latter-day Saint professionals, it may be more important how we are persuaded rather than how we persuade. For, while changing our mind is important in learning, the opening of our hearts is critical to our salvation.

May we be better able to engage the wide range of perspectives and discourse as Christians in the broader world around us—and become better citizens, diplomats, and professionals as well.

NOTES

1. Martin Hickman, "Diplomatic Relations," in *Encyclopedia of Mormonism*, ed. Daniel H. Ludlow (New York: Macmillan, 1992), 1:383.
2. Doctrine and Covenants 121:36.
3. Dieter F. Uchtdorf, "Your Potential, Your Privilege," *Ensign*, May 2011, 59.
4. *Teachings of Presidents of the Church: Heber J. Grant* (Salt Lake City: The Church of Jesus Christ of Latter-day Saints, 2002), 107.
5. Doctrine and Covenants 121:41–42.
6. 1 Nephi 3:10–14.
7. 1 Nephi 3:15.
8. 1 Nephi 3:21.
9. See 1 Nephi 7:1–3.
10. See 1 Nephi 3:28–30.
11. Jay Conger, "The Necessary Art of Persuasion," *Harvard Business Review* (May–June 1998): 86; emphasis added.
12. Hugh Nibley, "Beyond Politics," *BYU Studies* 15, no. 1 (Autumn 1974): 3–28.
13. See Moroni 7:17.
14. Orson Scott Card, "No Nation Is Devoid of Error," *Deseret News*, 2 July 2009.
15. Henry David Thoreau, *Walden* (Boston: Houghton Mifflin, 1893), 477.
16. Doctrine and Covenants 121:43.
17. Ezra Taft Benson, "Beware of Pride," *Ensign*, May 1989, 6.

18. *Teachings of Presidents of the Church: Joseph Smith* (Salt Lake City: The Church of Jesus Christ of Latter-day Saints, 2007), 330–48.
19. Neal A. Maxwell, "Meekly Drenched in Destiny," *BYU Speeches*, 5 September 1982.
20. "Listening Beyond Life and Choice," radio interview of Frances Kissling by Krista Tippett, *On Being*, 20 January 2011, http://www.onbeing.org/program/listening-beyond-life-and-choice/transcript/504.
21. Dieter F. Uchtdorf, "Pride and the Priesthood," *Ensign*, November 2010, 56.
22. *12 Angry Men*, directed by Sidney Lumet (1957; Orion-Nova Productions). Adapted from *Twelve Angry Men*, a teleplay by Reginald Rose (1954; Studio One).

10

INTERNATIONAL DIPLOMACY AND THE CHURCH

ELDER ROBERT S. WOOD

Elder Robert S. Wood, then a released member of the Second Quorum of the Seventy of The Church of Jesus Christ of Latter-day Saints, presented this essay at "The Church and International Diplomacy," the International Society's twenty-fourth annual conference, April 2013, Brigham Young University, Provo, Utah.

THE GREAT COMMISSION

In the prefatory section of the Doctrine and Covenants, the Lord declared, "And the voice of warning shall be unto all people, by the mouth of my disciples, whom I have chosen in these last days."[1] The foundation of the Church's international diplomacy is the great commission given to His faithful Apostles by the resurrected Lord: "Go ye therefore, and teach all nations, baptizing them in the name of the Father, and of the Son, and of the Holy Ghost: Teaching them to observe all things whatsoever I have commanded you: and lo, I am with you alway even unto the end of the world."[2] This commission was renewed with the restoration of the priesthood and Church and is preeminently in the hands and under the direction of the living Apostles.

In the Doctrine and Covenants, the Lord specifies the responsibility of the Apostles:

> The twelve traveling councilors are called to be the Twelve Apostles, or special witnesses of the name of Christ in all the world—thus differing from other officers in the church in the duties of their calling. . . . The Twelve are a Traveling Presiding High Council, to officiate in the name of the Lord, under the direction of the Presidency of the Church, agreeable to the institution of heaven; to build up the church, and regulate all the affairs of the same in all nations, first unto the Gentiles and secondly unto the Jews. . . . The Twelve being sent out, holding the keys, to open the door by the proclamation of the gospel of Jesus Christ.[3]

In this responsibility, they are to call upon and to be assisted by the Seventy.

Although the restored Church was initially small and concentrated within the United States, from the beginning, the Apostles were sent outside the center of the Church and beyond the borders of the United States. Even during the trouble in Kirtland in 1837, they and others were sent to Great Britain, and in the summer of 1839, during the construction of Nauvoo, seven members of the Twelve went to England. The building of Zion in the Great Basin was strengthened by the flood of immigrants from Great Britain, northern Europe, and finally elsewhere—a process that continued well into the twentieth century. The apostolic commission to proclaim the gospel and the early community building laid the foundation for the diplomatic role of the Church in the twenty-first century.

INDEPENDENT ABOVE ALL OTHER CREATURES

As I approach this subject, I think of the general subject of diplomacy itself. Diplomacy in the popular sense simply refers to words and behaviors calculated to soothe feelings and improve social intercourse. In the technical sense, it refers to the representation of sovereign powers, including the gathering of information, the communication of attitudes and policies, and the process of winning assent to particular policy objectives. This latter function has not always been portrayed in flattering terms. Indeed, the best-known quip about diplomatic representation was given by the seventeenth-century ambassador Sir Henry Wotton, who observed that a diplomat is "an honest man sent to lie abroad for the good of his country."[4]

This sentiment, it should be noted, did not sit well with his sovereign James I of England. However, for much of history, diplomats engaged in a range of chicanery from interception of diplomatic dispatches to bribery to stealing to even more nefarious acts. The British diplomat and historian Sir Harold Nicolson argued that diplomatic behavior improved by the mid-nineteenth century as public opinion played a greater role in the affairs of nations and as a sense of international community developed. As one scans news reports today, one is not entirely convinced that diplomacy's reputation has been entirely redeemed.

I hasten to add that these reflections on the darker side of diplomacy have nothing to do with the Church's diplomatic role. But I would argue the Church does occupy, in an important sense, a global position of "sovereign independence," and the theory and practice of diplomacy traditionally defined does apply to its mission and roles.

In a revelation counseling the Saints to organize and establish a storehouse and to make wise use of their properties, the Lord declared all things be done that "the church may stand independent above all other creatures beneath the celestial world."[5] From the earliest days of the Church, there has been a concern for establishing not only the spiritual but the temporal foundations of this independence. This was concretely manifest in community building in Ohio, Missouri, Illinois, and later in the Great Basin. The integration of the Church into the broader American society and the extension of its fellowship to the world as a whole have largely superseded these early attempts at constructing independent communities. Nonetheless, the Church still maintains its claim to an agency separate and independent of any earthly authority and shapes its policies to defend its independence of action. In a broad sense, this attitude and the historical evolution are not entirely dissimilar from that of the Roman Catholic Church.

The papacy has long maintained not only that there are separate temporal and spiritual spheres, but that, among the rulers of the earth, the Roman Catholic Church stands as an independent authority. This claim was initially underpinned by the Papal States and other political jurisdictions. Since the unification of Italy, this territorial jurisdiction has been reduced to the tiny Vatican state, but the sovereign claim remains.

Similarly, while the restored Church is not organized into a separate territorially based political jurisdiction, it remains concerned for the integrity of the Church, its governance, its doctrine, and its mission to proclaim the gospel. Moreover, while it seeks to use its influence to favor legislative and administrative norms in harmony with its teaching on Christian behavior, it is also active in supporting broad norms favorable to freedom of religious conscience and practice.

The Church, as the visible kingdom of God on the earth, does embody concerns for its independence and institutional integrity that make the application of the term "diplomacy" apt not only in a popular but in a technical sense as well. Joseph Smith and the early Brethren saw the Church not as simply a denomination but as a Zion society that would ultimately form the basis of a millennial government.[6] If the nineteenth-century projects of independent community building and an active discourse concerning a millennial political community have passed, the unique status of the Church as an independent entity under the sovereignty of heaven remains.

In 1993, I gave a keynote address on BYU campus to a symposium on moral perspectives on American security policy and mentioned the notion of raison d'etat, or reason of state. I noted that it is not a concept that applies exclusively to the state but to any group or organization for whom security or survival is a fundamental need. It arises whenever a group reaches a stage wherein it can assert its right to exist independently in the face of other powerful forces. Indeed, the Jesuits essentially used a reason-of-state argument in defense of the Catholic Church, whose existence and institutional health were seen as critical to the salvation of the individual.

Reason of state is the doctrine that the preservation of the group is so critical to the maintenance of such important values that the individuals responsible for the group will take the necessary measures to secure and advance the group. Some, such as Machiavelli, argued that they may even be compelled to take measures contrary to the normal standard of personal ethics. A godly society, however, does not have the option of separating institutional ethics from personal ethics. Although the Church is to endure, even to the filling of the earth, its stewards, disciples of the living Christ, represent a kingdom not of the worldly mind but must act in accord with celestial norms.

The mastery of diplomacy in its grandest sense is essential to its mission, and the counsel of Christ to His early Apostles remains true: "Behold, I send you forth as sheep in the midst of wolves: be ye therefore wise as serpents, and harmless as doves."[7] In latter days, in another context, the Lord added an assurance and a promise to this mandate: "Therefore, be ye as wise as serpents and yet without sin; and I will order all things for your good, as fast as ye are able to receive them."[8]

Perhaps I may lay out some general thought on the conduct of diplomacy useful to those charged with the wisdom of serpents and the gentleness of doves. Cardinal Richelieu, first minister of France from 1624 to 1642 and in most respects the founder of modern statecraft, was certainly not the most pious member of the Catholic hierarchy. At his passing, Pope Urban VIII remarked, "If there is a God, the Cardinal de Richelieu will have much to answer for. If not . . . , well, he had a successful life."[9] Whatever his defects of character and duplicity in the service of his sovereign, he had an uncanny grasp of the essentials of international relations. One of the wisest—and perhaps for our purposes the most relevant counsel he gave—was that diplomacy should not aim at ephemeral or opportunistic arrangements but at creating solid and durable relations.

THE KINGDOM OF GOD AND ALL THE KINGDOMS OF THE EARTH

Although the universal implications of the Restoration and the relation of the Church to foreign governments were early recognized, for over a century, the most pressing issue was to establish such a solid and durable relation with the United States and its subordinate jurisdictions. In a real sense, the twelfth article of faith and the 134th section of the Doctrine and Covenants represent the ground principles upon which this relationship was to be built.

The twelfth article of faith states the Latter-day Saint general attitude toward the relationship of the Church and its members, on the one hand, and the state, on the other: "We believe in being subject to kings, presidents, rulers, and magistrates, in obeying, honoring, and sustaining the law."[10] In a fundamental way, this restates the New Testament understanding that the state is in fact legitimate and is owed general deference. It recognized, as Jesus did, that there are both divine obligations and temporal political obligations incumbent upon us. If we must render unto God His due, we are obliged to render unto Caesar his.[11]

The Apostle Paul counseled in his first epistle to Timothy that we pray "for kings, and for all that are in authority; that we may lead a quiet and peaceable life in all godliness and honesty."[12] To Titus, Paul wrote that he should counsel the Saints "to be subject to principalities and powers, to obey magistrates, to be ready for every good work."[13] In this vein, the Apostle Peter admonished the Saints, "Submit yourselves to every ordinance of man for the Lord's sake: whether it be to the king, as supreme; or unto governors, as unto them that are sent by him for the punishment of evildoers, and for the praise of them that do well. For so is the will of God, that with well doing ye may put to silence the ignorance of foolish men: as free, and not using your liberty for a cloak of maliciousness, but as the servants of God."[14] Respecting even the institution of slavery, Peter, as also Paul, counseled servants to "be subject to your masters with all fear; not only to the good and gentle, but also to the froward [wicked]. For this is thankworthy, if a man for conscience toward God endure grief, suffering wrongfully."[15] Of course, the ancient Apostles counseled forbearance on the part of the master, but it is clear they were not interested in fomenting rebellion even as they sought to realize their apostolic mandate. And so it is in latter days.

Mindful of the renewal of this apostolic mandate to preach the gospel, declare repentance, and baptize, the Twelve Apostles of The Church of Jesus Christ of Latter-day Saints issued in April 1845 a proclamation drafted by Wilford Woodruff "to all the Kings of the World; to the President of the United States of America; to the Governors of the several States; and to the Rulers and People of all Nations."[16] In that remarkable though not widely distributed statement, the latter-day Apostles, looking forward to the millennial day and emphasizing the mission of the restored Church, extended an invitation to the political authorities of the world: "Come, then, to the help of the Lord and let us have your aid and protection—and your willing and hearty cooperation, in this greatest of all revolutions. . . .

Open your church doors and hearts for the truth. Hear the Apostles and elders of the church of the Saints, when they come into your cities and your neighborhoods."[17] It invited them to exemplify the spirit of Cyrus, "to aid and bless the people of God," or of Ruth, "who joined with the people of Israel."[18] The proclamation saw a great division between those rulers and peoples who take "a lively interest with the Saints of the Most High, and the covenant people of the Lord" and those others who become "their inveterate enemy, and oppose them by every means in [their] power."[19] To those nations—specifically the United States—that remove obstacles to the latter-day work, the proclamation promises a prosperous and enlarged dominion constituting "one great, powerful and peaceful empire of Liberty and Union."[20]

In 2002, while serving in Recife, Brazil, I was invited along with the Brazil South Area President to attend a solemn assembly in Brasilia sponsored by the House of Deputies (the House of Representatives of the Brazilian Congress). In attendance were senators and deputies. Their whole purpose was to honor the Latter-day Saints in Brazil. The other Area President and I sat upon the dais while one congressman after the other got up and said truly remarkable and complimentary things about the Church. As I sat there, I thought to myself, "These people are really going to receive the blessings pronounced in that earlier nineteenth-century proclamation." One of the deputies got up and said, "You know the old story that Brazil is the country of the future and always will be. But I want to tell you that I believe the future has arrived. And it has arrived to a substantial degree because of the Latter-day Saints. As they've gone to the various communities throughout Brazil, they have spread a spirit of optimism and a different set of expectations and values and a desire for improvement, which is filtering throughout our society. And I pay tribute to what they are doing in our society."

I was most impressed by a deputy from Recife—I believe the longest-serving member of the House of Deputies. He said, "Before I became a member of Congress, I was a professor of civil engineering at the University of São Paulo, and I noticed something—that none of my friends who were professors in the School of Theology and Religion believed in the miracles of the Bible, including the miracle of the Resurrection. But then I came across a book which I have now read." He held it up, and it was the Book of Mormon. He continued, "Having read this book, I have concluded that this book [the Book of Mormon]," and then holding up the Bible, "has established once again the truthfulness of this book, deepening my faith in the resurrected Lord as never before."

We did meet with him thereafter. He never did join the Church as far as I know, but he certainly gave a witness to the central work of the gospel. And that is precisely what the Apostles in 1845 had in mind when they issued that proclamation.

As you can imagine, of central concern in the proclamation was the plight of the Latter-day Saints within the United States. It called upon the political authority to "Protect the Saints; give them their rights; extend the broad banner of the Constitution and law over their homes, cities, firesides, wives and children; that they may CEASE to be BUTCHERED, MARTYRED, ROBBED, PLUNDERED, AND DRIVEN [emphasis in original], and may peacefully proceed in the work assigned them by their God."[21]

The proclamation petitioned the political authority both to allow the peaceful propagation of the gospel and to redress the ills visited upon the Saints. In its scope, it was a powerful statement of the reality of the Restoration and of the duty of the Church to boldly carry forth the apostolic mandate. However, like the ancient church, it resisted any call for rebellion in order to sustain just claims and resist unjust deprivations.

In the Doctrine and Covenants, the Lord counsels broad obedience to the political authority even in the face of outrageous persecution. Although laws are given by the Lord to govern the Church, He declares within the broader political community, "Let no man break the laws of the land, for he that keepeth the laws of God hath no need to break the laws of the land. Wherefore, be subject to the powers that be, until he reigns whose right it is to reign, and subdues all enemies under his feet."[22] The Lord explicitly justified the constitutional order of the land and counseled the Saints to seek redress under its banner and through its democratic processes, while acknowledging that "when the wicked rule the people mourn."[23]

It is of note as well that the Lord also saw the American constitutional order as providing, in a broad sense, a universal standard: "And as pertaining to law of man, whatsoever is more or less than this, cometh of evil."[24] This statement suggests the broad set of principles on the proper relation between the Church and the political authority enunciated in the 1835 "declaration of belief regarding governments and laws in general."[25]

As the histories of the early Christian church and the restored Church demonstrate, there is inevitably a tension between the apostolic mandate and integrity of the Church and the profession of fealty to the political authority. In the epistle of Peter cited previously, a juxtaposition of two exhortations suggests that tension: "Fear God. Honour the king."[26] The tension and open conflict between the Church and the federal authority in the late nineteenth century illustrates the extraordinary difficulty on occasion of both following the commandments of God and abiding by the commands of Caesar. The lessons derived from that experience are not irrelevant to the diplomatic role of the Church as it operates upon a much broader stage today. If that experience can be said to have shaped our understanding of church-state relations, so section 134 provides the basic principles by which we formulate the stance we seek to take as we operate in different political jurisdictions.

While recognizing that "all men are bound to sustain and uphold the respective governments in which they reside," the 1835 declaration adds the clause "while protected in their inherent and inalienable rights by the laws of such governments." It continues, "And that sedition and rebellion are unbecoming every citizen thus protected, and should be punished accordingly; and that all governments have a right to enact such laws as in their own judgments are best calculated to secure the public interest; at the same time, however, holding sacred the freedom of conscience."[27] It further asserts that "no government can exist in peace, except such laws are framed and held inviolate as will secure to each individual the free exercise of conscience, the right and control of property, and the protection of life."[28]

The Church further believes that there should not be such a comingling of civil and religious authority as to foster or proscribe free religious practice. Moreover, each religious society should be left free to determine its membership and preach the gospel without assuming civil power or disrupting the established order of the civil society.[29] It should be obvious that to weave a path through these requirements and desiderata will require a high level of skill and at times subtlety on the part of the representatives of the Church.

The sentiments expressed in section 134 echo those principles enunciated in the American Declaration of Independence, the American constitutional tradition, and James Madison's *Memorial and Remonstrance Against Religious Assessments*. And this tradition in turn reflects John Locke's *Second Treatise on Government* and *A Letter Concerning Toleration*. However, the authors of these political treatises were keenly concerned about maintaining the stability of the civil order. Disobedience to even unjust laws and practices, as John Locke wrote, is not to be taken lightly. Only a "long train of abuse, prevarications, and artifices, all tending the same way . . . , much worse than the state of nature or pure anarchy," would justify, and even then within the bounds of prudence, acts of rebellion.[30] If this circumspection is evident directly in the arena of political commentary and action, even greater circumspection has always prevailed in the church of Christ as it pursues its universal mission.

Such circumspection is particularly evident in times of upheaval and war. Perhaps the most comprehensive statement on the relationship of the Church and its members to political authority was given in a message of the First Presidency at the general conference of the Church on 6 April 1942. As might be expected in a time of global war, it gave reassurance to the Saints and reasserted the fundamental tenets and mission of the restored Church. While decrying war and proclaiming the gospel of love, it also condemned "false political -isms" and reiterated the words of the 134th section that "no government can exist in peace, except such laws are framed and held inviolate as will secure to each individual the free exercise of conscience, the right and control of property, and the protection of life."[31]

While stating again the injunction to the Church to "renounce war and proclaim peace,"[32] the First Presidency reemphasized that "the Church membership are citizens or subjects of sovereignties over which the Church has no control" and that the members on all sides of the conflict are subject to the commands of their governments. While counseling all its members to eschew hatred even in the midst of conflict and to act honorably, it reassured those engaged in the conflict that the Lord "will not hold the innocent instrumentalities of the war, our brethren in arms, responsible for the conflict. . . . For it would be a cruel God that would punish His children as moral sinners for acts done by them as the innocent instrumentalities of a sovereign whom He has told them to obey and whose will they were powerless to resist."[33]

Within this context, the First Presidency restated again the basic relationship between the Church and the state. In so doing, and in counseling obedience by its members to political authority, it reasserted the independent mission of the Church and subtly put its members on the side of free institutions. As they stated,

> The Church has no civil political function. As the church may not assume the functions of the state, so the state may not assume the functions of the church. The church is responsible for and must carry on the work of the Lord. . . . The state is responsible for the civil control of its citizens or subjects, for the political welfare, and for the carrying forward of political policies, domestic and foreign, of the body politic. For these policies, their success or failure, the state is alone responsible and it must carry its burdens. . . . But the Church itself, as such, has no responsibility for these policies as to which it has no means of doing more than urging its members fully to render their loyalty to their country and to free institutions which the loftiest patriotism calls for.

In that clause, the First Presidency, while counseling obedience, also put itself and its members on the side of free institutions as outlined in the 134th section—demonstrating once again the narrow and sophisticated path the Church must weave in its relationship with the powers of the earth.[34]

More contemporaneously, President Gordon B. Hinckley, in the April 2003 general conference, essentially reiterated the principles of the 1942 First Presidency statement and added that "self-defense" is justified and may transcend simply responding to a direct attack: "There are times and circumstances when nations are justified, in fact have an obligation, to fight for family, for liberty, and against tyranny, threat, and oppression."[35]

DURABLE RELATIONS AND SETTLED PRINCIPLES

All that I have said is preliminary to the broad principles undergirding the Church's attempt to create solid and durable relations with the nations of the earth and that are the foundations of its diplomatic role. In 1999, Elders Dallin H. Oaks and Lance B. Wickman contributed a chapter to a book entitled *Sharing the Book: Religious Perspectives on the Rights and Wrongs of Mission*. It is a comprehensive and, I would judge, definitive statement on the Church's missionary role. Near the conclusion of that piece, they have a section entitled "Relations with Governments," with the subtopics of "A Commitment to Obey, Honor, and Sustain the Law" and "Government's Duty to Guarantee the Right to Worship." In that section, they state seven minimal requirements in the Church's relationship with government.

It is often stated that the Church's relationship with government will be transparent and supportive of obedience to law and respect for the rights of all people. The intent is to promote harmony and understanding and not to undermine the trust essential to civil society and public peace. In terms of fulfilling the great commission to preach the gospel and to establish Zion, it is said that we "enter by the front door," that is, with the assent of the political authority. This will protect the integrity of both the Church and the state. Hence, Elders Oaks and Wickman stated seven desiderata undergirding the Church's request to enter or to continue within a political jurisdiction. It may be worth including in full those criteria:

> 1. The right to worship. Church members should have the right to practice their religion without interference by the agencies of government.
>
> 2. The right to meet together. Church members should have the right to meet together in public and in private in adequate facilities and without government scrutiny. The right of assembly is basic to religious freedom.
>
> 3. The right to self-government. The Church claims the right to noninterference by government in its internal affairs. Church doctrine and practices should be free from government regulation.

> The Church has the right to determine who will serve as its officers, how long they will serve, and how the affairs of the Church will be conducted.
>
> 4. The right to communicate with Church members. Church members should have the right to regular communication with Church leaders and other members, whether in person, in writing, or electronically. Such communications should not be prohibited, impeded, monitored, or otherwise interfered with.
>
> 5. The right to legal entity status and action. While the Church respects the right of government to establish reasonable requirements for churches to become recognized as a legal entity, it asserts that it has a right to legal recognition upon reasonable conditions. Thus recognized, the Church should be able to acquire, hold, and dispose of property, to open bank accounts, and to transact business necessary to Church operations.
>
> 6. The right to declare beliefs publicly. Church missionaries should have the right to proclaim the gospel individually or before assemblies of people. This should include the right to print and distribute literature explaining the teachings and doctrines of the Church; the right to display videos, tape recordings, and other electronic or graphic presentations concerning the Church and its beliefs; and the right of reasonable access to the public press, radio, and television to disseminate messages and information concerning the Church and its teachings.
>
> 7. The right to travel freely. Church members should have the right to travel freely to attend Church meetings and activities and to visit with other members. Similarly, full-time missionaries and other Church representatives, even if citizens of another nation, should have the right, consistent with reasonable government regulations, to enter the government's jurisdiction and to proclaim the gospel and participate in Church meetings and activities.[36]

It is clear that, while these principles define the framework within which the Church approaches political authorities, the actual activities of the Church may be more restricted than these criteria prescribe. Nonetheless, they define general parameters far beyond what the Church cannot and will not operate. For those regimes that will not allow either the assembly of our members or our proselytism, the Church may carry out more restricted roles, such as humanitarian assistance or cultural contacts. However, I believe the seven points well delineate the settled, long-term policy of the Church in its dealings with political authority.

THE MISSION OF THE CHURCH AND THE PERPLEXITIES OF NATIONS

Let me conclude with some observations on the contemporary international role of the Church. As the Church has become established throughout the world, the complexity of its relations with civic authority has been magnified, as has its sophistication of approach. Moreover, as many commentators have noted, throughout much of the world, including in North America and Europe, a hostile political and legal environment is developing against the free exercise of religion. Some of this stems from heightened secularism. Some of it stems from religious fanaticism itself and what Alma would recognize as priestcraft. This has called forth multifaceted and long-term approaches, joining in greater coordination the resources of Church headquarters and of those laboring in the field.

In one form or another and under the direction of the First Presidency and the Quorum of the Twelve, there has developed at headquarters various instrumentalities to facilitate communication and coordination on international matters and to identify issues or opportunities in the global arena that should be brought to the attention of the senior Brethren. This involves all the key departments. I would highlight not only the various functional divisions—such as missionary or temple activities, welfare services, the Priesthood Department—but the central role of the Public Affairs Department, the Office of General Counsel, the Presidency of the Seventy, and the Presiding Bishopric. An important forum in which these matters are often discussed, with decisions deferred to the regular meetings of the First Presidency and the Twelve, is the Area Committee, which is composed of the Twelve Apostles, the seven Presidents of the Seventy, the Presiding Bishopric, several other members of the Seventy, and others that might be invited from time to time.

Within the United States and Canada, the Presidency of the Seventy, as agents of the Apostles, exercises oversight of those matters that bear not only upon the internal operations of the Church but its external role as well. In other areas of the world, Area Presidencies, composed of General Authorities and Area Seventies, exercise that oversight, again under the direction of the Apostles and the seven Presidents of the Seventy. The various jurisdictions throughout the world have been directed to develop government-relations plans and organize government-relations councils. The purpose of this planning and organizing is to identify and develop relationships of trust and understanding with government and civic leaders and associations, as well as to define and achieve both short- and long-term objectives and maintain continuity across those assigned to each Area Presidency.

The spectrum of diplomatic activities is both vast and diverse, and some Area Presidencies are extraordinarily busy. The issues can range from establishing relationships with key decision makers and opinion leaders to regularizing the Church's legal status to visa problems to humanitarian assistance to the basic principles underpinning Church activities. Some matters are of such sensitivity that they are handled directly from Salt Lake, and in any event, the travel of the members of the First Presidency, the Twelve, and the Presidency of the Seventy inevitably involve meeting with key political and civic leaders. Harking back to the observation of Richelieu, in seeking to carry out the mission of the Church, its representatives are increasingly engaged in a focused, continuous, and varied role of establishing solid and durable relations that transcend changes of government and personalities. Given that we live in a world always in flux and often in turmoil, this is becoming ever more demanding.

In addition to specific church-government relations, the Church now has continuous representation at the UN in New York and Geneva and at the EU in Brussels. In addition, there are active hosting operations in Salt Lake; Washington, DC; and elsewhere. The number of occasions for senior Church officers to interact with foreign dignitaries both in this country and abroad has expanded enormously, and many important events are designed to include government officials and ambassadors.

Flagship institutions such as Brigham Young University are consciously employed both as venues and sponsors of important meetings with a range of citizens and officials of countries around the world. Notable in this regard is the annual International Religious Liberty Symposium held at the time of the October general conference of the Church. Working closely with senior Church officers and Area Presidencies, government officials and advisors, judges, academics, attorneys, writers, and commentators from around the world are invited to a symposium in Provo and Salt Lake. The symposium addresses a range of questions affecting religious liberty around the globe, including the Church's mission and role pertaining to this vital foundation for church-state relations. A closing lunch is held with the First Presidency, the Twelve, and other senior Brethren.

Many crucial church-state issues have reached a successful conclusion through the forging of relations and understanding through these multiple forums, as well as personal contacts by individual Church members. For instance, the registration of the Church in Slovakia was the result of fifteen years of Church diplomacy. As in many other things, the activities of the Church throughout the world depend both on the continual forging and strengthening of personal ties and on the development of formal understandings that transcend these contacts.

Elder Neal A. Maxwell once observed that we do not move up and down in the Church, but we move around—pointing to a key component of Church diplomacy. This is a lay Church. The bulk of Church leadership comes from people who are engaged in a vast range of occupations and professions both in the public and the private sector, as well as homemakers. In every country, the Church is not divided into clerics and laity. A very small percentage of Church leaders and, therefore, representatives, are engaged in full-time Church service. And often the governments with which the Church deals include members of the Church who may also be bishops, stake presidents, or Relief Society presidents, as well as others who may hold other Church callings. The Quorums of the Seventy represent a powerful contemporary example. Those who have been called to serve as a Seventy throughout the world are often prominent members of their nations and communities. The Church hierarchy is, therefore, something that is never entirely external or separate from the nations, kindreds, tongues, and peoples into which the world is divided. In an extended sense, the local members represent the Church not only to their immediate neighbors but to their country and its political authority. This gives an even more powerful meaning to the exhortation to be an example of the believers.[37] Continual and positive participation by local members in civic and political activities provides both a context and a potential key to the success of more formal diplomatic activities.

Former secretary of state Madeleine Albright once commented that she often told foreign ministers and other officials that they should welcome Mormon missionaries into their country, as these missionaries would thereby become lifelong friends of their people and country, in effect informal representatives of the countries from which missionaries came. As she later wrote, they also happen to represent to the countries where they serve some of the best traits of this country: "By the early 1900s, tens of thousands of American missionaries were established in foreign countries. They came from virtually every Christian denomination, with heavy representation from a movement that began in the United States, the Church of Jesus Christ of Latter-day Saints, referred to commonly as the Mormons. The missionaries carried with them both the good news of the gospel and the democratizing influence of American values and culture. Missionaries were among the nation's first experts on foreign customs and the first to learn foreign languages."[38] While missionaries are not sent forth to represent the countries from which they come, Secretary Albright's point is well taken and applies not only to missionaries but also to Latter-day Saint citizens throughout the world. Their activities profoundly shape the more formal and explicit diplomatic activities of the Church.

CONCLUSION: ARM AND SHIELD

Today, as in times past, the diplomatic role of the Church stems from its position as the earthly embodiment of the kingdom of God, mandated to preach the gospel and to bring forth and establish Zion. Its success depends not simply on the skill and sophistication of its leaders and people but is ultimately vouchsafed by the Lord, from whom the divine commission came. As He declared: "Wherefore, I call upon the weak things of the world, those who are unlearned and despised, to thresh the nations by the power of my Spirit; and their arm shall be my arm, and I will be their shield and their buckler; and I will gird up their loins, and they shall fight manfully for me; and their enemies shall be under their feet; and I will let fall the sword in their behalf, and by the fire of mine indignation will I preserve them."[39] To recall the words of the Prophet Joseph Smith in another context, "shall we not go on in so great a cause?"[40]

NOTES

1. Doctrine and Covenants 1:4.
2. Matthew 28:19–20.
3. Doctrine and Covenants 107:23, 33, 35.
4. Henry Wotton, written in the album of Christopher Fleckmore, 1604.
5. Doctrine and Covenants 78:14.
6. See Hyrum L. Andrus, *Joseph Smith and World Government* (Salt Lake City: Hawkes, 1972).
7. Matthew 10:16.
8. Doctrine and Covenants 111:11.
9. Henry Kissinger, *Diplomacy* (New York: Simon and Schuster, 2011), 58.
10. Articles of Faith 1:12.
11. See Matthew 22:21.
12. 1 Timothy 2:1–2.
13. Titus 3:1.
14. 1 Peter 2:13–16.
15. 1 Peter 2:18–19; see also Ephesians 6:5–8; Colossians 3:22; 1 Timothy 6:1–2; Titus 2:9–10.
16. *Messages of the First Presidency*, comp. James R. Clark (Salt Lake City: Bookcraft, 1965), 1:252–66.
17. Clark, *Messages of the First Presidency*, 1:256.
18. Clark, *Messages of the First Presidency*, 1:257.
19. Clark, *Messages of the First Presidency*, 1:257.
20. Clark, *Messages of the First Presidency*, 1:262.
21. Clark, *Messages of the First Presidency*, 1:261.

22. Doctrine and Covenants 58:21–22.
23. Doctrine and Covenants 98:4–10.
24. Doctrine and Covenants 98:7.
25. Doctrine and Covenants 134.
26. 1 Peter 2:17.
27. Doctrine and Covenants 134:5.
28. Doctrine and Covenants 134:2.
29. See Doctrine and Covenants 134:10–12.
30. See Locke, *Second Treatise*, 224.
31. Clark, *Messages of the First Presidency*, 6:148–63.
32. Doctrine and Covenants 98:16.
33. Clark, *Messages of the First Presidency*, 6:148–63.
34. Clark, *Messages of the First Presidency*, 6:148–63.
35. Gordon B. Hinckley, "War and Peace," *Ensign*, May 2003, 80.
36. Dallin H. Oaks and Lance B. Wickman, *Sharing the Book: Religious Perspectives on the Rights and Wrongs of Mission*, ed. John Witte Jr. and Richard C. Martin (Maryknoll, NY: Orbis Books, 1999), 247–78.
37. See 1 Timothy 4:12.
38. Madeleine Albright with Bill Woodward, *The Mighty and the Almighty* (New York: Harper Perennial, 2007), 26.
39. Doctrine and Covenants 35:13–14.
40. Doctrine and Covenants 128:22.

The first weapon of peace women are using is to write about peace. Their writings are providing vivid definitions of what peace is and what it would be like to live in a peaceful place. (Courtesy of Intellectual Reserve, Inc.)

11

WOMEN'S WEAPONS OF PEACE

BONNIE BALLIF-SPANVILL

Bonnie Ballif-Spanvill, then a professor emerita of psychology at Brigham Young University, presented this essay at "'Blessed Are the Peacemakers': Peace Is Possible," the International Society's twenty-sixth annual conference, April 2015, Brigham Young University, Provo, Utah.

First, I want to acknowledge the contributions of my colleagues and research assistants who have contributed to this work from Fordham University Graduate School at Lincoln Center, New York City; the former Women's Research Institute, Brigham Young University; the Women's Research Institute of Utah, Salt Lake City; and the PEACEABILITIES Board. Findings from this research have identified five major weapons women are using to increase peace throughout the world.

WOMEN ARE WRITING ABOUT PEACE

The first weapon of peace women are using is to write about peace. Their writings are providing vivid definitions of what peace is and what it would be like to live in a peaceful place—understandings that are essential to strategically accomplishing peace.

Through women's writings, ideas of peace are spreading and giving hope to people everywhere who are tired of conflict and war and longing for the possibility of peace. Their writings are critical because it is impossible to increase peace if you do not know what peace is or believe that peace is possible. Although many definitions of peace exist, most have not included women's views, which are necessary in order to paint a robust definition that both women and men can embrace.

In one study done at the Stone Center at Wellesley College, wives and husbands were asked what would bring peace into their homes at the end of the day. Women generally said they would like to sit down and talk to their husbands about all the things they had been worrying about. Men were more likely to say they would like to sit down in front of the TV with control of the remote. Perhaps a plan that included a time to talk and a time to unwind, incorporating both female and male views, would most likely be successful in bringing harmony. Clearly, women's perspectives on peace are needed to complement men's definitions of peace in order to fully understand what peace is for all people.

Our first research question was "What are women writing about peace, and how are they defining it?" We wanted to include what women from all over the world were saying about peace. We wanted contemporary women living in the world as it is to tell us what they think about peace. We wanted to know what the most articulate women we could find were saying, women who would have the skills necessary to express the essence of peace. And we wanted women who were acknowledged in their own countries as having expressed thoughts that were important to their people. Only women poets fit all of these criteria.

My colleagues Marilyn Arnold and Kristen Tracy and I began reading hundreds of women's poems. The poems were about victims of war and oppression, bewildered and brutalized children, bereft wives and mothers, raped and mutilated women, and tormented prisoners and soldiers. But these poets also talked about peace. They declared that peace is a tangible power, a presence, something more than the absence of conflict. Some of them offered only a glimpse of hopefulness; some showed snatches of their dream of a peaceful society. Others offered a full-blown vision of peace and harmony among people, of a world in which forgiveness has replaced blame, generosity has replaced greed, and healing has replaced pain. I would like to read two of these poems and invite you to not only listen to the words these poets use to describe the essence of peace but to also picture the scenes they paint that tell us how it would feel to live in a peaceful place. The first poem, "Springwater, Part 105," comes from the Chinese poet Bing Xin:

Creator,
If in eternal life
Only one wish is granted,
I will plead in all sincerity:
Let me be in my mother's arms,
Let Mother be in a small boat,
Let the small boat be on a moonlit sea.

The second poem, "Rocking," is by Chilean poet Gabriela Mistral:

The sea rocks her thousands of waves
The sea is divine.
Hearing the loving sea
I rock my son.
The wind wandering by night
Rocks the wheat.
Hearing the loving wind
I rock my son.
God, the Father, soundlessly rocks
His thousands of worlds.
Feeling His hand in the shadow
I rock my son.

These poems portray nature calmly surrounding gentle human relationships. A moonlit sea, wind rocking wheat, the Father rocking his thousands of worlds, a daughter in the arms of her mother, and a mother holding her son and feeling the presence of her God nearby. We published these poems in *A Chorus for Peace: A Global Anthology of Poetry by Women.*[1] Together, the collection constitutes a women's chorus of gifted, global voices blending in a heartbreaking plea for peace and telling us that it is our task as women to give birth to peace out of the ashes of war and violence.

WOMEN ARE ORGANIZING FOR PEACE

Armed with vivid definitions of peace, we next asked, "What are women doing to accomplish the peace they desire?" Here we found the second weapon that women are using to promote peace. Women are organizing. They are joining together with unique solidarity, specifically to bring about peace.

Regardless of whether they are women of poverty or plenty; whether they are African, Chinese, or Chilean; whether they are well educated or barely literate; or whether they are old or young, women are demonstrating great unity as they work for a more peaceful place to raise their children.

The following is an example of how these organizations are being formed. It is the story of a Nigerian pastor, Esther Ibanga. Observe excerpts from her own words as she describes how she found a way to bring together an unlikely organization:

> My life as a Christian preacher was rarely easy, but I enjoyed a good deal of comfort. . . .
>
> That all changed when more than 500 Christians were massacred in a village near my house, in an explosion of violence involving our Muslim neighbors.
>
> Armed with machetes, Islamic militants showed no mercy as they slaughtered women and children, including an infant only four days old.
>
> I gathered with friends and we wept for days. We were used to periodic violence between Christians and Muslims, sometimes perpetrated by angry mobs. . . . But this time, violence had invaded women's bedrooms, where they were roused from sleep and killed.
>
> The atrocities shook us to the core. Witnessing our grief, my husband challenged us, "Is that all you women are going to do? Cry?" His challenge inspired me to lead a march to protest the violence—100,000 women in the streets, a real show of strength. We let our leaders know that we would no longer remain silent.
>
> Then we learned that this massacre was a response to an attack by Christians against Muslims in another village. And after that brutal assault, Muslim women had also organized and poured into the streets to demonstrate. The men in power ignored both marches. And the killings continued.

> I decided that the only hope was to forge an alliance between Christian and Muslim women. . . . This was no easy task. . . .
>
> After lengthy prayers and hard work within my soul, I eventually was able to look Muslims in the eye, and truly forgive and love them. . . . I knew that peace had to begin with me, from within.
>
> I reached out to my counterpart, Khadija Hawaja, who had led the Muslim women's march. Our first meetings were secret, and could not be held in either my community or hers because we would have risked attack. But we persevered and co-founded our nation's first organization of Muslim and Christian women, called Women Without Walls Initiative.
>
> Together we engaged in a wide range of activities from caring for orphans to encouraging the voices of mothers as a force for moderation in families. . . .
>
> We work in poor, volatile neighborhoods that are breeding grounds for foot soldiers and other young people prone to violence. We say to them: "Think of us as your mothers." No one else takes the time to engage with them, so they are receptive and open to changing their ways. That is how the cycle of violence is disrupted—one soul at a time. . . .
>
> Violence between Muslims and Christians still rocks our nation. . . . But let there be no doubt. Both faiths embrace the principle of peace, as do all of the world's religions.[2]

Pastor Ibanga is recipient of the 2015 Niwano Peace Prize in recognition of her work promoting peaceful coexistence.

Inspired by such women, we began identifying other women's organizations for peace, organizations from all over the world. We wanted to find out who they were and what they were doing to increase peace. For each of the organizations, we sought information regarding how and when they were started, their mission statements and ideologies, and their membership, activities, and budgets. We included organizations that represented independent grassroots movements as well as organizations that were working for peace but that were part of a larger umbrella organization whose primary objective was not necessarily peace related.

After tracking down every lead, we obtained information from several hundred organizations. The information we obtained was spotty, with less than fifty women providing answers to all of the requested questions. Many responded simply with a request for money. Here is a summary of some of our findings about these women's organizations for peace: There were twenty-six ideologies represented by these organizations, giving rise to many approaches to working for peace. The majority of their goals were focused on political participation, information exchange, peaceful coexistence, and human rights. Other goals addressed a wide array of factors involved in establishing peace, including dealing with poverty, development, discrimination, domestic violence, education, economic issues, and more. The fact that these organizations are engaged in an array of approaches demonstrates women's awareness of the complexities of the issues that need attention to bring about peace and highlights the unique problems facing local communities as well as the areas of public life that allow access to women.

The next step was to determine what these women's peace organizations actually do. Once again, we found that they are engaged in a number of activities. Over half of the activities consist of collaborating and networking, publishing information, and conducting a range of education programs that cover skill training, participating in political systems, changing policy, lobbying, and the like.

Funding for the more established organizations ranged from $100,000 to $400,000, with financial resources coming from member dues and donations. The monies were used for activities and not management. It should also be noted that money absolutely determines the survival of these organizations, and lack of money prevents many from having much influence on the national or global level. The most frequently reported membership in these organizations was less than twenty-five thousand, with 25 percent having fewer than five hundred members. We also found evidence of many grassroots organizations that we could not contact directly, and we have obtained only secondhand fragmentary information about them. Hard evidence of the effectiveness of the activities of these organizations was impossible to obtain. At best, a few evaluative self-reports were available that indicated whether an activity was well attended or completed as planned. However, we did find that those organizations that used the media and involved men in their cause were more likely to believe they were effective.[3]

Recently, the members of the Women's International League for Peace and Freedom issued a 2015 manifesto on the centenary of their foundation. They paid tribute to the farsighted women who brought their movement into being amid the carnage of the First World War. They also renewed their commitment to eradicating war by addressing its root causes. Some of these root causes have been identified as the conditions in which women live.[4]

WOMEN ARE IDENTIFYING SPECIFIC STEPS THAT IF TAKEN WOULD INCREASE PEACE

The third weapon of peace women are using is identifying specific steps that, if taken, would improve the conditions in which they live and would increase peace. Women are encouraging efforts to implement these specific conditions from the top down in order to increase state security and peace.

The creation of the WomanStats database allowed us to study the specific conditions in which women live and the relationship between those conditions and peaceful states. The database is currently the most comprehensive database on women available anywhere.[5] In our book *Sex and World Peace*, which I coauthored with Valerie Hudson, Mary Caprioli, and Chad Emmett, we demonstrate that societies with greater violence against women have greater incidence of conflict and war.[6] Thus, efforts to establish greater peace and security throughout the world would be more effective if governments worked on eliminating the violence that occurs against women.

Because we identified and had data on the exact variables that represent the conditions women experience, we used those variables to predict whether a state would be peaceful or not. Having a list of laws and practices is invaluable in working on improving the conditions of women. It is not enough to say we must make conditions for women better; we know what the specific laws and practices are that need to be changed. With knowledge of the steps that could be instrumental in improving chances for peace, women are encouraging states and large organizations who possess resources and capabilities that are simply not available to grassroots women's peace organizations to engage in top-down efforts, making progress faster and far reaching. The specific conditions that need addressing are many. They include making national family law equitable, putting women's priorities on the state's list of priorities, enacting pro-women legislation, including women in decision making, and keeping caregiving economically rational.

The following examples illustrate the incredible influence of strategies when they come from the top down: Recognizing that conditions for women, including marriage laws, needed to be revised, King Mohammed VI of Morocco gave a historic speech in 1999 in which he asked how society can progress "while women, who represent half the nation, see their rights violated and suffer as a result of injustice, violence and marginalization."[7] During the next few years, he shepherded an overhaul of family law in Morocco, giving women extraordinary rights compared to their sisters in other Islamic societies. Among these specific reforms were those related to raising the legal age of marriage and virtually doing away with polygamy.

Another example of specific conditions in women's lives that have been addressed with effective top-down strategies comes from the work of Albert Bandura. He has applied his social learning theory around the world to encourage literacy and to raise the status of women in societies where they are marginalized. He does this through televised mini-dramas. These dramatic productions are not fanciful stories; they portray people's everyday lives and help them see a better future. These productions also provide people with strategies and incentives that enable them to take steps forward.[8] In Mexico, nearly one million people enrolled in a study program to learn to read after watching a drama that promoted national literacy. Another example comes from a Mexican television executive, Miguel Sabido, who created a drama centered on the lives of adults enrolled in a literacy class. The show drew large audiences, and new enrollments in adult literacy programs were nine times greater that year. After one of the shows mentioned that the national distribution center provided free literacy booklets, twenty-five thousand people showed up the next day to get their copies.[9] A major advantage of modeling through media is that it can reach vast populations simultaneously in widely dispersed areas. In a radio serial drama in India, with forty-five million listening, a female model resists restrictive cultural norms and pursues an education. This drama inspired teenage listeners to start a school of their own, which they held around a village water well.

Armed with knowledge of the specific conditions that need to be addressed, states and organizations and women and men can develop top-down strategies that have the potential to greatly improve conditions for women and hence contribute to greater peace.

WOMEN ARE HELPING YOUNG PEOPLE REDUCE VIOLENCE

The fourth women's weapon of peace is teaching. Women are using education to help young people prevent and reduce violence.

While only 12 percent of the women's organizations for peace are involved in education, there are many educational programs designed to reduce violence throughout the world involving substantial numbers of women. Because so many women are involved, we turn now to a brief analysis of worldwide antiviolence education programs.

Many women believe the most critical education for the twenty-first century is for people to learn how to get along with each other. This is particularly important for women because they are disproportionately victims of much of the violence. Twenty years after the landmark Beijing conference on gender equality, a new UN report states that violence against women around the world persists at alarmingly high levels in many forms.[10] It is not surprising that women have gotten involved in developing educational programs to reduce violence. The experience of one woman illustrates how and why many women have taken on this challenge. Bushra Qadim Hyder is a woman who had a little school in the city of Peshawar, Pakistan, which borders Afghanistan and is one of the most dangerous and unstable regions in the world. Last year, militants attacked the Army Public School, killing 150 children. Close to fifty thousand civilians and security personnel died as a result of roadside bombs and drone attacks. Bushra talks about watching as the girls in her school tore the limbs off their dolls, acting out the mayhem they saw around them. Her youngest students experienced heartbreaking feelings they could not articulate and expressed them in the pictures they would draw of guns, ambulances, and dead bodies. Bushra said she felt like her students felt and that she herself was, and is, often afraid. She asked herself how she could destroy fear.

With that desire, she decided to teach two additional topics in her little school: diversity and tolerance. She also selected two students from each class to be "peace angels" to help resolve small conflicts as they arose between the children. With that beginning, her curriculum has evolved. Today she is hard at work advocating for the inclusion of peace education in the provincial school curriculums throughout Pakistan, but her educational program was begun, as many others have, by a woman concerned about the children she was teaching.[11]

In our research, we gathered information on hundreds of educational programs both within the United States and throughout the world. We limited our search to programs designed for teenagers and children. We organized them by their target populations, theoretical base, program goals, methods they used, and any evidence of the effectiveness of their efforts. We were particularly interested in programs that had a track record indicating they were making a difference, but of these, there were very few. Analyses of these programs found that they fell into three basic types of programs: the largest number were violence-prevention programs, followed by many conflict-resolution programs, and finally a few peace programs.[12]

The objectives of each of these types of programs differ, and they are effective in different ways. Violence-prevention programs are designed to help children tolerate one another without aggression. These programs focus on repressing violent and antisocial behaviors. Usually they use some form of an external constraint, punishment, or the intimidation of authorities to suppress violent behavior. When these external threats are removed, however, violent behavior usually returns. While suppressing violence is only a small step toward creating peaceful relationships, it can be a useful first step in preventing physical harm when children are having difficulty controlling their aggression, thus buying a little time for relationship skills to be taught.[13]

The following programs illustrate these approaches. Hand in Hand: Center for Jewish-Arab Education in Israel is one example of a violence-prevention program. Both Jews and Arabs attend these schools in Israel and are taught both in Hebrew and Arabic. The schools are run by Jewish and Arabic co-principals, and the students are taught by Jewish and Arabic teachers in each classroom. The presence of dual authority figures suppresses students' tendencies to lash out against each other, making it clear that living and working together without fighting is possible in a multicultural environment.

Conflict-resolution programs go a step beyond violence-prevention programs by actually teaching how to keep conflicts from escalating into violence. In these programs, students are trained on what to say and do when they find themselves in a conflict. Essentially, conflict-resolution programs help the young defuse conflicts once they have occurred through the use of memorized scripts and preprogrammed patterns of behavior. If the conflicts evolve in ways that deviate from the scripts that have been learned, however, it is difficult for youth to continue to defuse the conflict. The Seeds of Peace program was designed to help youth in the Middle East resolve conflicts by increasing their communication skills to work through conflicts. It sponsors camps and workshops where youth can learn how to respond in a variety of ways that are usually capable of defusing conflicts.[14]

In both violence-prevention and conflict-resolution programs, the focus is on conflict itself—first preventing conflict and then reducing it. The assumption behind both of these types of programs is that the absence of antisocial behavior guarantees that prosocial behavior will just appear. That is not so. Such programs do not develop the specific thinking patterns that will enable children to interact peacefully. Peace is much more than the absence of violence. Peaceful strategies, values, and feelings must be developed; they do not just emerge. A few peace-education programs are trying to encourage peace, but in general their objectives are broadly defined and often vague.

One example of a peace-education program is sponsored by the PeaceJam Foundation. It makes it possible for youth to study with Nobel Peace laureates, so they can become familiar with world leaders' views on how to create peace. The youth are then required to apply what they have learned in local community service-learning activities. More than five hundred thousand youth have participated in this program since 1996, and they have completed over three hundred thousand service projects.[15] Creating an atmosphere in which youth can understand and experience peace is an essential element of peace education; youth need good examples of nonviolent living to counter the prevalence of violent images all around them. Without awareness of the benefits peace brings and the belief that peace can be achieved, the young will not have the necessary motivation to seek after and practice living peacefully with others. Although this program provides good models that can be imitated, it cannot guarantee that simply watching these models will be sufficient to ensure that their peaceful ways will be passed on, nor does it guarantee that the models will display the specific skills individuals need to build peaceful relationships. Desperately needed are programs that focus directly on developing the specific abilities in children that will help them get along with others, such as the ability to forgive, to be kind, to be just, and to treat others with respect and equity. So we created one.

WOMEN ARE EMPOWERING CHILDREN WITH ABILITIES TO BE PEACEFUL

This is the fifth weapon of peace being used by women. Women are empowering children by helping them develop internal abilities they need to live peacefully with each other. To do this, they are using the PEACEABILITIES program.

After gleaning insights from all of the programs, we studied and searched through hundreds of books for stories and art that would teach children the principles that would enable them to govern themselves. We created the PEACEABILITIES program.[16] This program focuses on developing the internal strengths and understandings that empower children to prevent their own behavior from becoming violent, to resolve conflicts, and to create peaceful relationships. It is based on the belief that violence begins in individual minds long before weapons are fired or abuse is inflicted. Therefore, preventing violence and creating peace must also take place in individual minds. We believe that skills can be developed to repel aggressive thoughts and choose peaceful alternatives and to overcome ideas that fuel inequality and self-interest in favor of desires to be kind, forgive, and respect selves and others. We collected compelling stories and activities, including children's books, well-known art depicting peace, movie clips, and original music. We have already placed a large number of these materials on our website for all to use freely. We encourage everyone to use PEACEABILITIES for families, schools, neighborhoods, churches, villages, etc. It is also our hope that women all over the world will gather activities and stories of their own, perhaps using PEACEABILITIES as a model of those skills that are critical to establish peace. Once again, children will not mature into peacefulness if they do not have the opportunity to cultivate kindness, respect, justice, and compassion. They will not become peaceful on their own, nor can they be forced to do so. PEACEABILITIES teaches children step-by-step how to care about each other.

Each of the eighteen chapters in PEACEABILITIES contains a number of activities and stories, with each chapter building upon the one before. The child progresses from controlling anger to learning to listen, getting the facts, trusting, caring, including others, winning with kindness, building friendships, loving, and finally, creating peace. Each of the activities and stories has been designed to precisely teach a specific skill. For example, by participating in the activity "Facts and Assumptions," children learn the precise skill required to not jump to assumptions about the actions of those around them. False conclusions can hurt feelings and increase contention and are avoided only by getting the facts. Here is one of the exercises to show the difference between facts and assumptions:

> Samantha didn't meet Amy and Elise at the store. (Fact)
>
> Amy and Elise think Samantha doesn't want to go shopping with them. (Assumption)
>
> Samantha didn't get the message from Amy and Elise to meet at the store. (Fact)
>
> Samantha thinks Amy and Elise left her out. (Assumption)

The children are then taught how to gather facts before making assumptions.

Because it is important for children to learn and benefit from wisdom that has accumulated over centuries of time, PEACEABILITIES includes compelling pieces of work from many ancient and modern sources, as well as material from different cultures. Here is an example of an Ethiopian story called "Lion's Whiskers":

> Bizunesh, a woman of the African highlands, married a man of the lowlands. When she went to the house of her new husband she found that he had a son who was very sad because his mother had died of the fever. The woman and her new son were often alone together because her husband was a merchant and traveled with mule caravans to distant cities. Bizunesh would speak to her son

very kindly. "I have always wanted a small son. Now God has given me one. I love you very much." But the boy would shout in a cross voice, "I do not love you. You are not my real mother. My mother is dead. I do not love you. I hate you." When the woman cooked, her son would not eat. When she mended his robes, he would run through the thorn bushes and tear them. When she tried to kiss him, he would run away from her. Often she cried alone in her room.

One day Bizunesh went to the cave of a very famous wise man. She told the wise man about her new son who did not love her and asked for a magic love powder so that her son would love her. The wise man answered, "To make such a powder I must have the chin whiskers of an old and ferocious lion who walks in the black-rock desert beyond the river. Bring the whiskers to me." The woman protested that the lion would kill her, but the wise man insisted that that was the only way.

Because she loved her son so much, she decided that she would try to get the whiskers and crossed the river to the black-rock desert and looked at the lion from afar. The lion was fierce and roared so loudly that she ran away. The next day she came from her house carrying food. She placed the food on a rock a mile away from the lion and ran. On the following day she brought food and left it only a half-mile from the lion, and the next day a quarter of a mile, and she stayed to watch the lion while he ate. Each day she continued to get a little closer, until finally Bizunesh left the food 100 yards away from the fierce lion, who saw her and growled in a friendly way. She stayed while the lion ate the food. And then one day she went right up to the lion and fed him. She watched the lion's great jaw fly open and heard his teeth tearing through the meat. She was terrified, but she shut her eyes and snatched whiskers from the lion's chin. She ran as fast as she could to the wise man's cave and asked for the love powder so that her son would love her.

"I will not make you any love powder," the wise man said. "You learned how to approach the lion—slowly. Do the same with your son, and he will surely learn to love you."[17]

We also use fine arts in PEACEABILITIES because there is power in accumulated cultural expressions and different mediums make peaceful ideas more accessible to children with different styles of learning. One example of art we have included is the painting *Dance of Youth*, by Picasso. In this painting, colorful figures are holding hands and dancing in a circle with a dove of peace in the center. This painting needs no extensive preparation to present it or lengthy discussions for the children to "get" the message. It, like the other stories and activities in PEACEABILITIES, speaks for itself. Children just need to hear the stories or participate in the activities as many times as possible.

In our further research, we found evidence that participating in PEACEABILITIES helps children see themselves as more peaceful. Before participating in the program, children with violent backgrounds saw themselves as doing everything they could do to be peaceful, but they did not know what to do, and they felt inferior and vulnerable to violence. As a result of participating in PEACEABILITIES, aggressive children made significant gains in becoming less violent. PEACEABILITIES helped all children see themselves as more peaceful.

We devised several instruments to evaluate the effectiveness of PEACEABILITIES in developing peaceful behavior. These were not pencil-and-paper tests. We used many little situations to see what the children would actually do. For example, to see how a child would act in a conflict situation in which there were limited resources, we put three paper plates on a table in an empty room along with five cookies. The child was told that they could keep one plate and the other two plates were for other children who would be coming in soon. The child was then left alone to divide the cookies between the three children. Some children broke the cookies up in tiny pieces in a desperate effort to ensure that each child had the exact same amount. Others gave two to each of the absent children, and kept one. A few gave one to each of the absent children, and kept three. And one kept all of the cookies. The children's actions were then scored on the Structure of Violence and Peace Scale—a twelve-point continuum from altruistic, forgiving, and compassionate behavior to behavior that is violent and vengeful and that expends others for gain. The exciting results came not only from scores on our scales but from the spontaneous peaceful activities the children initiated themselves. In a second-grade class that had completed the PEACEABILITIES program, the children, on their own initiative, used their recesses to form a club they called Think Kind Thoughts, Do Kind Deeds. Members of the club were called Troubleshooters, and the rules for the club required that the members must always be on duty and never allow other children to cry, be left alone, or fight.

Today, I have briefly outlined five weapons of peace women are currently using:

1. Women are writing about peace.

2. Women are organizing for peace.

3. Women are identifying specific steps that if taken would increase peace.

4. Women are helping young people reduce violence.

5. Women are empowering children with abilities to be peaceful.

Help women use these weapons and develop new weapons. Use these weapons yourselves. Success is greater when women and men work together. The establishment of peace cannot be left to negotiations, treaties, and wars alone. While important, they only suppress violence; they do not teach the principles that create peace. Only when children of all ages learn to be peaceful from within will we break intergenerational cycles of violence.

Women are in a unique position to teach children to be peaceful before they become socialized into the culture of violence that exists around them. It is my dream that women everywhere will begin to tell stories that teach the principles of peace to their children. Remember the success of microcredit loans when placed in the hands of women—entire families benefited from their work. Educating women also benefited families. It is time to engage women in empowering their children to create peace. Together, women could give the next generation abilities to value themselves and one another equally, to respect the rights of others, and to share their resources, in this way fulfilling the dream of Richard Martin, the little boy killed in the Boston bombings, when he wrote, "No more hurting people. Peace."

I would like to tell you about an experience I had some years ago. I lived in the middle of New York City for many years, one block west of Tiffany's and one block east of Carnegie Hall. The city never slept in midtown Manhattan. Lights were always flashing, cabs honking, and people laughing. One morning my husband and I awoke to total silence—no honking horns, talking people, sirens, or dogs barking. We were stunned. Not a sound could be heard. We got up and looked out our window at a city buried in deep snow. We went out. There were no cars moving on the street to obey the ever-faithful traffic lights turning red, yellow, and green again, and again. The department stores and restaurants were closed, Wall Street was closed, and schools and universities were closed. There was not a soul anywhere in sight. Snow had brought this enormous city to its knees. As we walked along the benches in Central Park, soaking in the quiet, I caught one little snowflake on my finger and watched it quickly melt before my eyes. I wondered how such a vulnerable little snowflake could have such power over this magnificent city. Then I realized it was not just one snowflake that humbled New York, there were millions of snowflakes that together had taken over this city.

It is not just one story told to one child that will establish peace, nor one game, nor one song that will help children care for each other. But if we can get dozens of women to tell stories and do the activities that will develop peace abilities in their children, then hundreds, thousands, and some day millions of women to empower their children to be peaceful, we can bring down the use of violence. And as we do, momentum will build and peace will ripple through families, villages, and even countries.

NOTES

1. Marilyn Arnold, Bonnie Ballif-Spanvill, and Kristen Tracy, eds., *A Chorus for Peace: A Global Anthology of Poetry by Women* (Iowa City: University of Iowa Press, 2002).
2. Esther Ibanga, "Uniting Christian and Muslim Women in Nigeria Is Imperative for Building a Bridge toward Peace," *Global Post,* 19 March 2015, www.globalpost.com/dispatches/globalpost-blogs/commentary/uniting-christian-and-muslim-women-nigeria-imperative-build-b.

3. Bonnie Ballif-Spanvill and R. Jones, "Women's Peace Organizations" (Women's Research Institute, Brigham Young University, 2008).
4. "WILPF 2015 Manifesto," www.womenstopwar.org/wp-content/uploads/2015/02/Draft-6-edited_1.pdf.
5. Mary Caprioli et al., "The WomanStats Project Database: Advancing an Empirical Research Agenda," *Journal of Peace Research* 46, no. 6 (2009): 1–13.
6. Valerie M. Hudson et al., *Sex and World Peace* (New York: Columbia University Press, 2012).
7. Hudson et al., *Sex and World Peace.*
8. Albert Bandura, "Going Global with Social Cognitive Theory: From Prospect to Paydirt" (paper presented at the annual meetings of the American Psychological Association, Honolulu, HI, 2004).
9. "Theory Supporting Sabido," Population Media Center, www.populationmedia.org/product/sabido-theory/.
10. *Summary Report: The Beijing Declaration and Platform for Action Turns 20,* (n.p.: UN Women, 2015), http://www.unwomen.org/en/digital-library/publications/2015/02/beijing-synthesis-report.
11. Bushra Qadim Hyder, "Pakistan–Peace Curriculum Teaches Hope in Dangerous Peshawar," New America, weeklywonk.newamerica.net/articles/fear-hope-peshawar/.
12. Claudia J. Clayton, Bonnie Ballif-Spanvill, and Melanie D. Hunsaker, "Preventing Violence and Teaching Peace: A Review of Promising and Effective Antiviolence, Conflict-Resolution, and Peace Programs for Elementary School Children," *Journal of Applied and Preventive Psychology* 10 (2001): 1–13.
13. Clayton, Ballif-Spanvill, and Hunsaker, "Preventing Violence and Teaching Peace," 1–13.
14. Bonnie Ballif-Spanvill and H. Farrell, "The Personalization of Peace Education" (paper presented at the Comparative and International Education Society, Baltimore, MD, February 2007).
15. Ballif-Spanvill and Farrell, "The Personalization of Peace Education."
16. "PEACEABILITIES," Brigham Young University, 2009, http://creativeworks.byu.edu/peace/overview.htm.
17. Brent Ashabranner and Russell Davis, *The Lion's Whiskers: Tales of High Africa* (Boston: Little, Brown, 1959), paraphrase of original story.

12

DIALOGUE: RELIGION AS PEACEMAKER

ROBERT A. REES AND GORDON C. THOMASSON

Robert A. Rees, visiting professor and director of Mormon studies at the Graduate Theological Union in Berkeley, and Gordon C. Thomasson, professor emeritus of history, philosophy, and social sciences at State University of New York at Broome, presented this dialogue at "'Blessed Are the Peacemakers': Peace Is Possible," the International Society's twenty-sixth annual conference, April 2015, Brigham Young University, Provo, Utah.

ROBERT A. REES

Gordon Thomasson and I have been friends and colleagues for many years. Our hope in this dialogue is to have an exchange of ideas about war and peace as it relates to Mormonism. We would like to frame this conversation in light of the Jewish concept of *Tikkun olam*, which means "repairing the world," an ethic also found in the Latter-day Saint tradition. The origin of *Tikkun olam* can be traced to the sixteenth-century Kabbalist Isaac Luria, who taught that when God created the world, he sought to light it by shaping special lamps or vessels to hold his light. "But as God poured the Light into the vessels, they catastrophically shattered, tumbling down toward the realm of matter [that is, the earth]. Thus, our world consists of countless shards of the original vessels entrapping sparks of the Divine Light. Humanity's great task involves helping God by freeing and reuniting the scattered Light, raising the sparks back to Divinity and restoring the broken world."[1] One of the ways in which we can participate in "freeing and reuniting the scattered Light" is by working for peace. Making and keeping peace is the shared, sacred work of God and humans.

As followers of the Prince of Peace, peacemaking is our collective calling. The face of peace is dramatically different from the face of war, as I try to illustrate in the following poem, titled "The Face of War," based on a photograph I saw in the newspaper many years into our current war in the Middle East:

> On a sunny day in Basra or Baghdad,
> a child's face is fractured beyond
> anything human, as if God
> shaping an image of himself
> had dropped the clay on stones:
> eyeless and a bloody rupture
> where a mouth had been.
> The child's face gone
> and with it all we count
> of ourselves so long
> out of the arroyos and savannahs:
> our songs and sonnets,
> our cantatas and cathedrals,
> skyscrapers and spaceships,
> our science and our psalms—
> all are nothing without
> the face of this child.

I have admired Gordon Thomasson for many years. Gordon has been one of the most incisive, penetrating, and thoughtful thinkers in LDS culture over the past half-century. He is a scholar whose faith and intellect have made a significant contribution to Mormon intellectual and spiritual life. Gordon and I worked together during the sixties when both of us experienced opprobrium from some of our fellow Latter-day Saints over our opposition to the war in Vietnam. Gordon assembled and edited a collection titled *War, Conscription, Conscience, and Mormonism*, which helped a number of Latter-day Saints who considered becoming or who became conscientious objectors during that misbegotten war.

GORDON C. THOMASSON

I was privileged to learn from and study with Hugh Nibley. One of Hugh's greatest contributions was to remind the Saints of our obligation, in the words of the Doctrine and Covenants, to both "renounce war and proclaim peace."[2] Few here might remember the controversy that erupted during that time over Nibley's open opposition to war, which was unpopular among the majority of Latter-day Saints but profoundly influential on a few, including me. Others who influenced my ethic of peace include two of my professors at UC–Santa Barbara—the Roman Catholic scholar Thomas O'Day and the Methodist pacifist minister Robert Michelson. Both of them respected and sustained me in my own faith as well as enriched my understanding of what it means to be a Christian peacemaker in a world that seems always to be waging war. I am thankful for the fact that there are people of that sort today at various colleges and universities who are looking out for our children in the way these men looked out for me. As members of the Latter-day Saint community, we need to recognize and be thankful for the good men and women of the earth who work for peace. It is a real blessing we enjoy, and we do not mention it often enough to each other or in our prayers of thanksgiving.

My career includes Southeast Asian studies. I have also worked in Mexico and sub-Saharan Africa, especially in Liberia and in southern Sudan. As a result, I have seen enough conflict to last a lifetime. There were military involvements all around me when I served as a missionary in Mexico in the early 1960s but much more so in southern Sudan and other places I have lived. We have been blessed in the United States to be protected from the worst of those kinds of conflicts. We really have little sense of what it means to live in an environment torn by war with no place to turn for escape or safety.

Occasionally, one hears the sentiment that religion is the greatest cause of war. Historically speaking, that is nonsense. It makes religion a scapegoat for humanity's problems. To me, the greatest cause of war is greed. Greed for wealth, for territory, and for power. The fact is that whatever else is involved, religion has been much more of an ameliorating force than a causal force of the world's problems. Whenever I have studied so-called "wars of religion," I have found people using religion to justify their own agendas, which were anything but religious. One needs to be very distrustful of such a simplistic explanation, because it goes against the fundamental principles of the world's religions.

It is popular today to demonize our Muslim brothers and sisters as warlike because a small group of Muslims have waged what they call *Jihad* against the United States. The Muslims with whom I have been familiar over the years have been adamant that *Jihad* really refers to self-mastery and to putting oneself in harmony with God, not to attacking others. The fact is that most of the people of the earth desire peace and wish to love their brothers and sisters regardless of their faith and tradition.

The most important questions any of us can ask are, "What can I do personally to make peace?" and "How can I work with others in building and sustaining peace?" I have found that there is an enormous hunger among people of all faiths for a better world, a world that is promised if we take care to see everyone as Heavenly Father's child.

ROBERT A. REES

I agree with what Gordon says about the impulse for peace one finds in other faith traditions. I teach at a theological university and also at a public university. My students come from many religious traditions, and it is wonderful to learn from them. I also learn much about peace from colleagues and friends of other faiths. In a recent lecture titled "Reimagining the Restoration," I asked those in attendance, "If you could change one thing about the Church, what would you change?" In this conference devoted to peace, I reframe the question: "If you could change one thing about the world that would lead to peace, what would it be?" My own answer is that we would have a better chance of creating a peaceful world if more of the leaders of nations were women. That is not said in jest. I believe that women are much more inclined to solve problems through peaceful means than by waging war than are men.

In 1976, Latter-day Saints were somewhat surprised to hear President Spencer W. Kimball refer to us as "a warlike people, easily distracted from our assignment of preparing for the coming of the Lord." Speaking of Americans in general and by implication Latter-day Saints, President Kimball was even more specific: "When enemies rise up, we commit vast resources to the fabrications of gods of stone and steel—ships, planes, missiles, fortifications. . . . When threatened, we become anti-enemy instead of pro-kingdom of God."[3]

It is interesting that President Kimball characterized Latter-day Saints as warlike, implying we are more eager to support war than to oppose it. Many Latter-day Saints may not be aware of the fact that during both the first and second world wars, respective First Presidencies issued strong declarations against the United States entering those wars. In truth, both ancient and modern prophets have consistently opposed war.

In the Doctrine and Covenants, we are commanded to "renounce war and proclaim peace." Hugh Nibley said, "'Renounce' is a very strong word. We are not to try to win peace by war or merely call a truce but to renounce war itself, to disdain it as a policy by proclaiming peace without reservation."[4] We often hear that truth is the first casualty of war, but peace is really the first and also the last casualty of war.

Historically, one of the attitudes that leads to war is exceptionalism—the belief that we are a chosen people. This attitude is something we are susceptible to as both Mormons and Americans. Exceptionalism can easily seduce us into thinking of ourselves as better than others, as more favored of God and as more entitled than others. Exceptionalism can lead to the belief that we are justified in going to war and in doing so are always serving the cause of truth and justice. The following is a poem, titled "Famine and Scarcity," about one of my grandchildren, and it exemplifies a nonexceptional attitude about war:

> My grandson, seven,
> head bent over his crustless peanut-
> butter and honey sandwich,
> bowl of grapes
> and cup of juice,
> says these very words:
> "Heavenly Father,

bless that there will be no war, famine
or scarcity in the land."
And I wonder where this
pocket prophet, this junior Jeremiah
heard such a biblical phrase
and how in his sabbath year
he seems to understand.
On the evening news I see
bone piles of the vultures of war
and beneath a tangled bush in Africa,
a woman holding her ghost child—
a collapsed puppet.
At night I say my clichés
for the wrecked and wretched of the earth
who speak holy words
to the world's vast darkness.

GORDON C. THOMASSON

In 1970, my body was in no shape or form draftable. I had some forty fractures in my face and skull from multiple accidents—always as a passenger. If you ride in a car I am riding in, your insurance premiums go up! Thus, I was witness to and the subject of a great deal of injury. Because of the power of priesthood blessings, I was brought back to life and healed in ways I still marvel at. That said, my suffering was insignificant in comparison with the suffering of others in the hospital.

In one accident, my best friend died. My testimony that he was in a better place did not change the fact that his parents were suffering terribly over the loss of their son. When I knew I was going to live, my attention turned immediately to others affected by the accident—and other accidents and maladies and the myriad conflicts raging across the world. Surviving those accidents renewed my desire to make a better world for the Lord's children, and that led me increasingly to become involved in international studies and to work for peace.

When you spend time in a place like southern Sudan, it does not take long for you to recognize how blessed your life is. Being there and in similar countries made me much more aware of my own personal blessings, but it also led me to focus on how I could bless others, including the people who live in such places. It also led to larger questions about how to spend my time and money, how to best serve others and how to better devote my life to the Prince of Peace.

Many argue that war is necessary for attaining peace. Ultimately, such an argument leads to the logic that there can be no peace without war, and that leads us to do what President Kimball warned us against: devoting so much of our resources to building and enhancing the machinery of war.

ROBERT A. REES

One of the things I appreciate about Gordon is the extent to which he has studied the Book of Mormon, including what it teaches us about war and peace. It is not uncommon for Latter-day Saints to justify war from the pages of the Book of Mormon. Hugh Nibley was clear that the essential message of the Book of Mormon is that war is not only hell, it is outer darkness. One of the great lessons about war in the Book of Mormon is found in the attitude of the Nephites toward the Lamanites. As much as the Lamanites try to destroy the Nephites, the Nephites continue to refer to them as their "beloved brethren."[5] I wonder how many of us could say that about our enemies, including those in ISIS who are so bent on our destruction.

I have been thinking about a seminar I have been invited to participate in at BYU this summer on "Developing a Latter-day Saint Ethic of War and Peace." It seems to me that consideration of such an ethic should begin and end with the twenty-fifth chapter of Matthew. The imperative of that scripture is that we see those whom we consider least in the world as if they were Christ himself. By and large we do not think about this parable when it comes to war. The reality is that today in the Middle East there are hundreds of thousands of people, many of them innocent civilians, who are victims of our bombs and bullets. There are many children whose lives are completely shattered as a consequence of our going to war. In Matthew's gospel, Christ asks us to imagine an Iraqi child killed or maimed by one of our drones as if it were him, or to imagine a Syrian family displaced

Christ is the world's greatest example of the virtues we need in order to make peace. (Harry Anderson, The Second Coming. *Courtesy of Intellectual Reserve, Inc.)*

by the war that is devouring that country as if it were our family or his family. I always feel condemned before this particular scripture because it is extremely difficult to do what Christ asks us to do—to consider everyone as if he or she were Christ. In other words, He is saying, "Inasmuch as you have failed to make peace with others, you have chosen to make war with me."

I would like to conclude with a story that illustrates what I am trying to say about love—and about forgiveness. Raymond Carver's "A Small Good Thing" is a story of a couple, the Weisses, and the birthday celebration they are planning for their only son, Scotty. The mother orders a cake from the local bakery. On the day of the party, the boy is hit by a car and lapses into a coma. The parents wait anxiously by the bedside day and night, but their son never awakens and, after a few days, he dies. The baker, unaware of the accident, continues to call the parents to come and pick up their cake. Grieving, they do not return his calls. He continues to call and becomes abusive and even threatening. Finally, one night they go to the bakery to express their outrage at the baker's behavior. When they tell him that their son is dead, he is embarrassed and ashamed. A simple man, he does the only thing he can think of—he offers them some of his fresh-baked bread and rolls. As they sit in the darkened bakery eating, he reveals his own life of loneliness, of being childless, of working sixteen hours a day baking thousands of wedding and birthday cakes and imagining the celebrations surrounding them, none of which ever touch him personally.

Not knowing what else to do, he takes a fresh loaf of dark bread from the oven, breaks it open and offers them some. "Smell this," he says. "It's a heavy bread but rich." Carver writes, "They smelled it, then he had them taste it. It had the taste of molasses and coarse grains. They listened to him. They ate what they could. They swallowed the dark bread. It was like daylight under the florescent trays of light. They talked on into the early morning, the high, pale cast of light in the windows, and they did not think of leaving."[6]

This is a powerful story of loss, grief, death, conflict, forgiveness, and redemption. It is also a story about empathy, sympathy, and compassion. The association in the story of bread with light reminds us of Christ, who is both the Bread of Life and the Light of the World and who is the world's greatest example of the virtues we need in order to make peace, as Gordon and I have discussed. Partaking of the bread of life each week, we too taste of his light. It is a small, good thing we do every Sunday and is akin to all of the other small gifts of kindness, generosity, and forgiveness we give to one another. Those acts of love, it seems to me, have their genesis in the Light of Christ, which is in every one of us.

I feel fortunate that while I did spend some time in the military, I did not have to go to war. My father was not so fortunate. He was in some of the worst battles of the Pacific and saw death and destruction that plagued him the rest of his life. Visiting the Pearl Harbor Memorial in Hawaii recently, I thought of my father and all those others, Americans, Japanese, and others who lost their lives or were wounded in that and other wars. On the way home, I wrote the following poem:

Pearl Harbor

"Those are pearls that were his eyes."
[Shakespeare, *The Tempest*]

Beneath these waters
their bones lie in repose,
buried
in an instant
by bombs and torpedoes.
At that moment, in a small Arizona town,
my father,
fresh from milking,
sits down to late breakfast
and listens to the radio.
We are too young to
understand
but recognize
a fear we know
from dreams.
Later their voices erupt,
strafing the night.
She begs him not to go, but
my father's fierce will
is adamant.

Soon he sails
from San Francisco
to islands of death
across the Pacific.
In the museum I look up
at the plane
suspended from
the ceiling
and remember the story:
a Kamikaze bomber
heading straight
for my father's ship
at the last moment
changes course
to hit a nearby destroyer.
There is nothing he can do
while eternity is suspended in time.
My father sees blood and fire,
bodies in the water,
a severed arm,
Images no whisky
can wash away.
Looking at the placid sea,
I bow my head
for all that unfolded
from that day
when I was six
and the world
twisted on its axis
to this.

Had that plane not changed directions at the last moment, I would not be here today. My father came home from that war and rescued me from a foster home and taught me the gospel of Jesus Christ. It changed my life dramatically and indelibly. At the memorial, I thought of all of those children whose fathers did not come home from the war and all of those children whose fathers might go to war at some future time. It is not inevitable that they will be required to do so—peace is always a choice. Working for peace, making peace, is something we all can do. Stopping war is a choice we always have. The Beatitudes do not say, "Blessed are the peace lovers" but rather, "Blessed are the peacemakers: for they shall be called the children of God."[7] The shards of light that Isaac Luria spoke about as being in all of us can help us transform the darkness of war into the light of peace. It is a choice we always have. It is a choice I believe Christ calls us to make as members of his peaceable kingdom.

NOTES

1. Joseph Naft, "Tikkun Olam: The Spiritual Purpose of Life," http://www.innerfrontier.org/Practices/TikkunOlam.htm.
2. Doctrine and Covenants 98:16.
3. Spencer W. Kimball, "The False Gods We Worship," *Ensign*, June 1976, 6.
4. Hugh Nibley, "Renounce War!" *BYU Daily Universe*, 26 March 1971.
5. See Jacob 4:2–3.
6. Raymond Carver, "A Small Good Thing," *Where I'm Calling From: New and Selected Stories* (New York: Vintage Books, 2009), 376–405.
7. Matthew 5:9.

Part 4

RELIGIOUS FREEDOM AND OPPRESSION

Family at Buenos Aires Argentina Temple. (Courtesy of Intellectual Reserve, Inc.)

13

"LET THEM WORSHIP HOW, WHERE, OR WHAT THEY MAY"

WILLIAM F. ATKIN

William F. Atkin, then associate general counsel at The Church of Jesus Christ of Latter-day Saints, presented this essay at "International Challenges Facing the Church," the International Society's seventeenth annual conference, April 2006, Brigham Young University, Provo, Utah.

Elder Lance B. Wickman, who is a member of the First Quorum of the Seventy and is the general counsel of The Church of Jesus Christ of Latter-day Saints, has observed that the most serious challenges to the Church in the United States and internationally are the attacks on religious liberty. Religious rights are being restricted and narrowed by legislatures and governments globally. Religious liberty is being diminished due to official indifference caused by rampant secularism in various "enlightened" countries. Freedom to worship is being decimated in the name of God by the reassertion of dominant religions.

An example of this concern is the plight of Abdul Rahman, an Afghani who more than fifteen years ago converted to Christianity. I think we have all been appalled the past several weeks to follow his story. Based on his conversion, Rahman was being prosecuted by the Afghani government for his conversion, a criminal act under Islamic law that carried with it the possibility of a death penalty. All of this transpired notwithstanding a provision in the 2004 Afghani constitution that provides for religious liberty. While I believe that the answer is obvious, I would like to review the importance to us as Latter-day Saints of religious liberty to all people.

When I was a child, my mother recounted to me the story of my third great-grandfather—a story that illustrates the intolerance and hatred that has repeated itself over and over during the history of the world for those who believe differently than the majority. The setting of this story was, ironically, a Missouri village named Independence. On a hot, muggy July evening in 1833, a local mob sought out the home of Bishop Edward Partridge. Bishop Partridge retells this event as follows:

> July 20, 1833. George Simpson and two other mobbers entered my house (while I was sitting with my wife, who was quite feeble, my youngest child being then about three weeks old) and compelled me to go with him. Soon after leaving my house, I was surrounded by about fifty mobbers, who escorted me about half a mile to the public square, where I was surrounded by about two or three hundred more. Russell Hicks, Esq., appeared to be the head man of the mob; he told me that his word was the law of the county, and that I must agree to leave the county or suffer the consequences. I answered that if I must suffer for my religion it was no more than others had done before me; that I was not conscious of having injured any one in the county, therefore I would not consent to leave it. Mr. Hicks then proceeded to strip off my clothes and was disposed to strip them all off. I strongly protested against being stripped naked in the street, when some, more humane than the rest, interfered, and I was permitted to wear my shirt and pantaloons. Tar and feathers were then brought, and a man by the name of Davies, with the help of another, daubed me with tar from the crown of my head to my feet, after which feathers were thrown over me.[2]

Bishop Partridge's daughter wrote in her journal that as they waited anxiously for their father's return, they saw a young family acquaintance approaching their home with a person who they thought was an American Indian because of his dark covering. They ran upstairs in fear. They discovered that the dark figure was their father, covered with tar and feathers.[3] They, together with their mother, stayed up late into the night pouring hot water on the tar to soften the tar in attempts to remove it. As they did so, strips of Bishop Partridge's flesh were torn off together with the tar. One Church historian described this event as follows: "This dastardly outrage, with others of still greater enormity, [was] committed under the broad sunlight of American liberty, with the executive of the State looking on and in secret league with these mobocratic wretches."[4] Commenting on the life of Bishop Partridge, B. H. Roberts observed, "Stripped of his earthly possessions and broken in health, he reached Commerce, but the trials through which he had passed had proven too much for his constitution, which was never robust, and he passed away, a victim to the intolerance and religious bigotry of his generation."[5]

Religious liberty and tolerance of belief have been emphasized as a basic tenet of the Church from the very beginning of its history, a theme reemphasized by President Gordon B. Hinckley with his heartfelt plea for tolerance and love of all, regardless of race or creed.[6]

The following are a few examples of modern prophets' teachings about religious liberty and tolerance.

Elder Wilford Woodruff: "We claim no religious liberty that we are unwilling to accord to others."[7]

The First Presidency in 1907: "The religion of the Latter-day Saints stands for the rights of all men, whatever their standing may be in society. It teaches tolerance to those of all other religions or no religion."[8]

Elder John A. Widtsoe: "Among the principles of beauty and power which make up the Gospel, none is more conducive to peace than the Mormon doctrine of tolerance. We are taught to give due respect to the opinions and mode of life of our fellow beings."[9]

Elder J. Reuben Clark: "We are universal in our tolerance and in our respect for the opinions of others. We feel we may rightfully ask for the same consideration for ourselves."[10]

Elder James E. Talmage referred to religious liberty as "the unbounded liberality and tolerance with which The Church of Jesus Christ of Latter-day Saints regards other religious denominations."[11]

Elder Russell M. Nelson: "The noble expression of religious tolerance found in the 11th Article of Faith is particularly poignant in light of the fact that its author, Joseph Smith, suffered persecution and finally martyrdom at the hands of the intolerant."[12]

Joseph Smith declared the following:

> [I] want the liberty of thinking and believing as I please. It feels so good not to be trammeled. . . . The ideal of tolerance at its best is hospitality to new ideas. Genuine tolerance weighs carefully opposing views. Above all, it allows those with opposing or conflicting views their right to private judgment. And even more important, the person who is genuinely tolerant will rise above his differences into the fullest fellowship and the noblest friendships. Mormonism represents such tolerance. It is deeply opposed to coercion or compulsion of any kind. If ever an organization depended wholly upon the voluntary spirit of man, fellowship that rises above individual differences, and divine love that unites the body of the Church, it is the religion called Mormonism. Intolerance is a sure sign of weakness. And someone said, "Only the confident can afford to be calm and kindly; only the fearful must defame and exclude."[13]

Religious liberty is not just another teaching of the Church; it is perhaps the core of all Church doctrine. Our Heavenly Father lost one-third of his children in the premortal existence due to their opposition to freedom of conscience. Elder Bruce R. McConkie said,

> Freedom of worship is one of the basic doctrines of the gospel. Indeed, in one manner of speaking *it is the most basic of all doctrines*, even taking precedence over the nature and kind of being that God is, or the atoning sacrifice of the Son of God, or the vesting of priesthood and keys and saving power in the one true church. *By this we mean that if there were not freedom of worship, there would be no God, no redemption, and no salvation in the kingdom of God.*[14]

What is our responsibility, both institutionally and individually, in defending this principle globally? The Prophet Joseph Smith stated our obligations very clearly:

> The Saints can testify whether I am willing to lay down my life for my brethren. If it has been demonstrated that I have been willing to die for a Mormon, I am bold to declare before heaven that I am just as ready to die in defending the rights of a Presbyterian, a Baptist, or a good man of any denomination; for the same principle which would trample upon the rights of the Latter-day Saints would trample upon the rights of the Roman Catholics, or of any other denomination who may be unpopular and too weak to defend themselves.[15]

Are we as willing to do the same? Are we willing to lay down our lives to defend the rights of those "who may be unpopular and too weak to defend themselves?" Is it enough for us to be satisfied if the Church benefits while the rights of others are trampled?

In early October 2001, I visited Washington, DC, with a Jewish friend of mine. Because of 11 September 2001, the city seemed almost vacant. Early on Saturday morning, we visited the Holocaust Memorial Museum. For those of you who have never visited the museum, let me briefly describe the experience. The tour progresses chronologically, starting with the Nazis' rise to power. A visitor sees how the Nazis started slowly with the imposition of measures that, at first, benignly segregated Jews from other citizens. The severity of the segregation and other restrictions imposed on the Jews increased gradually until a visitor is face-to-face with the horrendous results of the Nazis' so-called Final Solution, the extermination of all Jews in Europe. At this point, my soul was terribly depressed with the darkness and evil imposed by men and women on their fellow beings. However, the last portion of the museum consists of a chest-high wall that lists alphabetically by country and surname the "rescuers" of Jews, the men and women who put their own lives at risk on behalf of the Jews, examples of hope for the goodness of some men and women.

Upon leaving the museum, I pondered these questions: Who were these individuals who were listed on the wall? What made them act differently in defense and protection of their Jewish friends and neighbors, while others stood passively aside and permitted the horrors to occur? In seeking an answer to these questions, I found a study conducted by two psychologists at Columbia University that explored these very questions.

Their conclusions are as follows:

> The primary focus of the rescuers was on others and not on self.
>
> Pity, compassion, concern, and affection for others were the common vocabulary of rescuers.
>
> Rescuers emphasized the need to be helpful, hospitable, concerned, and loving toward others.
>
> Their ethical values extended to all human beings (e.g., "We all came from the same God"; "All men are equal and are free and equal by right").
>
> Unlike the resistance fighters, the rescuers were motivated by concern and love for others, not hatred for the Nazis.
>
> For rescuers, their religious beliefs involved action, not merely knowledge and theoretical love of neighbor.
>
> Their driving concern for others and their understanding that all are children of God were values taught to them in their homes by their parents.
>
> Finally, they believed that care and love of others was not a spectator's sport; it compelled action.[16]

In summary and in gospel terms, I believe that the rescuers had developed charity, the pure love of Christ, and this charity motivated their actions. What about us? One cannot help but make the self-inquiry, "What would I have done?" While this leads to important self-reflection, the more telling question is "What will I do to promote religious liberty and tolerance in my neighborhood, my community, and the world?"

The Church has its institutional response to the attacks on religious liberty. However, what about you and me individually? Are we content to enjoy the blessings of the religious liberty in our wards and stakes in the United States while our neighbors in minority or unpopular religions are being persecuted? Or while Saints around the world struggle to enjoy the full blessings of the restored gospel in their homelands because of restrictions on their freedom of conscience and belief?

As covenant people, we are committed to our Heavenly Father to use our time, talents, and resources to build his kingdom. My hope and prayer is that we will use our time, talents, and resources to promote and defend religious liberty and freedom of belief for all, particularly for those who are weak, disenfranchised, or otherwise defenseless.

NOTES

1. The eleventh article of faith reads, "We claim the privilege of worshipping Almighty God according to the dictates of our own conscience, and allow all men the same privilege, let them worship how, where, or what they may."
2. Andrew Jenson, *Latter-day Saint Biographical Encyclopedia: A Compilation of Biographical Sketches of Prominent Men and Women in The Church of Jesus Christ of Latter-day Saints*, vol. 1 (Salt Lake City: The Andrew Jenson History Company, 1901), 220.
3. Emily Dow Partridge Young, *Reminiscences of Emily Dow Partridge Young* (Salt Lake City, 1884), 12.
4. Jenson, *Latter-day Saint Biographical Encyclopedia*, 1: 220.
5. B. H. Roberts, *A Comprehensive History of the Church of Jesus Christ of Latter-day Saints*, vol. 2 (Provo, UT: Brigham Young University Press, 1965), 40–41.
6. Peggy Fletcher Stack, "Hinckley Plea: End Divisive Attitudes," *Salt Lake Tribune*, 2 April 2006.
7. G. Homer Durham, comp., *The Discourses of Wilford Woodruff*, Durham (Salt Lake City: Bookcraft, 1946), 195.
8. James R. Clark, comp., *Messages of the First Presidency* (Salt Lake City: Bookcraft, 1965), 4:156–57.
9. John A. Widtsoe, in Conference Report, April 1941, 115.
10. J. Reuben Clark Jr., in Conference Report, April 1935, 92.
11. James E. Talmage, *The Articles of Faith*, 12th ed. (Salt Lake City: Deseret Book, 1924), 404.
12. Russell M. Nelson, "True Brotherhood Develops Bridges of Understanding," *Church News*, 9 April 1994.
13. Obert C. Tanner, *Christ's Ideals for Living* (Salt Lake City: The Obert C. and Grace A. Tanner Foundation, 1981), 370 –71.
14. Bruce R. McConkie, *A New Witness for the Articles of Faith* (Salt Lake City: Deseret Book, 1985), 655; emphasis added.

15. Joseph Fielding Smith, comp., *Teachings of the Prophet Joseph Smith* (Salt Lake City: Deseret Book, 1976), 313.
16. Samuel P. Oliner and Pearl M. Oliner, *The Altruistic Personality: Rescuers of Jews in Nazi Europe* (New York: Free Press, 1988).

14

PROTECTION OF RELIGIOUS LIBERTIES

Current Initiatives

COLE DURHAM

Cole Durham, then professor of law at Brigham Young University, presented this essay at "The Church and the Global Community," the International Society's twentieth annual conference, April 2009, Brigham Young University, Provo, Utah.

Today I want to talk about some of the challenges and initiatives going on with religious freedom. Let me start with the challenges and headlines I've picked up—some from the last week or so:

> India: Supreme court rules against a Muslim schoolboy. (They don't want the Taliban coming to India.)
>
> Egypt: Bahá'í villagers attacked in their homes.
>
> Saudi Arabia: Shi'ite cleric threatens secession over treatment of Saudi Shi'ites.
>
> Morocco: Government clamps down on Shi'ite Islam. Five foreign Christian women deported for proselytizing.

> China: China cracks down on Muslims in the western provinces. (Of course, they've been doing this with Tibet.)
>
> Armenia: New draft law in Armenia requires five hundred adult members for registration of religious organization.
>
> Uzbekistan: Four Protestants jailed and three detained for impermissibly gathering for religious purposes. (They admitted to going into someone's home to talk about religion.)

Headlines like those are coming in, and we're trying to develop a website that can easily serve as an umbrella clearinghouse for them. If you get stories, send them to us. I don't have our site address, but you can find it easily. Look up "law and religion" on Google, and we're usually in the top five or six results.

We saw an extraordinary opening of the world to religious freedom in 1990, particularly with the collapse of most of the Communist world. What we're seeing now is a significant retrenchment, although it's somewhat of a mixed picture. It's interesting to bear in mind that there are free countries, or countries with high degrees of religious freedom, on every continent. Based on some rankings done by Freedom House and the Hudson Institute, you can come up with analyses of different places.

In Asia, we have Japan, South Korea, and Mongolia. In Latin America, there are several countries: Argentina, Brazil, Chile, and Guatemala. The African countries are Botswana, Mali, Namibia, Senegal, and South Africa. More interesting in the rankings by Freedom House and the Hudson Institute are that some of the foregoing countries score higher than Belgium, France, Germany, and Greece. (Greece is less surprising if you know about Greece.)

One of the implications about this is that, to quote Paul A. Marshall, "there are absolutely no grounds for thinking that religious freedom is an exclusively Western concern or achievement." Now there is no doubt that some of the basic ideas and constitutional history started in the West. But this is, with great credibility, an issue about which there is universality—particularly among those who feel they need the protection.

Religious freedom is not a "quasi-luxury" that needs to be advanced "only after more basic needs such as food and shelter have been achieved."

For example, Senegal is not exactly a rich country; it's a Muslim country and a place where there is substantial religious freedom.

Another quote from Marshall: "It is a moral travesty of the highest order to maintain that because people are hungry or cold, it is legitimate to repress their beliefs as well." That's an important thing to bear in mind, because sometimes people make the argument that religious freedom, civil rights, or human rights are things that one can add on later. It turns out that people who are hungry and cold often care about religion—often more than others. Indeed, one thing I've thought a lot about is the many ways we can give service—through humanitarian aid and other ways that open doorways. Remember how significant religious freedom is to people. We are saving many lives from measles and from various kinds of infant diseases, while many of the children in these countries will grow up without religious freedom. You have to think about priorities and what is ultimately going to be important.

It turns out that it's worth looking at the relationship of religious freedom and what the prevailing religion is in the country. Not surprisingly, there's a high correlation between countries with Christianity as a prevailing religion or culture and religious freedom. One particular study surveyed about half of the countries in the world, and of the countries rated as "religiously free," thirty-five are traditionally Christian. Only two Christian countries (Cuba and Belarus) are listed on the "not free" list in the analysis. Other free countries include Israel and countries with largely Buddhist backgrounds, such as Japan, Mongolia, and Thailand. Buddhist countries with weak religious freedom typically have a communist or nationalist background, such as China, Tibet, Laos, North Korea, Vietnam, and Myanmar. It will not come as a surprise that some of the countries without religious freedom are often Islamic, but not always; as indicated, there are exceptions. Of the twenty "un-free" countries surveyed, twelve are Muslim. It's worth noting that there are Muslim countries with a high or moderate degree of religious freedom, like Senegal and Indonesia. Religious freedom is stronger in Muslim areas outside of the Arab world and the Middle East. There is a diaspora effect, and I know that some of the areas we have been focusing on are the diaspora areas of Islam. Often, constraints on religious freedom do not reflect governmental will to regulate, but they do reflect communal tensions, widespread societal religious violence, and religiously based terrorism. This is an issue in many countries that have real security problems, and it is faced by a lot of countries in the world as they wrestle with how to deal with the upswing of religious extremism.

Then we come to the veneer of liberty. One thing that is interesting and important to remember is how fast things can turn. I remember in the early '90s going to dinner one night with a friend from Yugoslavia, who I taught with for many years. He and his wife remembered the civil war breaking out in Yugoslavia, and they were talking about watching their country unravel right before their eyes—seeing friends suddenly become enemies. Proposition 8 is obviously not on the same scale, but many of us have been surprised to see the intensity of the reaction. I know for me that it's the first time in my life that I started feeling that there might be risks of mob violence that I had only read about growing up in the early history of the Church. I had an article in the Salt Lake Tribune published about me about a week or so ago, and I read some of the comments that came in on the website. What was amazing to me was how virulent they were. We need to bear in mind the veneer.

In March, the Organization for Security and Co-operation in Europe had a special meeting on the persecution of Christians. We tend to not think of that as a major problem, but in many parts of the world it is a major problem. Significantly, much of the persecution is not Muslim versus Christian persecution, but a Christian versus Christian persecution. So this is not altogether a wonderful story. But these are legitimate realities.

I tend to think that religious freedom faces constant forces of attrition—like a mountain peak exposed to wind and weather and unrelenting forces of erosion. The erosion starts happening all of the time for a lot of different reasons—these are the things we are seeing. Let me describe the different types of problems.

A very typical problem legally around many parts of the world is getting initial registration of the legal entities through which religious organizations do their work. One of the very significant developments in the past decade, at least in European space, has been the emergence of a series of European court decisions that make it very clear that religious communities have a right to legal entity status. I've been involved with the Organization for Security and Co-operation in Europe in reviewing a lot of other legislation in central Asia. Some of these places don't think about that; they think they are free of regulation in these organizations—the way they always have been. This has been a big problem; it's a practical matter when we talk about opening the doors of nations, and it really means getting legal registration for legal entity status.

I would say another major wave of issues coming has to do with land-use issues. These problems arise everywhere. We certainly have them in the United States. We never have a temple project go forward anywhere that doesn't encounter opposition that will take this kind of form. These issues are going to become more significant and more complex because they are always local and are managed at the local level. Think about the fact that we have sixty-seven thousand municipalities in the United States. You don't pass one zoning ordinance in the United States; you have sixty-seven thousand of them. This is true for every other major country. This means there is a constant and immense challenge. And very often, religious communities—especially unpopular ones—are the ones that face risks. This will be hidden in various ways; there are a lot of phone calls from churches and from other people. We are also seeing, particularly in Asia, proliferation of antiproselytizing laws.

There are huge issues in the field of education with respect to both the religious and educational impact that is on children with minority backgrounds. There are issues of religious clothing that people can wear, in cases about headscarves in Turkey, France, and elsewhere.

Another recurrent problem, particularly for small religious groups, is disruption of religious services. Discrimination in all forms is significant. Interestingly, there was a case last week in the European court holding that Austria had discriminated against the Jehovah's Witnesses because the Jehovah's Witnesses didn't get a higher form of recognition in the country—a form of recognition that the LDS Church has in Austria. Their ministers could not get ministerial exemptions, and this was a form of discrimination. This is actually quite significant because it means that some of the discrimination coming from the multichurch recognition systems that are very prevalent in Europe may be challenged.

The following are some general trends that I want to highlight—some things happening that we need to watch for.

FREE EXERCISE REDUCTIONISM

There is an increasing tendency in a lot of countries to argue that we don't really need religious freedom anymore. We can stretch freedom of speech, freedom of association, and nondiscrimination norms, and if we add those up, we certainly don't need religious freedom anymore. My sense is that the stretching of the other norms is not going to be the same; moreover, there is something about the age and long-term legitimacy in something like the religious freedom norms that makes it very significant. But this is a trend that is happening that needs to be watched.

SECURITY PROBLEMS WITH ISLAMIC EXTREMISM

Another problem is the tension between religious freedom and security. No one doubts that there are situations where security is concerned that threaten the physical safety or health of public workers. One thing that happened after 9/11 is this kind of an excuse for overreactions that virtually always have the effect of making life more difficult for religious groups. In central Asia, there are legitimate concerns about groups who are calling for the overthrow of governments based on religious means. It's a little hard to know what this means. There are groups calling for the restoration of the Caliphate returning to early Muslim history. Most of us believe there will be a Second Coming, and that will change governments. We would hope that the government officials are not going to use that as a claim that we are trying to undermine the country. But the nexus is a little closer with some of these Muslim groups, and this creates difficult problems; it's in the background for people working on legislation.

DEFAMATION OF RELIGION

Some of you will be aware that the UN has just passed a resolution on defamation of religion. In principle, defaming or speaking ill of other religions is not a thing to be encouraged. We try to train our missionaries to be respectful of others. But this is a more insidious problem. In effect, a number of the Muslim countries—and there have been resolutions like this going on for about ten years now—in which resolutions call for countries to impose penal sanctions for defamation of religion. Number one, with defamation you can have the tort of defamation of a person. It's a lot harder to know what it means when you are defaming a religion. The real risk is that this will be used particularly in a lot of Muslim countries to restrict speech about religion from both people outside the Muslim tradition and from the Nordic roots within the Muslim tradition. So there are tremendous risks that this will undermine a variety of freedoms, including freedom of expression and freedom of religious expression.

FAILURE TO TAKE RELIGION SERIOUSLY

There is a book by an individual named Tom Farr, who was very involved in setting up the current regime of doing country reports on religion every year. But he has written a book in which he argues—among other things—that some of the basic schools of thought that shape the way we think about foreign policy in the United States are realism, international law or international idealism formulations, and also neoconservativism. All three of those defined the major approaches to thinking about foreign policy in various ways that filter out religion and tend to not take it seriously. This is in a world where it has become clear that the secularization thesis no longer holds—or if it does hold, it's only in Europe. Religion has emerged as a major force of public life, and to simply ignore it or not notice what a significant factor it is or to not be in a position to deal with that effectively is a problem.

LOSS OF PRESUMPTION IN FAVOR OF RELIGION

We are seeing charges of extremism and narrowness. The abuse scandals undermine the credibility of religion; mounting forces on the atheist side are questioning religion. All of these things are having a cultural effect—a kind of presumption in favor of religion that helps to anchor. Religious freedom is being undermined.

These are some of the problems. It's worth underscoring how significant religious freedom is to us as members of The Church of Jesus Christ of Latter-day Saints but also to people of many other faiths. I have always thought the following statement by Elder Bruce R. McConkie was a fairly radical one, and only someone like Elder McConkie could have said it: "Freedom of worship is one of the basic doctrines of the gospel. Indeed, in one manner of speaking it is the most basic of all doctrines, even taking precedence over the nature and kind of being that God is, or the atoning sacrifice of the Son of God, or the vesting of priesthood and keys and saving power in the one true church. By this we mean that if there were no freedom of worship, there would be no God, no redemption, and no salvation in the kingdom of God."[1]

That's pretty strong. Now, he did not say it's the most important doctrine. Any of those on the list are more important. He said that it's the most basic doctrine, because without freedom, none of the other things can be done. And that is one of the fundamental things that we need to bear in mind.

RELIGIOUS FREEDOM AND THE GROWTH OF THE KINGDOM

On a belt across the middle of the world of Islam and out into China, there is no constitutional protection and religious freedom protected. Not surprising are the countries where we have little or no formal LDS presence. This is because we believe in going through the front door, as President Gordon B. Hinckley used to say. As I remember, Jim Toronto used to say, "In a lot of the Muslim countries there isn't a front door, or a back door, or even a tunnel." But again, this emphasizes the significance of religious freedom. One of the LDS members in Brussels right now spoke to me once about how religious freedom is a forerunner carrying the gospel to all nations. It's needed to protect from persecution, but more than that, it's important in ways that are not obvious for the general well-being of society. There has been a lot of empirical work going on over the past few years validating the significance of religious freedom to societies at large.

I have a chart intended to show that there is a high degree of correlation between religious freedom and a number of other social goods.

Now, it is no surprise that religious freedom will line up with things like freedom of speech, freedom of association, and other typical civil liberties because these things overlap in intimate ways. What is less obvious is that religious freedom also has high degrees of correlation with better health and education. With the consolidation of democracy, recipient democracies tend to correlate with better incomes for women—and for men as well, by the way. With economic freedom comes a reduction in conflicts. Some of this is stating things in another way, but there is strong correlation with the presence of other fundamental freedoms. The longevity of democracy—if you look at how long democracy lasts in places—helps anchor democracy. Where religious freedom is high, there are fewer incidences of armed conflict, there are better health outcomes, higher levels of earned income, better educational opportunities, and higher overall human development as measured by UN human development indexes.

Now, correlation is not the same as causation, but there are a lot of reasons for thinking that religious freedom is a causal contributor for other social goods. Religious competition results in increased religious participation. Religious participation levels lead to a variety of positive outcomes.

Brian Grim is one of the leading figures in international religious freedom research. He talks about the religious freedom cycle, in which religious freedom leads to broader participation, which in turn leads to various positive contributions that makes things work better in societies. What follows are examples of things that have been researched in 143 countries that show religious violence is lower if there are no barriers to religious competition. Countries without restrictions on conversion have higher levels of fundamental freedoms.

SOCIAL CAPITAL

Members and regular attendees of religious congregations, either membership or people who actually go to religious meetings regularly, give larger amounts to charities. Not surprisingly, they give larger amounts to religious organizations, but they also give to other secular organizations. The same is true for volunteer activities. One thing that religion seems to be associated with is greater social capital. On the flip side, there is the religious violence cycle. If you have social restrictions on religion, it leads to government restrictions, and this often exacerbates tensions and leads to more restrictions. If you have the opposite of religious liberty, you will have negative overall effectiveness on social capital.

CURRENT INITIATIVES

Let me shift and talk about initiatives. First, let me talk about general things that are going on. One thing that is quite interesting is this new process of Universal Periodic Reviews. George Jarvis, who has been one of the people working on government relations issues in Geneva, did a study that helped track and see what was happening in this Universal Periodic Review, which is a new process. Every five years, every country in the UN gets reviewed for their human rights record. What you have to understand is that this review puts countries under scrutiny, and in many ways it's that kind of scrutiny and public press that the critics of government get involved in and have had some of the maximum human rights compliance effects in. That's a significant development to see the kind of role that someone from here is contributing.

Similarly, we're seeing more countries accept the jurisdiction of the Human Rights Committee—if there are human rights violations, cases go there. The European Court of Human Rights has jurisdiction stretching from Ireland to Vladivostok, and that is a pretty effective jurisdiction. This is the major human rights court of the world and has tremendous persuasive authority beyond its jurisdictional limits.

Another organization less known is the Organization for Security and Co-operation in Europe. I serve on an advisory council for freedom of religion and most of the legislation on religion issues, particularly focused east of Vienna. In general, everything from Vancouver to Vladivostok comes before our panel to review.

At a practical level here, let me give you a quick picture of some of the things we've been doing. The International Center for Law and Religion Studies was established on 1 January 2000. We thought this would be a good millennial date. We didn't have any meetings. The budget kicked in on that day, and it's a memorable date. This institutionalized the activities of a number of us working on these issues. A permanent endowment has been authorized, and we are making good progress on that—although that's good in this past year, as you can imagine.

The mission of the center is to "help secure the blessings of freedom of religion and belief for all people by expanding, deepening, and disseminating knowledge and expertise regarding the interrelationship of law and religion; facilitating the growth of networks of scholars, experts, and policy makers involved in the field of religion and law; and contributing to law reform processes and broader implementation of principles of religious freedom worldwide." One of the things we have learned is that worldwide there is a very restricted set of people who work all the time on these issues. These are people who are in formal offices, people with "the stamp," as Elder Wickman said—the people that actually give approvals. There are academics who give reports that will train the people with the stamp, or give those reports and recommendations. When we think of countries, we often speak of about fifty leaders per country or ten thousand globally. I don't know what the actual number is, but this is a relatively finite number of people. And one of the things that we've been working on is developing a network and relationships and doing the kind of scholarly and academic research that can be of service to these people.

If you think about the gateways to nations, there are legal gateways—that is, religious association laws and visa regulations—and there are the gatekeepers—officials, religious leaders, human rights workers, and academics. And if we can reach those people, we can have a very significant effect on world religion policy.

Many of you are aware that we hold an annual conference here every fall. We typically bring in seventy to eighty officials from different countries. Some are academics, and some are government officials. This has an extraordinary effect. We've brought about seven hundred people, so we are getting close to a tenth of that ten thousand. These people rotate in office, so it will be an ongoing issue. If I hadn't seen the impact this has on people's lives, it would be hard to believe. What comes to my mind is the following story. My son was a missionary in Albania. One year, we had the head of religious affairs from Albania with us. It was the year the LDS Conference Center was opened, and we took him to general conference.

Afterward, this person said, "In my country, people line up for bread. I've never seen people line up for religion before." In a lot of ways, people are moved. I have a friend from Romania who was the head of religious affairs. In his country, we worked on a number of drafts with him. He came to our conference, and he has gone to some of the conferences in Europe. One time, he took me into his home, and I saw that he was a devout Orthodox believer. His wall was covered with Orthodox icons. He took one down and gave it to me. It was an iconic graphic representation of the Mount of Transfiguration. He said, "This is what working with the center has meant to me."

We do a lot of other conferences. Over the past three years, the center has helped sponsor and has participated in over seventy conferences in all parts of the world. It's too expensive to bring everyone here. We can do a lot of regional training; we've had a lot of experience in doing that in different parts of the world. One thing we are working on is trying to build a global religious freedom community. And with modern web tools—as we move from the 1.0 world, which was sort of static databases, to the more interactive world that we're seeing with the next generation, which is social networking and other kinds of software—we have a potential for getting in touch with, staying in touch with, and being of service to this sort of elite group who really shapes and molds religion policy in the world.

We think this will enhance the ability of law and religion specialists to improve local implementation of international religious freedom standards. It will gather and disseminate information that will enhance public awareness of religious freedom issues. And, as a practical matter, it will help us to stay in touch with people, building a global community where people can talk with each other in improved performance.

One of the realities of religious freedom is that there are some very dark forces working against us. However, we have allies that are honorable and just people on this earth. My experience is that many of them find their ways in these offices—not all. Some are hardcore, problematic characters working for the other side. But there are a lot of wonderful people that can be shown better ways of doing things.

Let me give a couple of other examples of things that we are doing to interact internationally. We just got back from Nepal, where we've been working on the new constitution that is being drafted there. It was a fairly incredible experience. We had about three hundred people come to a conference, some of whom had to walk a couple of days to get to an airport where they could then fly into Katmandu, where the conference was. One of the things we've done is set up a website that's using a common format. It's sort of a common front page that can have local identity, and ultimately this is going to be coordinated with people at a law school in Katmandu. But in the meantime, it's a place where we can make information available to those working on the constitution.

Another similar initiative is in the European Court of Human Rights where you can intervene in cases if you are an affected party or if you have some special expertise, but there is nothing like the amicus practice that is very common in the United States. If you have a big church-state case in this country, you'll get a stack of briefs—more than any Supreme Court judge wants to read, I'm sure. Some of these are more valuable than others, but a lot of them are valuable. When the Turkish headscarf case was argued in the European Court of Human Rights, the Turkish regime in power at that time was more sympathetic to religion. They wanted to lose the case, so they told their counsel to describe the facts and sit down. The woman involved was a medical student, and she didn't have money for expensive lawyers. The court got very little guidance and decided the case on the basis, I would say, of some French stereotypes. Coming out of that experience, a number of us, mostly Europeans (I happened to be involved because I am on a panel with some other people involved) came to the conclusion that we ought to find a way that we could make academic, higher-level commentary available in an expedited manner—much faster than you can usually get things in law reviews that might be helpful to resolve cases like this. One of the next grounds is going on right now. There is a bevy of cases in Germany involving religious employment. One of the cases is a Mormon case; there are a couple of Catholic cases, a Salvation Army case, and a couple of Protestant cases. These cases will affect religious employment from Ireland to Vladivostok, and this is profoundly important to us. We are in the process of doing similar things that we hope will have an impact. We've already had meetings with some of the people arguing the cases, and this is a significant initiative.

We are expanding our ability to take advantage of volunteers, and some of you here may be in a position to be helpful. We need interdisciplinary area studies experts. We know we have some legal expertise, but it needs to be matched with people who have in-depth knowledge of what is going on in countries and cultures. We have a tremendous need for help with computer technology that can lift us into the next generation so that we can really find the tools to be in steady contact with the religion experts of the world. But, of course, the computers alone can't do it. What we are, in effect, working on, as I see it, is helping to befriend country after country, and we need people to nurture those relationships.

Now let me speak of another level of initiatives. For me, this comes out of listening to general conference. I remember early in my career going to a talk that Elder Maxwell gave to a small group in Salt Lake City on the Prophet Joseph Smith's birthday. He talked about all the things the Prophet went through in his life, all the persecutions. Then Elder Maxwell talked about some of the hardships of the early Saints, like the Martin handcart company. And then he said, "All the easy things have been done. What lies ahead are times of high adventure. And the new high adventure will be more cerebral; it will be different. But it will be equally hard and challenging and intensive." Some of the work we've been doing is part of that high adventure. Many of you are doing it in other aspects of your lives. One of the other initiatives we heard over the past weekend is people calling us to move to another level. It's like the "lengthen your stride" speech from President Kimball's era.

Elder Andersen said, "We live in a day of destiny." He talked about new pioneers. Elder Christofferson talked about covenant power. President Uchtdorf talked about focus. Elder Bednar talked about the fire of the covenant. We will not do what needs to be done without drawing on higher power. One of the initiatives we've all heard that is going on is the call for us to do the things so that we can have access to the higher powers that are going to be needed. In a priesthood meeting, I was sitting by Bill Atkin, and he pointed out the following scripture: "Behold there are save two churches only; the one is the church of the Lamb of God, and the other is the church of the devil; wherefore, whoso belongeth not to the church of the Lamb of God belongeth to that great church, which is the mother of abominations."[2] I remember going to an institute class that was taught by Elder Marion D. Hanks in which he made it quite clear that there are a lot of Mormons who are going to be surprised at whose church they are in. It was pretty sobering. In 1 Nephi it states, "I beheld that the church of the Lamb, who were the saints of God, were also upon all the face of the earth; and their dominions . . . were small, because of the wickedness of the great whore."[3]

The religious liberty situation we as Latter-day Saints are in is described exactly in that verse. We are small; we are less than one thousandth of the population in most parts of the world. We are likely to remain small even if we grow at the staggering rates Rodney Stark has projected. We are going to need religious freedom, and we are going to need to work with others to preserve it.

The following verse is a little further on in the same chapter in 1 Nephi: "And it came to pass that I, Nephi, beheld the power of the Lamb of God, that it descended upon the saints of the church of the Lamb, and upon the covenant people of the Lord, who were scattered upon all the face of the earth; and they were armed with righteousness and with the power of God in great glory."[4] When we see that, we will be a part of it—if we live for it. I read recently the book that Kim Clark has done called *Armor*. It has meant a lot to me because I've known Kim since college days. The book is about putting on the whole armor of God. It's about people like Kim Clark six to seven years ago, before he left Harvard Business School for BYU–Idaho. He was relatively busy—a bishop, dean of Harvard Business School, leader of a funding campaign—and realized he needed greater spiritual depth in his life. He woke up one morning and read the following scripture: "Put on the whole armour of God, that ye may be able to stand against the wiles of the devil. For we wrestle not against flesh and blood, but against principalities, against powers, against the rulers of the darkness of this world, against spiritual wickedness in high places."[5]

There is darkness out there, but there are also people who we can work with. One of the things the International Society in particular knows about is the Ammon model. I remember early as a young law professor being impressed that some of our students—not all, but some—would go out to difficult places to live. I've known some of them; I know the people who opened Kazakhstan. I know some of the people of these other countries. I got to know many of you out in some of those places, so I know you know what I'm talking about. Those of us who have felt the high adventure of international work know what it means for the Church to have a special responsibility.

A few years ago, I climbed Mount Timpanogos in Utah. This may have been a mistake; I'm very glad I took my children with me. It turns out I have an acute fear of heights, so this was a very hard day. But I remember going by a waterfall and remarking to my kids, "You know, life is a lot like that. The Lord has waterfalls for us, and we can't absorb it."

The Doctrine and Covenants states, "God shall give unto you knowledge by his Holy Spirit, yea, by the unspeakable gift of the Holy Ghost, that has not been revealed since the world was until now. . . . As well might man stretch forth his puny arm to stop the Missouri river in its decreed course, or to turn it up stream, as to hinder the Almighty from pouring down knowledge from heaven upon the heads of the Latter-day Saints."[6]

One of my favorite scriptures is this passage at the end of the Words of Mormon: "And there were many holy men in the land, and they did speak the word of God with power and with authority. . . . Wherefore, with the help of these, king Benjamin . . . did once more establish peace in the land."[7]

This is another example that I like, found in 3 Nephi: "And there began to be men inspired from heaven and sent forth, standing among the people in all the land, preaching and testifying boldly."[8]

I don't know all the ways we are supposed to do things. I've learned something about the importance of religious freedom and the initiatives that we can take in very practical ways that will make a global difference. I believe that we will see many people in the kingdom find different ways to do that, and I am convinced—and it's been one of the reasons I've been such a supporter of the International Society—that the people who have international experience in the Church will play a deep role in making that go forward. And this is one of the powerful initiatives. I pray that we'll be recommitted to push ourselves to deepen our commitments so that we will have access to the powers that we are going to need to move forward with these great things.

NOTES

1. Bruce R. McConkie, *A New Witness for the Articles of Faith* (Salt Lake City: Deseret Book, 1985), 655.
2. 1 Nephi 14:10.
3. 1 Nephi 14:12.
4. 1 Nephi 14:14.
5. Ephesians 6:11–12.
6. Doctrine and Covenants 121:26, 33.
7. Words of Mormon 1:17–18.
8. 3 Nephi 6:20.

The spiritual path being pursued by young Americans is more like meditation; they are not looking to religion for ultimate truths.

15

EROSION OF RELIGIOUS FREEDOM

Impact on Churches

MICHAEL K. YOUNG

Michael K. Young, then president and chancellor of the University of Utah, presented this essay at "The Erosion of Religious Liberties—Impact on the International Church," the International Society's twenty-second annual conference, April 2011, Brigham Young University, Provo, Utah.

I read something in the paper not too long ago that was looking at trend data for what people are doing with respect to churches in the United States—what they believe and how they feel. The conclusion of the article essentially was that within a couple of generations, we will very likely have no churches in America. As you can imagine, that was a very startling realization, and there was some reason they were identifying that.

The first observation was not that young people were essentially unspiritual or uninterested in spiritual things or things that relate to the Spirit, but just the opposite—young people were interested in spiritual matters but not interested in organized religion. This fact is already reflected in a very significant decline in the participation of young people in organized religion. As the article described, they were spiritual but "unchurched."

The second observation made was that the spiritual path being pursued by young Americans is more like meditation; they are not looking to religion for ultimate truths but are seeking truths that are true to them. Their conclusions are as follows: Your truth is fine, my truth is fine, and his truth is fine. Everyone's truth may be different, but they are all equally acceptable. These conclusions have created a very significant movement away from organized religions—particularly religions that seem to have some foundational set of beliefs that are unalterable. Looking at these trends, we see the likelihood of Americans moving in directions that would ultimately undermine the stability, the presence, and the need for churches. That is really unsettling.

I think most of you are familiar with Elder Oaks and the wonderful talk he gave at BYU–Idaho. One of the things he said was that a writer for the *Christian Science Monitor* had predicted the coming century will be "very secular and religiously antagonistic," with "intolerance of Christianity [rising] to levels many of us have not believed possible in our lifetimes."[1] So those sets of concerns, coupled with an opportunity through a Church assignment I had, have turned my interest to the United States.

WHY FOCUS ON THE UNITED STATES?

I would like to talk about the United States today for a number of reasons. First of all, the United States is just as important as any other country in the world. I have talked for many years about the importance of religious liberties to people and how foundationally important it is as they ask these important questions in their life: Who am I? Where am I from? Why am I here? How should I behave? What should I teach my children? How should I treat my fellowman? Where do I go? Those are the kinds of really important questions that motivate literally billions of people around the world, but they motivate and engage Americans every bit as much.

Historically, when I was serving on the US Commission on International Religious Freedom, we were often asked, "Well, why are you not looking at the United States?" Part of the reason was that in an era of limited resources and time, you looked at the most horrific abuses, and we did not have those in the United States. In the United States, we were not arresting, torturing, and killing people for their religious beliefs. We were not discriminating, generally speaking, against them in terms of jobs and other sorts of things. And so there was no reason to look there.

As time has gone along, what is happening in the United States has begun to interest me for many reasons. This is the heart of our Church. This is where the headquarters of the Church is located. We need this view in America to see the Church develop and progress in the way it can serve not only the members here but, indeed, the members worldwide.

It is as important to Americans as it is anybody else. But I think, importantly, it is also a profound foundational right. A new book was recently published that does some statistical work suggesting a relationship between religious liberties and other liberties, not only civil rights but economic development, income disparities, rights for men and women, economic rights, and lack of conflict.[2] All of those things are highly correlated in statistically significant ways with the presence of freedom of religion in a country. It becomes important in that regard and with things like the gross domestic product, employment rights, and so forth.

From my perspective, one of the things I learned serving on the US commission is that at the end of the day, no country is likely to have more religious liberties than the United States does. We are a bellwether; we are a model. Our capacity to argue persuasively and intelligently on behalf of religious liberty around the world and to make this part of our foreign policy has a kind of credibility because of our own behavior. And to the extent liberty begins to erode here in the United States, it will inevitably have significant ripple effects around the world. Looking at what happens in the United States, in my judgment, becomes significant and important.

ARE WE AT RISK?

The question is, "Are we at risk in the United States?" As a country essentially founded on religious principles, founded by many people who were themselves escaping religious persecution, is religious liberty at risk here? This chapter will have a little bit of "lawyerly dimensions" to it, for which I apologize in advance to the non-lawyers. I am trying to repent from being a lawyer, but it still bubbles up from time to time.

We do have an event I think the lawyers in the audience worry about: *Smith v. Division of Employment* in the early 1990s. This is a significant case that fundamentally took away a lot of the special judicial protection we have understood historically for two hundred years to be afforded to religion. Essentially, the *Smith* case concluded that any law of general applicability that is neutral on its face can apply to religion as well as to everything else. Now, there were exceptions, but that case was one of those epical events.

What worries me more is the gradual erosion. Major events such as the *Smith* case certainly come along from time to time, and one needs to be attentive. And, indeed, I think people generally are attentive to those major erosions. What worries me more is a very profound sense I have that there is a sort of gradual erosion of religious freedoms in the United States. I think of the old story of the pot of water with the frogs in it, and if you drop a frog in a boiling pot of water, it jumps out. But if you put it in the pot and slowly bring it to a boil, it will simply stay there and be boiled to death. That is what I worry about: the water is gradually warming up and up and up.

Let me give you another example. I want to be very clear because I do not want this example to be misunderstood, and I will explain why in a minute. Have you had the chance to visit the Holocaust Memorial Museum in Washington, DC? The most unsettling part of the Holocaust Memorial Museum to me is the initial portion that describes chronologically the gradual introduction of the Nuremburg Laws. In the beginning, these laws were, on their face, quite benign—not so bad. I might have disagreed, but also I might have been willing to vote in favor of these first laws. And then, the second law was a little worse, but it was just a little amendment to this first law. And the third law, well, it went just a little bit further—and a little bit further and a little bit further, until they were putting people on trains and sending them to gas chambers. It was unsettling in a profound way to see the initial lack of concern among the lawyers about the gradual erosion of the rights of Jewish people and how such apathy ultimately resulted in "laws" ordering the extermination of more than six million people.

Maybe Hitler started out that way, but the lawyers did not start out that way. They started out in a very different way, saying, "Well, we have got a little bit of a social problem here, and we just need to tinker with it a little." That tinkering occurred again and again and again and again. Now, please do not misunderstand this example. I am not saying the people who are behind these incursions on religious liberties here in the United States are anything like or similar to the Nazis. Please do not misunderstand that example. The point is that laws can accrete in very subtle ways over time and create very serious problems you would never have anticipated, agreed with, participated in, or been willing to credit or understand at the beginning—this is a reality and not a historically unprecedented reality. It is very important for us to understand, and that unsettles me quite a bit.

During the time of the founding of our country almost two centuries ago, we really did have a fundamental confidence in and appreciation for religion. Look at what Alexis de Tocqueville wrote in the nineteenth century: "Religion in America takes no direct part in the government of society, but it must be regarded as the first of their political institutions. . . . I do not know whether all the Americans have a sincere faith in their religion, . . . but I am certain that they hold it to be indispensable to the maintenance of republican institutions. . . . The Americans combine the notions of Christianity and of liberty so intimately in their minds, that it is impossible to make them conceive the one without the other."[3]

So the understanding that religion should be free and is necessary to a republic is important foundationally for this country. Even if we were sometimes inconsistent in our application of that principle, there was a general adherence to it and very little erosion.

ARGUMENTS UNDERMINING RELIGIOUS LIBERTY

Today one senses the consensus that has guided us for so many years may be eroding in fundamental ways. The notion of whether religion is unique, good, important, or even necessary in a just society is up for question in our society. And the debate increasingly challenges what role, if any, religion should have in the public square. Let me give you a few examples of that increasing challenge. For me, the arguments tend to coalesce around three broad arguments. I do not think, for the most part—and I am going to say "for the most part" because there is a little footnote to this statement—these people are necessarily ill-intentioned. I do not think they are out there saying, "Let us see if we can suppress a religion today." Again, that is not what is going on.

Religion Is Not Special

Let me give you the first set of arguments asserting that religion is actually not special. These arguments do not deny the goodness of religion, but they claim religions do not hold a monopoly on virtuous conduct, and that is absolutely true. They go on to say that, therefore, all good and moral organizations should be recognized and treated equally. That is to say, religions have no special place. Religions are just one of a number of good organizations, like the Humane Society and Mothers Against Drunk Driving, which are both good organizations. The idea is that essentially they are all equivalent. There is a moral equivalency and an institutional equivalency between all these, and religions really deserve no more protection than those organizations deserve—no less but no more.

Now, what does that mean? It means if you are going to build a house of worship somewhere, why should that receive a special zoning exception or any other particular land-use requirement waiver or exemption any more than any other charitable relief house or any other kind of organization that does good in society? That is an increasingly profound and important argument that you hear again and again at the local level, at the state level, and even at the national level. This argument asserts that religious claims for special treatment should be evaluated on their merits, just as everybody else's claims should be. If we are not willing to give an exemption for union members, for teachers, for members of any charitable organization or any organization that is itself designed to accomplish some social good, why should we give an exemption to people of a religious organization or to the religious organization? Religion is like everything else. It is sort of a hobby, an interest group that people have, a particular faith, and an endeavor. But somebody else may want to make the highway safe for bicycles, and these two interest groups are really pretty much equivalent. So religious organizations are not entitled to any more protection than, say, the Sierra Club.

Now, the logical corollary of this argument is that religions have to compete with other political and economic values in every instance that they come in conflict with each other. So requirements that a church employee must adhere to standards of that church must compete with equal employment and nondiscrimination laws. Tax exemptions have to compete with arguments of tax equality and tax fairness. Land-use restrictions have to be pitted against the desire of a church to build a chapel. And that list goes on and on and on.

In each individual case, the social value might be seen to be very great and the incursion on the right to worship relatively small. And time after time, religion loses. And it may indeed be that in that particular case, the harm to religion may be minimal. But the gradual accumulation of these adverse decisions ultimately, profoundly, and unalterably destroys the right to freedom of religion just as if we had repealed the First Amendment in the first place. The accretion of harm, while barely perceptible at the moment, ultimately undermines freedom of religion in a way that would have been impossible had you simply posed the ultimate question of the importance of religion and that had been front and center in the decision in the first place.

From this perspective, religion is simply another example of a do-good organization that is fulfilling some social purpose, with people who are guiding themselves by whatever light they choose to guide themselves. Every time, the issue of freedom of religion gets pitted against that social value, and every time, the interest group in interest of that social value is likely to be more powerful than the religious group, so time after time, you will see accretion beginning to occur.

We see this somewhat in the *Smith* case. The *Smith* case basically said that any law of general applicability applied equally to religion as well. We see an interesting variation of that even more recently in the case called *Christian Legal Society v. Martinez*. That case involved a chapter of the Christian Legal Society on the campus of Hastings College of the Law in California. The law school had a nondiscrimination policy that included sexual preference as well as ethnicity, religion, etc. The organization received a certain number of small benefits from the school. This lawsuit was lodged because the Christian Legal Society did not permit people to assume leadership positions unless they were willing to adhere to the tenents of the Christian Legal Society, which was largely evangelical based and, therefore, it was not comfortable with the notion of gay rights. At least some range of those who were avowedly practicing homosexuals were not permitted to run for offices in this particular organization.

The Supreme Court held that if the institution received a public benefit—which it did in modest ways, but a public benefit nonetheless—the school may require adherence to its nondiscrimination policy. It did not answer the questions as to whether it *must* require adherence, although there is a footnote in the case that at least leaves that possibility open. Let me give you some immediate problems that the ruling raises. What do we do with the Latter-day Saint Student Association if schools require it to take a pledge of nondiscrimination, a pledge of nondiscrimination based not merely on the way it treats people but on what its members believe? It has not happened yet; it may not happen. But you can see we are not a far distance from something like that. If you look at this progression of cases—small cases and small movements—they are potentially significant. The court did not say the school must require adherence or that they must have such a policy. But that question was raised, and I think Justice Kennedy, who is the swing vote in these rulings, seems to be inclined to be in a position where he says in essence, "If it is for the public good at the end of the day, they may require and they must require in certain circumstances those nondiscrimination policies."

If such an exemption is not required by the First Amendment, then we are subject to the local whims of state legislatures and of local governments, all of which are passing laws, many that are being debated around the point of whether there is a religious exemption or an employment requirement. But I can give you the even more extreme example in which the court granted certiorari just a few weeks ago in a case that involves what is called the "ministerial exemption."[4] The ministerial exemption really permits people from a church to pick their clergy regardless of any requirements relating to state and federal laws. The ministerial exemption has been a bedrock in US jurisprudence for hundreds of years. All of the US circuit courts of appeal acknowledge that.

In this new case, the real question raised for review by the lower courts was the degree to which a particular job was either secular or sectarian. One lower court decided it was sufficiently sectarian that the local employment laws would apply. And another court concluded it was not sufficiently secular, so the local laws would apply. And yet another court concluded it was sufficiently sectarian, so the ministerial exemption prevailed. The court took certiorari in those cases. Normally, the court may simply decide that the two lower courts got the balance right. That would be an odd thing for the Supreme Court to decide. The court does not usually do that; it usually decides the fundamental question. And the ministerial exemption has never been decided by the Supreme Court before. So you can imagine at present what it would be like if you had to apply all the employment laws as you are picking bishops, stake presidents, and all the leaders we call out of the lay members in our Church. These cases are unsettling and potentially far-reaching if, in fact, they take what is now a relatively short step from that perspective.

Other examples of this trend include a photographer in New Mexico who was fined for his unwillingness to take pictures of a gay wedding. The Department of Health and Human Services is now revising its standards for the conscience exemptions for doctors who are uncomfortable performing abortions because they go against their religious beliefs. Licensing and accrediting agencies, especially in the field of psychology, are increasingly requiring all lifestyles be taught as equally acceptable and equally appropriate and equally personally sound. Now it may in the end be true, but at the end of the day they are requiring the teaching of these lifestyles not as a matter of scientific research but as a matter of accrediting, and if you are an accredited psychologist coming out of these programs, you may have to adhere to standards in terms of counseling of that sort. The head of the Equal Employment Opportunity Commission recently argued that sexual orientation liberty could become the type of right that should prevail over competing religious belief liberty. I think we are seeing—or beginning to see—these kinds of arguments prevail: Religion is a nice thing, and we are amused you believe it, and good for you if it causes you to do good charitable work. That is terrific, but it is no different than being a member of a union, being a member of PETA, no different than being a member of the Sierra Club. As a religious organization, you are going to get all the rights they are entitled to but no more.

Religion Is a Private Affair

The second argument I can see prevailing, which is gaining a great deal of currency in the popular mind, is that religion is a good thing, but it is essentially a private affair and should be entirely excluded from the public square. That is the argument advanced by many of the opponents of Proposition 8 in California.

As one scholar wrote, "Religious participation in the political process can produce dangerous results." He asserts that fervent beliefs fueled by suppressed fear are easily transformed into movements of intolerance, repression, hate, and persecution. There are, in short, in his view, substantial reasons for exercising caution with respect to religious involvement in the public square.[5]

Another opponent of Proposition 8 put it slightly differently but with the same intent. He said, in essence, that while he thought religious folks were good people, they should get out of politics and go back to their primary work of helping the victims of Katrina. Now this is interesting because it suggests not only that religions, religiously motivated dialogue, and religiously moved people do not deserve special treatment but that they should be disadvantaged in the public square. Normally, they should not have a favored place in our constitutional order, but they should not even be afforded the free-speech protections every other citizen in our nation is guaranteed.

The first time I heard this set of arguments, it was jaw-dropping. I thought nobody could seriously make those arguments, much less take those arguments seriously. In fact, for textualists, in the Constitution there is a theory hard to ignore—the First Amendment. And even Justice Scalia had an enormous difficulty seeing it. He managed to read the First Amendment out of the Constitution. I did not think the bulk of people could do that, but lo and behold, the judge did. In this case, which is now under appeal, the district court judge said, in essence, at the end of the day, they were not entitled to argue in favor of this. If this was the basis, then they would not be entitled to use that as a basis or justification for this law.

What are the implications of this? Well, if we are subject to all discrimination laws and are not permitted to argue against them based on some religious set of tenets, then we might be in a position where the state really is not allowed to give us those protections to which we historically had been entitled. This sounds a little farfetched. How could this possibly happen? Well, a judge has already done so. But let me extend this scenario just a bit further as we think about it. How then does the government force us to adhere to these discrimination laws if we are not permitted to talk about it in the public square? How do they do that? Well, one way they do is through the interstate-commerce laws, but more importantly, you have to remember that all religions not only survive but thrive based on the bestowal of a number of benefits: the right to register—that gives you the right to own or transmit land—and the right to publish and to distribute information. These are rights often in jeopardy in a foreign country. As Cole Durham will tell you so brilliantly, these rights are often where the rubber hits the road. It is not that they are rounding people up and arresting them, but they are not allowing them to register, they are not allowing them to publish materials, they are not allowing them to witness, and they are not allowing them to proselytize. In short, they are not allowing them to do those things that are so essential to so many religions. And in the process, not allowing them to do that fundamentally undermines their ability to function.

Think about our church. What if we have an incapacity to register, if we were not tax-exempt, so our activities were all taxed, not just our commercial activities but every activity we engaged in? Or what if your charitable donations to the Church were no longer tax exempt? In the latter case, I think you would still pay your tithes and offerings to the Church, but it would cost you a lot more to do so. If such were the case, the Church would be not only equivalent to the Sierra Club and other such organizations with respect to tax exemption, it would be significantly and demonstrably disadvantaged. And that is where this argument leads. It necessarily leads to the notion that you thought you were equivalent to the Sierra Club, but you are not. You are actually more dangerous than the Sierra Club, and your dialogue is sufficiently irrational that we are not going to let you even participate in public dialogue. You might think this does not make any sense. How can the government do that? Well, they have already done that. This is the *Reynolds* case, which we all know dealt with polygamy, but this is also the case of Bob Jones University. Bob Jones University is a religiously based institution that had a principle that forbade blacks and whites from dating. The Internal Revenue Service essentially said this principle so fundamentally violated public policy that the IRS withdrew Bob Jones University's tax-exempt status. And that happened in our lifetime.

Let me give you another example. There are two cases that have recently decided to challenge the constitutionality of the Defense of Marriage Act (DOMA), the federal law that protects traditional marriage. DOMA does not require states to recognize a marriage between two people of the same gender that is performed in another state. It also has some federal implications in that the federal government does not recognize same-gender marriages for pension purposes, tax-exempt purposes, and so forth.

A judge in Massachusetts has declared DOMA unconstitutional on two grounds. One argument used by the judge is the Tenth Amendment, which the judge interprets as saying that marriage itself is left entirely up to the states. That is a pretty silly argument, particularly given that DOMA deals with federal benefits. But setting that aside, the other argument is that DOMA violates equal protection. Now you can understand that argument if in fact you say members of the LGBT community are a particularly protected class, because then the level of scrutiny for protected classes goes way up; courts will give strict scrutiny to any laws that might discriminate against a group in a protected class. Nothing ever survives strict scrutiny.

Okay, so that is the way the judge could have decided. What was interesting is the judge did not do that. The judge ruled DOMA is unconstitutional because it violates the equal-protection clause. He reached that conclusion not on the basis that members of the LGBT community are a suspect classification but on the basis that there is no rational basis for DOMA—no rational basis at all. In essence, the judge concluded that Congress was essentially out of its mind when it passed DOMA and did so without any rational basis. Admittedly, Congress is often out of its mind, and that is fair enough. But on this particular seventeen-year-old law, the judge concluded Congress had no rational basis when it enacted DOMA. It is presumed Congress always has a rational basis—it may be a margin of rationality, to be sure, but it always has a rational basis. Nothing ever fails that test. But this judge concluded DOMA failed the rationality test.

Again, you might think the Massachusetts court's decision is pretty extraordinary, except about six months later, the Department of Justice and the Office of the Attorney General said the US government's executive branch will no longer defend DOMA. Historically, there are only two reasons why the executive branch cannot defend a law. One reason is that the law is an unconstitutional incursion on executive power, and the second reason is that there is no reasonable constitutional argument in its favor. Essentially, the Department of Justice is now agreeing with the judge that there is no rational basis, no reasonable argument for that particular law. These are small moves—but again, moves with potential significance.

Religion Is a Bad Influence

Let me give you the third argument that religion has a negative impact on society. There are a few examples in which one would see this trend manifest itself. Many believe that there is no place for the Ten Commandments in parks, buildings, or public places because a public manifestation of those beliefs must be kept in the closet and cannot be out in the public square. It would be unconstitutional for the government to proclaim a national day of prayer. It would be impermissible for people of faith to advocate religious doctrine or beliefs in their campaign for supporting any law, including Proposition 8.

This is an area in which there is growing sentiment against religion. The arguments in this category complain that religion has a negative impact in society. This argument moves from a neutral view of religion to an aggressive attitude against religion and religious believers that says to keep religious believers in the closet if we can—keep them quiet; keep them in their homes, where they can talk about religion all they want, but do not let them out in public, because they might scare others with their religious nonsense.

> The argument is that religious bodies are like corporate entities—usually motivated by money, power, and prestige. And as such, they are prone to just the same socially harmful behavior and misconduct and need similar regulation. The following is what one observer wrote on the subject: "Religious organizations really are no different than large corporations. The whole range of destructive behavior can be seen in both: fraud, extortion, misappropriation of funds, lying, deceit, covering up scandals like child abuse or doctoring financial records for the sake of the organization's image,

> and the list goes on. If religious actors are not deterred and punished for bad acts, they wreak great wrongs."[6]

According to this argument, religious organizations essentially endanger social justice, diversity, and harmony. They threaten secularism, pluralism, diversity, and social equality—so goes the argument. As another put it: "Religious participation in the political process can produce dangerous results: fervent beliefs fueled by suppressed fear are easily transformed into movements of intolerance, repression, hate, and persecution. There are, in short, substantial reasons for exercising caution with respect to religious involvement in the public square."[7]

We have not ourselves been immune from this kind of criticism. One observer states that religious entities often create an environment "that is propitious for those who would abuse children and disabled adults, or who would cover up such abuse to protect power, image, and wealth."[8] This argument has also been directed against the Church: "The [Latter-day Saint] system is constructed so that abuse stays internal, victims have no escape route, and perpetrators can have a field day."[9] And they go on to say religious beliefs are antiquated—out of touch with modern-day science.

As one famous atheist wrote, "Religion is about turning untested belief into unshakable truth through the power of institutions and the passage of time."[10] In that context, religion should be particularly disadvantaged because it is capable of causing particular harm.

You can see these three arguments gradually move little by little from the position that religions and religious believers are no longer protected to the point where their enemies actually get affirmative engagement on the part of the political system to control and repress religion. You can already see the manifestations of this in very practical ways.

Is there an alarm sounding? No evidence of that. In fact, to some extent the opposite is true. If you look at the polling data, the majority of Americans believe religion is important and essential and believe it in large numbers. But they are not particularly worried about the degree of religious freedom; they think it is just about rights.

To the extent they are worried, they are more worried about establishment clause issues. They are more worried that perhaps government is doing too much to promote or sustain religion, as manifested in issues such as public prayer at school, displays of the Ten Commandments, and similar things—all of which the public believes should be discouraged. The perception is not that there is some problem arising in this gradual way in the United States, but rather that everything is fine, or to the extent there is a problem it is to the other side—that government may be favoring religion.

WHAT TO DO?

Let me conclude with just a few thoughts. What do we do about this? I think others in this room are going to have much better insights and ideas, and I am very much looking forward to the panel that is going to follow because I think the brilliance they will bring to this will far exceed any ideas I have. But let me just make a few suggestions that occurred to me as I think about this.

First of all, I think we need to be attentive to the gradual erosion of religious freedom in the United States. This sounds very simple, but it is more complicated than it seems. I think a lot of the time we even sit back and rely on the Church and its institutional structures, such as the Church's Office of General Counsel and the terrific work that goes on out of Cole Durham's shop. We think they are going to spot this stuff, and we are okay. We just do not have to worry about it. The truth of the matter is that a tremendous amount of this is occurring at the local level, where we really do not have the kind of information, the work, or the capacity as an institution to do very much about it. And I think we need to be more attentive than that to watch local zoning decisions, to watch what city councils are doing with respect to employments laws, and all sorts of other protections and prohibitions that might be imposed. And I think this is something that is ultimately incumbent upon every member because there is no way institutionally that it can be observed and combatted.

However, that does lead to the second dimension: I think we need allies. I think this is an area in which we need not only to align with other faith-based organizations who share the same concerns with us but I think we need to reach out even more broadly. I am always struck by the extent to which freedom of religion is so profoundly connected to other civil liberties, and I think we need to link into those organizations that protect and are concerned about those and help weave into their thought process and their dialogue the notion of freedom of religion and how central and important that is. Conversely, we would need to carry our half of the burden, which is we need to be better champions of civil rights more broadly and human rights more broadly. Those kinds of alliances can be very important. We should be among the most passionate civil libertarians in the world. And as we do so, I think we get allies in this fight. These allies, if we could help them better understand that religion is not the threat, will be the saviors that the fight needs for a particularly profound set of reasons. And in turn we understand the other kinds of collateral civil liberties that need to surround it, and we will champion those. These are the important alliances that need to be made.

Third, we need to do this very much for the right reason—not just simply to save the world for Latter-day Saint missionaries, as laudable and important as that is, but we know how critical free will is and how essential it is to the gospel. Elder Bruce R. McConkie has described it as the most basic doctrine of the Church,[11] as Cole Durham described it a decade ago in his brilliant oration here at a BYU devotional.[12] Religious liberty is not necessarily the most important principle, but it is foundational. As Elder McConkie goes on to say, "If there were no freedom of worship, there would be no God, no redemption, and no salvation in the kingdom of God."[13] We have a profound moral obligation to protect this, not only on our behalf but on behalf of so many others around the world for whom it is such a passion. I was in Europe recently. When seeing the great art and visiting the great cathedrals and museums in Europe, you cannot do so without being struck at how profoundly important religion is to so many people around the world. Protecting their capacity to live that passion and to feel that passion seems to me an enormously noble and worthy goal. We need to think about its application in that context.

We need to not be defensive about this. What we are doing is actually not a rearguard action but is a wonderful, progressive, and important thing to do for the world. And the positive arguments in favor of this are positive for all—not only religious believers, but for those who do not believe. If you look at the correlation between this right and so many other goods it provides in society, it is incredibly profound. From that perspective, we ought to warmly engage and welcome our critics. The thing I love about our critics is they take us seriously. The thing that drives me nuts is when somebody says, "Oh, that is very nice. I am glad you believe that," or, "That is a cute thing you believe." I would rather someone really come at me, hammer and tongs: "How could you possibly believe that? That will destroy civilization as we know it." That person is taking me seriously. Those are the people we ought to embrace. Those are the people we ought to love and work together with. It is our critics who understand how important this is and are the ones who are most concerned and engaged. Those ought to be our best friends, because those are precisely the ones who are taking this every bit as seriously as we do.

Finally, I think we need to be vigilant and go back to where I started. This erosion to our religious freedom is happening frequently, consistently, and often at a level and pace that is just hard to discern where the tipping point is, but it is also happening so often at the local level. If we are engaged and committed and work to that end, I think our capacity to stem this tide, to raise the alarm, and to do what we need to do for our Church and for people everywhere is important.

I conclude as I suppose I always do about this: We need to trust in the Lord. If we care, if we try, if we do it for the right reasons, and if we are charitable and Christian in the way we do it and why we do it and what we do it and how we do it, then I believe we are on the Lord's errand. I believe he will use us in places where he needs us to be. I believe he is not going to let this Church and the center of religion fail on this earth, and we are on his errand. I appreciate the opportunity to talk a little bit about what I know with the International Society, but I do think we all have opportunities to look in both directions across the seas and a little closer to home as well.

NOTES

1. Michael Spencer, "The Coming Evangelical Collapse," *Christian Science Monitor*, 10 March 2009, http://www.csmonitor.com/ Commentary/Opinion/2009/0310/p09s01-coop.html.

2. Brian J. Grim and Roger Finke, *The Price of Freedom Denied: Religious Persecution and Conflict in the Twenty-First Century* (New York: Cambridge University Press, 2010).
3. Alexis de Tocqueville, *Democracy in America* (New York: Walter, 1847), 334–35.
4. EEOC v. Hosanna-Tabor Evangelical Lutheran Church and School, 597 F.3d 769 (2010).
5. William P. Marshall, "The Other Side of Religion," in *Law and Religion: A Critical Anthology* (New York: New York University Press, 1993), 44.
6. Marci A. Hamilton, "Church Autonomy Is Not a Better Path to 'Truth,'" *Journal of Law and Religion* 22, no. 1 (2006–07), 215–16.
7. Marshall, "The Other Side of Religion," 859.
8. Marci A. Hamilton, "The Rules Against Scandal and What They Mean for the First Amendment's Religion Clauses," *Maryland Law Review* 69, no. 1 (2009), 131, http://digitalcommons.law.umaryland.edu/mlr/vol69/iss1/11.
9. Marci A. Hamilton, "How Other Religious Organizations Echo the Roman Catholic Church's Rule Against Scandal—A Precept that Entrenches and Perpetuates Cycles of Child Sex Abuse: Church of Jesus Christ of Latter-Day Saints," FindLaw.com, http://writ.lp.findlaw.com/hamilton/20100415.html.
10. Richard Dawkins, "The Root of All Evil," *Channel 4 UK*, 2006, http://www.quotationspage.com/quote/38908.html.
11. Bruce R. McConkie, *A New Witness for the Articles of Faith* (Salt Lake City: Deseret Book, 1985), 655.
12. Cole Durham Jr., "The Doctrine of Religious Freedom," *BYU Speeches*, https://speeches.byu.edu/talks/w-cole-durham-jr_doctrine-religious-freedom/.
13. McConkie, *A New Witness for the Articles of Faith*, 655.

RELIGIOUS LIBERTY INITIATIVES

Preserving the "First Freedom" at Home and Abroad

HANNAH CLAYSON SMITH

Hannah Clayson Smith, senior counsel at the Becket Fund for Religious Liberty, presented this essay at "The Erosion of Religious Liberties—Impact on the International Church," the International Society's twenty-second annual conference, April 2011, Brigham Young University, Provo, Utah.

For those unfamiliar with the Becket Fund for Religious Liberty,[1] allow me to tell you a little bit about who we are. The remainder of this presentation will be "a view from the trenches" of our current cases that defend this vitally important freedom.

The Becket Fund is a public interest law firm based in Washington, DC, that protects the free expression of all religious faiths. We have a fifteen-year record of defending religious liberty for all people, including Buddhists, Christians, Hindus, Jews, Native Americans, Sikhs, Muslims, and Zoroastrians. The Becket Fund works in the courts of law, courts of public opinion, and the academy. We do work both domestically and internationally. The Becket Fund was founded by a devout Catholic, and the people who work there represent a spectrum of religions. It is a wonderful place to work with colleagues of many different faiths.

I want to quote to you from an address given by Elder Dallin H. Oaks exactly two months ago at Chapman University in California:

> It is imperative that those of us who believe in God and in the reality of right and wrong unite more effectively to protect our religious freedoms to preach and practice our faith in God and the principles of right and wrong He has established. . . .
>
> All that is necessary for unity and a broad coalition along the lines I am suggesting is a common belief that there is right and wrong in human behavior that has been established by a Supreme Being. All who believe in that fundamental should unite more effectively to preserve and to strengthen the freedom to advocate and practice our religious beliefs, whatever they are. We must walk together for a ways on the same path in order to secure our freedom to pursue our separate ways when that is necessary according to our own belief.[2]

I believe that the work that we do at the Becket Fund answers that eloquent call.

I was asked to speak today about the various initiatives we work on at the Becket Fund. I'll provide an overview of trends and issues and several pending cases we are engaged in to illustrate some of the current assaults on religious liberty in this country and abroad.

First, I want to give you some domestic trends. As we began 2011, we saw a lot of commentary about important developments for religious liberty over the past decade. Some of these, particularly here at home in the United States, include (1) a partnership and development of social programs between government and faith-based institutions begun under President George W. Bush and continued by President Obama, (2) the rise in anti-Muslim sentiment in America post-9/11, (3) the fight over marriage for same-sex partners, and (4) the rise of secularist organizations like Secular Coalition for America and the Freedom from Religion Foundation, which attempt to undermine the religious pillars of our culture and society.

As we look ahead, there are several trends to watch for in the coming year, including (1) battles over policies prohibiting discrimination on the basis of sexual orientation and the extent to which religious organizations are exempt from such policies and (2) the continued debate over conscience-clause issues in the healthcare arena, especially with the passage of the new healthcare law. How much room is there for people of faith to conscientiously object to some of the new mandates? I turn now to some of the current cases.

RELIGIOUS AUTONOMY

The first theme I want to address is religious autonomy for churches. One of the most exciting developments happened in March 2011, as the Supreme Court agreed to hear a case involving the ministerial exception.[3] On the side of the religious organization at issue, the Becket Fund is counsel in the case, with Professor Doug Laycock of the University of Virginia as lead counsel. The ministerial exception is a doctrine that is derived from the First Amendment that prohibits courts from reviewing firing and hiring decisions from religious institutions involving their ministerial employees. The question is, who counts as a ministerial employee?

In that case, a Lutheran church in Michigan operates a religious school. The school's purpose is to provide a Christ-centered education based on biblical principles. The church dismissed a teacher (who had the title of a commissioned minister within the Lutheran Church) for insubordination and disruptive conduct in violation of the church's teachings. The teacher sued and asked the court to reinstate her. The Michigan federal district court ruled in the church's favor.[4] It held that the teacher's claim could not proceed because she was a licensed minister and led students in prayer, worship, and religious studies, which the court found was enough for her to fall under the ministerial exception. Not so, said the US Court of Appeals for the Sixth Circuit when it reversed and held that the teacher could pursue the claim.[5] Because she spent more minutes of the day on secular subjects than on religious ones, the ministerial exception did not apply. The test they used was focused on time: How many minutes of the day did the teacher spend teaching math or teaching reading?

We filed a petition for certiorari, asking the US Supreme Court to review the case with the scope of the ministerial exception at issue. This will be a landmark case. It is the first time the Supreme Court has heard arguments in a ministerial exception case. It will likely be of great significance to any religious organization that hires and fires people based on religious preferences. On a similar note, in September 2010, The Church of Jesus Christ of Latter-day Saints had a case before the European Court of Human Rights involving a public affairs director for the Church in Europe. That employee committed adultery, lost his temple recommend, and was fired. In the ensuing legal battle, the court held for the Church.[6] While this case was obviously decided in a different legal system than ours, we are optimistic the Supreme Court will recognize this fundamental right derived from the First Amendment of churches to decide who to hire and who to fire.

Another issue under the theme of religious autonomy relates to religious hiring preferences by faith-based organizations competing for federal grant awards. I mentioned before the relationship between the federal government and faith-based organizations in social welfare programs. The Justice Department is now "debating whether to reinterpret federal law so as to allow discrimination, when awarding federal grants, against faith-based organizations who engage in . . . religious hiring preferences."[7] During the Bush administration, the Department of Justice's Office of Legal Counsel (OLC) analyzed this issue. It determined the protection of religious exercise in the federal Religious Freedom Restoration Act (RFRA) is "reasonably construed to apply to religious organizations that accept federal grants,"[8] and "because requiring a religious organization to abandon its religious practice in order to receive a federal grant is a substantial burden on religious exercise, the government may not force a religious organization to abide by the non-discrimination rules as a condition of receiving a grant."[9] After President Obama was elected, various groups urged his administration to rescind this opinion and narrow the scope of RFRA's protection. This is an ongoing matter and one that would have a great impact on religious organizations who engage in preferential hiring, who want to engage in social welfare programs, and who want to receive federal grants to help them do so.

CONSCIENTIOUS OBJECTION

The second category of cases I'd like to discuss is conscientious objection. Our country has a long history of conscientious objection, including the refusal of eighteenth-century Quakers to bear arms[10] and the conscientious objection of twentieth-century Jehovah's Witnesses to pledge allegiance to the American flag.[11] We have long recognized that the government should not force people to choose between their livelihood and their religion.

We're working on several cases in this category: (1) an Amish group in the Northeast threatened by state prosecution for violating fire codes by not installing battery-operated smoke detectors because of their religious belief against using batteries and (2) in the Sixth Circuit, an MA student who was kicked out of her counseling program right before graduation because she objected on religious grounds to counseling homosexual couples in a way that approved of their conduct.

Perhaps the greatest potential area for concern in this category is in health care, particularly as our country deals with the new healthcare legislation. We represent a family-owned pharmacy called Ralph's Thriftway and two pharmacists who refuse to dispense Plan B contraceptives, also known as the "abortion pill" because it can destroy a fertilized egg, and they believe life begins at the moment of fertilization.[12] The outcome of this case could force these two pharmacists out of their professions solely because of their religious beliefs.

Let me give you some background. In 2006, the Washington State Board of Pharmacy unanimously supported a rule protecting conscience for pharmacy workers. The board voted to allow pharmacists with religious objections to refrain from dispensing Plan B and instead to refer people to other nearby dispensers—a very reasonable position. The board recognized the sincerely held religious beliefs of the pharmacists and essentially said to the pharmacists, "If you don't want to dispense this, then as long as you give customers adequate notice where they can find this contraception at another nearby pharmacy, it's okay." Things soon turned ugly, however, and the board reversed course. The board admitted it found no evidence that anyone in the state had been unable to obtain medication due to the religious objection of a pharmacist. Notwithstanding that lack of evidence, the board issued a regulation requiring the pharmacists to stock and dispense medication even when doing so violated their conscience. The two pharmacists sued to prevent the new regulation from forcing them out of their profession. They argued that forcing pharmacists to dispense Plan B contrary to their religiously held belief violated their constitutional right to the free exercise of their religion. The case is now poised for trial November 2011 and will set an important precedent.

Of course, this case has broader implications beyond pharmacists. It could potentially extend to all healthcare workers who object to performing abortions, who object to performing in vitro fertilization for same-sex couples, who object to providing sterilization, and who object to providing similarly morally troubling procedures. This is a very significant issue.

The second case under this category of conscientious objection deals with a religious university's right to refuse to provide contraceptive and abortion coverage in its employee insurance plan to remain true to that university's religious teachings.[13] Some background in this case: Belmont Abbey College is a small Roman Catholic liberal arts college in North Carolina. In December 2007, it removed coverage for abortion, contraception, and voluntary sterilization from its insurance plan after learning that coverage had been included accidentally in its plan. Several faculty members filed complaints of gender discrimination with the EEOC. In March 2009, the EEOC initially concluded there was no evidence of such discrimination. Just weeks later, the EEOC (presumably at the direction of the incoming Obama administration) rescinded that decision. Several months later, the EEOC issued a contrary decision. It reasoned that "by denying prescription contraceptive drugs, [Belmont Abbey College] is discriminating based on gender because only females take oral contraceptives. By denying coverage, men are not affected, only women."[14] The Becket Fund stepped up to defend Belmont Abbey's cause, joining its legal team and exposing the EEOC's actions in the press. We announced that because the EEOC's position is a direct assault on the principle of conscientious objection, we will resist it vigorously. The ball is now in the EEOC's court as it decides whether it will sue the college or not.

DEFAMATION OF RELIGION

Generally speaking, the "defamation of religion" agenda is an attempt, mostly by Islamic countries, to enshrine blasphemy laws in international human rights organizations. Such laws are commonly found in Pakistan, Saudi Arabia, and Iran to shield these Islamic states in their often violent attempts to silence religious minorities in their countries. In March of 2011 in the *National Review*, Nina Shea wrote about the anti-blasphemy measures in the UN.[15] I will attempt to summarize the efforts in the UN and how these anti-blasphemy laws play out in Islamic countries around the world.

Initiatives to oppose the so-called "defamation of religion" in UN human rights bodies followed the 1989 fatwa by Ayatollah Khomeini calling on Muslims to kill Salman Rushdie for his book *The Satanic Verses*.[16] The Organization of the Islamic Conference (OIC) is an organization of about fifty-six Muslim member states that seeks to impose on the UN the principle that "Western law should be subject to Muslim initiatives against apostasy and blasphemy."[17] It introduced annual UN resolutions on the issue. In 2005 and 2006, the resolution sponsors were emboldened by the incident involving the cartoons of Mohammed in Danish publications. Pakistan crafted the resolution carefully to appeal to Western liberal and multicultural sensibilities: "Unrestricted and disrespectful freedom of opinion creates hatred and is contrary to the spirit of peaceful dialogue and promotion of multiculturalism."[18]

Western states began to resist these resolutions in 2001, and by 2007 support within the UN Human Rights Council had greatly eroded. By 2010, the council passed the resolution by only a narrow margin, and this year the OIC didn't even introduce the resolution. The shift in the West is largely thanks to the Bush administration's lead in defending free speech. That lead has been joined by a large coalition including the EU, the US Commission on International Religious Freedom, members of the US Congress, and NGOs like the Becket Fund that lobbied vigorously against the defamation of religion resolution.[19] In 2011, instead of the usual defamation resolution, the UN Human Rights Council adopted one denouncing religious discrimination and violence but did not call for restrictions on free speech.[20] The change largely occurred at the urging of the Obama administration, which advocated "more speech" as the antidote for offensive expression.[21]

Notwithstanding the victory at the UN level, we continue to see blasphemy laws in individual Muslim countries applied to persecute members of minority religious faiths or those who defend them. Let me give you a couple of examples. In Indonesia, the world's most populous Muslim country, the government uses its forty-five-year-old blasphemy law—which was recently upheld against constitutional attack despite the strenuous efforts of Cole Durham and various NGOs around the world—to outlaw outright the religious groups that are not among the six officially sanctioned faiths in that country: Islam, Buddhism, Hinduism, Catholicism, Protestantism, and Confucianism.[22] That law had also been used to justify violent attacks against minority religious groups. In Pakistan in March 2011, the national minister of minorities, Shahbaz Bhatti, was murdered because he opposed his country's blasphemy laws.[23] This followed the assassination for the same reason of another high government official—Salman Taseer, governor of Punjab—and of a Christian mother of five whom Taseer had defended against charges of blasphemy and who was sentenced to death.[24] Similarly, a Pakistani youth has been arrested on blasphemy charges for statements he made in a school exam paper.[25] Police have refused to disclose what he wrote, arguing that repeating his statement would itself be blasphemy.[26] Islamic blasphemy laws and other defamation-of-religion initiatives remain a major human rights issue around the world.

RELIGION IN THE PUBLIC SQUARE

The fourth theme I want to cover is religion in the public square, specifically the Pledge of Allegiance cases. The Becket Fund defended the constitutionality of the words "under God" in the Pledge of Allegiance case in the US Court of Appeals for the Ninth Circuit. Michael Newdow is an atheist activist who campaigned to have the two words removed. We represented the school children and their parents, arguing that the phrase "under God" in the Pledge of Allegiance affirms a foundational premise in the American tradition of law and rights—namely, that human rights are not bestowed by the state but are rather derived from a source beyond the state's discretion. "Under God" does not unconstitutionally advance religion but rather reflects the deeply rooted political philosophy of the Founding Fathers, who believed these rights derived from a source greater than a government made of men.

The pledge was also defended by the Justice Department's lawyers but on different grounds. They defended the pledge on the usual grounds of ceremonial deism, a concept that has been developed in the Supreme Court case law on the subject. Ceremonial deism holds that the words "under God" have been repeated so frequently in a ceremonial way that they have lost all religious meaning.

After considering the case for almost two-and-a-half years, the Ninth Circuit reversed itself and kept the words "under God" in the Pledge of Allegiance.[27] In its reasoning, the Ninth Circuit showed it was persuaded by our political philosophy argument rather than the ceremonial deism argument.[28] We fully anticipated Newdow would take the case to the Supreme Court, but he did not meet the deadline for filing his petition, so the case is closed. We are happy to say that the pledge is now safely intact in the states within the Ninth Circuit. Though that was a major victory, Newdow has vowed to continue his fight to rid our country of the words "under God" in the Pledge of Allegiance. He has said he will find whatever judge will hear his case and will continue to travel around the country in his quest. The Becket Fund will be there to fight back.

RELIGIOUS DISCRIMINATION

Finally, the fifth theme is discrimination against religious groups. The primary example I want to address here is state Blaine Amendments. Between 1870 and 1900, forty-one states adopted Blaine Amendments to prevent public funds from going to any "sectarian institution."[29] At the time, "sectarian" was code for Catholic. The Blaine Amendments were largely a result of anti-Catholic nativism that was sweeping the country at the time. But Blaine Amendments are now used by states to forbid programs that otherwise comply with the federal Establishment Clause. More specifically, the federal Establishment Clause as interpreted in the last half-century permits religion-neutral support of programs with a predominantly secular purpose, provided they do not improperly advance religion. The Blaine Amendments, which are state constitutional amendments, often operate as a second wave of attack because they can forbid what the federal Establishment Clause permits. So in actual terms, the Blaine Amendments operate to impose a per se bar against funding to all religious organizations. We see the results in a wide variety of cases involving religious organizations, in funding to faith-based organizations, in contracts between a government and religious organizations, and in cases regarding religious schools' choices. There is an effort at the Becket Fund to challenge these state Blaine Amendments through the courts and through legislative repeal.

CONCLUSION

I hope from this overview today that you have seen that the attacks on religious liberty are serious and widespread. More importantly, we have many friends in this battle to uphold religious liberty in this country and abroad. I will close with a quote from Cardinal Francis George, then-president of the US Conference of Catholic Bishops, when he spoke at BYU last year. He delivered a message very similar to Elder Oaks's that I quoted at the beginning of my talk:

> In the coming years inter-religious coalitions formed to defend the rights of conscience for individuals and for religious institutions should become a vital bulwark against the tide of forces at work in our government and in our society to reduce religion to a purely private reality. At stake is whether or not the religious voice will maintain its right to be heard in the public square.[30]

NOTES

1. See the Becket Fund for Religious Liberty, 2010–16, http://www.becketfund.org.
2. Dallin H. Oaks, "Preserving Religious Freedom" (lecture, Chapman University School of Law, 4 February 2011), http://www.mormonnewsroom.org/article/elder-oaks-religious-freedom-Chapman-University.
3. See Hosanna-Tabor Evangelical Lutheran Church and School v. EEOC, et al. (Docket no. 10–553, granted 28 March 2011).

4. See EEOC v. Hosanna-Tabor Evangelical Lutheran Church and School, 582 F. Supp. 2d 881 (E. D. Mich. 2008).
5. See EEOC v. Hosanna-Tabor Evangelical Lutheran Church and School, 597 F.3d 769 (6th Cir. 2010).
6. See Obst v. Germany, European Court of Human Rights, no. 425/03, 23 September 2010.
7. Derek L. Gaubatz, "Will the Obama Administration Reinterpret Federal Law Re: Religious Discrimination When Awarding Federal Grants?," 11 February 2011, http://www.fed-soc.org/publications/detail/will-the.obama-administration-re-interpret-federal-law-re-religious.discrimination-when-awarding-federal-grants.
8. Gaubatz, "Will the Obama Administration Reinterpret Federal Law Re: Religious Discrimination When Awarding Federal Grants?"
9. Gaubatz, "Will the Obama Administration Reinterpret Federal Law Re: Religious Discrimination When Awarding Federal Grants?"
10. See Kevin Seamus Hasson, *The Right to Be Wrong* (San Francisco: Encounter Books, 2005), 45–67.
11. See West Virginia State Board of Education v. Barnette, 319 US 624 (1943).
12. See Stormans, Inc. v. Selecky, 524 F. Supp. 2d 1245 (W. D. Wash. 2007) and Stormans, Inc. v. Selecky, 586 F.3d 1109 (9th Cir. 2009).
13. See Belmont Abbey College, North Carolina, 2009, The Becket Fund for Religious Liberty, http://www.becketfund.org/belmont-abbey-college-north-carolina-2009.
14. See Belmont Abbey College, North Carolina, 2009, The Becket Fund for Religious Liberty, http://www. becketfund.org/belmont-abbey-college-north-carolina-2009.
15. See Nina Shea, "An Anti-Blasphemy Measure Laid to Rest," *National Review Online*, 31 March 2011, available at http://www.nationalreview.com/articles/print/263450.
16. Shea, "An Anti-Blasphemy Measure Laid to Rest."
17. Shea, "An Anti-Blasphemy Measure Laid to Rest."
18. Shea, "An Anti-Blasphemy Measure Laid to Rest."
19. Shea, "An Anti-Blasphemy Measure Laid to Rest."
20. Shea, "An Anti-Blasphemy Measure Laid to Rest."
21. Shea, "An Anti-Blasphemy Measure Laid to Rest."

22. See Peter Gelling, "Law Banning Blasphemy is Upheld in Indonesia," *New York Times*, 19 April 2010, http://www.nytimes.com/2010/04/20/world/asia/20indo.html.
23. See Shea, "An Anti-Blasphemy Measure Laid to Rest."
24. Shea, "An Anti-Blasphemy Measure Laid to Rest."
25. See Howard M. Friedman, "Pakistani Student Charged with Blasphemy for Remarks on Exam Paper," http://religionclause.blogspot.com/2011/02/pakistani-student-charged-with.html.
26. See Friedman, "Pakistani Student Charged with Blasphemy for Remarks on Exam Paper."
27. See Newdow v. Rio Linda Union School Dist., 597 F.3d 1007 (9th Cir. 2010).
28. See Ken Blackwell, "Living Under God," *American Spectator*, 18 March 2010, http://spectator.org/archives/2010/03/18/living-under-god.
29. See Meir Katz, "The State of Blaine: A Closer Look at the Blaine Amendments and Their Modern Application" (original in possession of author).
30. Cardinal Francis George, "Catholics and Latter-day Saints: Partners in the Defense of Religious Freedom," 23 February 2010, http://www.usccb.org/seia/catholics-latter-day.saints.pdf.

Part 5

GROWTH AND GLOBALIZATION

Early missionaries preached the doctrine of the gathering, but by the early twentieth century, members in foreign countries were encouraged to "stay home" and "build Zion" in their own country. (Courtesy of Intellectual Reserve, Inc.)

17

MIGRATION— IT'S IN OUR BLOOD

Implications for The Church of Jesus Christ of Latter-day Saints

TED E. LYON

Ted E. Lyon, then professor of Spanish at Brigham Young University, presented this essay at "'The Perplexities of Nations': Current Trends and the International Church," the International Society's eighteenth annual conference, April 2007, Brigham Young University, Provo, Utah.

The genesis of this paper stems from simple observation—The Church of Jesus Christ of Latter-day Saints is sending Spanish-speaking missionaries to every state in the United States, including unlikely spots such as Alaska, North Dakota, and Tennessee. Many of the missions in Canada receive young missionaries who will teach and baptize in Spanish. Members of the largest Church units in Stockholm, Sweden, speak little Swedish; Spanish is the language of the ward, and most are displaced Chileans and other Latin American émigrés.[1] But Hispanics are not the only immigrants hearing the gospel and joining the Church outside their native countries. Many Africans hear the gospel in Germany or Portugal; Chinese travel to Singapore to find work and often find the missionaries as well. Lebanese and Iraqi refugees seek asylum in Denmark and not only discover peace but also the gospel. Spain and Italy, often unwillingly, host North Africans, who hear and respond to the message of the Restoration in those foreign countries. In developed areas of the world, a large percentage of Latter-day Saint baptisms occur among immigrants to those countries. The percentage is higher, usually much higher, than the total number of immigrants in that country. Immigrants are joining and contributing to the Church.

Based on this initial observation, I began asking questions and seeking to know just how many of our Latter-day Saint converts were immigrants to the country in which they were baptized. I consulted with the Church offices and was informed, kindly, that data relating to national origin of converts is "proprietary and confidential."[2] I turned to Rodney Stark, a well- known sociologist of religion who has written a considerable amount on Latter-day Saints. I posed many detailed questions and explained my need for data on just who is being baptized into the Church. He wrote back immediately, stating, "Those are very interesting questions and I don't know the answers [at all] nor where to find data. If you discover anything useful, I would very much like to know about it. Sorry."[3] In short, he understood my research questions but had no data to share. For the above-noted reasons, my sources are limited to general fact books (the *CIA World Factbook* and other similar summaries), UN studies and documents on world migration, and scholarly studies dealing with immigration and religious conversion in general. I have also conducted interviews with Latter-day Saint mission presidents, missionaries, and recent converts in an attempt to establish a baseline percentage of how many converts are immigrants to the country in which they are baptized. These latter sources are both experiential and anecdotal.

MIGRATION: A WORLDWIDE PHENOMENON

In the year 2007, the estimated world population stood at 6.5 billion people. A small percentage of this large number, approximately 3 percent, live outside their country of origin.[4] Yet, 3 percent means 191 million people, more than the total population of France, Germany, Spain, Austria, Belgium, Holland, and a few other smaller European countries. These are people on the move, displaced by desire, by hope for a better economic future, by political strife; in short, these are people who were not content with their status or the situation into which they were thrust or born. It is obvious that these displaced, upward-seeking human beings are often susceptible to a new message, a message of hope, of future, of a new beginning. Conversion to the Church is dramatically and disproportionately high among these modern-day immigrants.

A related factor to the concept of religious conversion among the newly arrived is internal migration, typically urbanization within one's own country. This process of urbanization is occurring on every continent in the world. Philip Jenkins convincingly demonstrated the effect that urbanization has exerted on conversion to Christianity. "In its early days, African Christianity [for example] was conspicuously a youth movement, a token of vigor and fresh thinking," composed mainly of ambitious young adults who would travel to large cities and ports seeking work, where they also found Christian missionaries.[5] Conversion to a Christian religion was filled with energy, as the rural workers often returned to their native villages carrying on the evangelization with friends and relatives.

While this paper cannot explore the effects of internal migration on Latter-day Saint conversion rates, nearly every missionary knows that as people displace themselves from the stability of a rural area, they often open up to new ideas. In *Followers of the New Faith*, Emilio Willems demonstrates the power of urbanization and conversion in Brazil and Chile.[6] The newly arrived have usually broken ties with old friends, tradition, family pressures, and their native-born religion and are seeking for something better. New friends in the new city mean new contacts and possibilities for employment. Foreign missionaries and established members often provide a model for what a newly arrived city-dweller hopes to achieve. The hundreds of excellent Church employment resource centers around the world could wisely target and recruit this group, encouraging them to participate in the very successful ten-hour-workshop training program. Unfortunately, I will not be able to pursue urbanization as a source for Latter-day Saint baptisms, but it is truly a fertile field and one that should be studied in depth.

Political and economic refugees are yet another source of displacement in the contemporary scene. In 2005, worldwide political refugees numbered approximately 9.2 million. These dislocated people, often victims of violence and frequently living in extreme poverty, may also be open to the preaching of the Restoration. However, their most urgent needs will likely be met first by the Church's humanitarian services and other similar organizations. This paper cannot consider political refugees as a unique group—they, too, are migrants and exhibit even more spiritual and physical needs than do most other immigrants. They certainly make up a vital percentage of Latter-day Saint baptisms and contribute their unique experiences to their new church.

Neither can this paper discuss the problem of illegal immigration. A recent estimate calculates that each year in the world some four million people cross borders illegally to reside in another country.[7] The four million figure appears very low to me, based on the fact that most country borders are very porous, controls are generally inadequate, and counting illegal crossings is almost impossible. Reliable observers estimate that in the US alone there are now eleven to twelve million illegal immigrants. Of course this number represents a build-up from many years, but nevertheless, several million people a year cross into (and sometimes out of) the US. Latter-day Saint missionaries are instructed not to be concerned about the legality of their teaching contacts nor to pose such problematic questions during their lessons. In short, the problem exists for the host country but not for the missionaries nor for those who wish to join the Church.

In sum, worldwide migration is occurring at an increasing, not decreasing, rate. Migration should not be feared; it has been the lifeblood of many societies and nations. In 1776, the rebellious American colonies boasted three million people; today more than 300 million citizens call the US home, and legal immigration to the US continues to be the major source of growth, more than a rapidly expanding birthrate. For example, during the 1990s the nation's population grew by nearly 33 million, the largest ten-year increase ever; the great majority of this increase was foreign born.[8]

Obviously, migration creates problems in the host country—often a change in the status quo of that nation—but it also deepens and broadens that host culture. A simplistic but obvious example is that there are now more pizza outlets and more taco sites than hamburger "joints" in the US. Music, the visual arts, entertainment, and so forth in the United States are all richer because of the millions of twentieth-century immigrants who have made this country a center of invention and innovation.

Most of the immigrants throughout the world make their way to a new country to find work and to create a better economic life for themselves and their families. Thirty market democracies in the world form the Organization for Economic Cooperation and Development (OECD). One-fourth of the workforce in Austria, Switzerland, and Luxembourg are foreign-born; nearly 12 percent in the US are foreign born, and certainly the number is much higher when illegal workers are factored in. South Korea, Ireland, Austria, and Finland experienced more than a 100-percent increase of foreign-born workers in ten years. Every one of these thirty countries has witnessed increases. These thirty countries also demonstrate a high percentage of foreign-born Latter-day Saint converts.

MIGRATION TRADITIONS AND THE CHURCH OF JESUS CHRIST OF LATTER-DAY SAINTS

Quite obviously, the first converts to the Restoration were family, friends, and neighbors of Joseph Smith. But as that pool exhausted itself and local opposition deepened, Joseph sent the Quorum of the Twelve and a few others first to Canada and then to Great Britain. Even in Joseph's short lifetime, missionaries journeyed through Europe, to the Holy Land, to the Caribbean, and to the Pacific Islands. All of these early missionaries preached the doctrine of the gathering—emigrate or be damned. For sixty years, this doctrine infused life and new blood into Nauvoo, and later, into nearly three hundred developing communities in the Mountain West. By the early twentieth century, the doctrine changed, and members in foreign countries were encouraged to "stay home" and "build Zion" in their country of origin. Yet this preachment has not stopped the migration; each year, thousands of Latter-day Saint immigrants flow out of Africa, abandon Tonga and Samoa, and leave Argentina and Chile for good; they depart their homeland in Russia or the Ukraine and quit scores of other countries. Most of the Latter-day Saint immigrants come to the US if possible, and some go to Europe. They seek a better life, partially because they see new possibilities, new opportunities, and a chance to advance and make a better future for their children.

The migrating Latter-day Saints have scriptural precedent. The Book of Mormon is truly a story of migration. Lehi and his family were "called out" of the Old World to avoid impending violence and commanded to journey to a land of promise. Four hundred years later, Mosiah abandoned the comfortable old city of Nephi and made his way down to Zarahemla, where he found the descendants of another band of immigrants—the Mulekites. Alma had to escape the political oppression of his Lamanite tax masters and sought refuge in Zarahemla. In the next generation, the converted and immigrant people of Ammon so burdened the hospitality of the seven churches in Zarahemla that they were granted a nearby land of their own—Jershon. Zarahemla, which had been the haven to so many immigrant groups, soon became wicked, and the Church's leaders moved on to Bountiful, bringing the faithful with them. After too brief a period of peace and prosperity, war again broke out, and Mormon and Moroni escaped northward, becoming refugees from the tragic violence that ends the book. Truly, there is spiritual precedent for migration to avoid violence and unite with larger spiritual units.

In the developed and generally peaceful OECD countries, Latter-day Saint missionaries are finding, teaching, and baptizing a large number of immigrants, a much higher number than their proportion in the new country, and generally a higher percentage than that of native-born citizens of that same country. One single cosmopolitan mission may have missionaries who teach in eight or ten languages. The New York New York South Mission boasts some fourteen foreign languages among its missionaries. In 1990, the population of New York City was 28 percent foreign born. By 2000, that proportion had increased to 40 percent, and it continued to climb to approximately 45 percent in 2007. At the present time, 52 percent of the foreign-born in the US come from Latin America.[9] And Latter-day Saint missionaries are finding these fields; they are finding them "white already to harvest."[10]

The assistants to the mission president in Miami, Florida, reported to me that between 60 and 65 percent of their monthly baptisms come from the Hispanic population (not all of whom are foreign born, of course). My own son recently reported that in his mission in Anaheim, California, approximately half of the converts were Spanish-speaking and another

10–15 percent were from other foreign-language groups. Missionaries in the Utah Provo Mission inform me that 30–40 percent of their converts are natives of other countries; this includes many Asian students at BYU. Quite logically, 50 percent of the converts in the New York New York South Mission, with its multiple languages, are from abroad.

Similar statistics apply in many other developed countries in which the gospel is preached. Missionaries in one particular mission in Germany (Hamburg) baptized 118 new members in 2006. Of these 118 baptisms, 72 were native Germans, but the other 46 (39 percent) were foreign born. It is instructive to note that several of these baptisms come from China, Afghanistan, and Iran, countries in which there are currently no Latter-day Saint missionaries, nor an official Church presence. Others came from Ghana, Nigeria, Peru, the Philippines, Poland, and Romania. These types of international baptisms give the Church a worldwide flavor in most of the OECD countries.

Some might question Mexico's placement among the OECDs (there are only three Western Hemisphere countries on the list), yet it too receives thousands of immigrant workers and refugees from Cuba and from Central and South American countries. Newspaper articles and editorials in Mexico often lament the uncontrolled influx of poor foreigners and call for tighter border controls and higher fences. The Latter-day Saint missionaries in Mexico often meet these immigrants, teach them, and baptize them.

Foreign-born university students in OECD countries are discovering the Church and Christianity in general. A recent study has shown that during their first year in the US as foreign students or visiting professors, "about one-third of People's Republic of China students and scholars . . . had become Christian by the end of [their] research [year]."[11] The study's author lists reasons why such a high percentage of Chinese students, usually raised with little or no religious background, seek out Christian churches in the US.

He says they feel "marginality, rootlessness, amnesia, anger, frustration, alienation, and helplessness" in their new setting, and may discover that a community of Christians does indeed help alleviate these negative feelings.[12] This study does not deal exclusively with Chinese students who join The Church of Jesus Christ of Latter-day Saints, but experiences on BYU campuses demonstrate that every year, scores of Chinese nationals prepare for and receive baptism in the Church. This paper postulates that, similar to the 33 percent of Chinese students who join Christian churches in the US, in most developed countries, between 30 and 40 percent of the Church's baptisms occur among immigrants to that country.

A recent letter from a Latter-day Saint sister missionary serving in Macau details the conversion of a large family from China:

> Last Saturday and Sunday we were so busy to teach eight people from mainland China. We taught them from 11:00 to 6:00; after that they had the interview. Then they could be baptized on next day. In Macau, I have many opportunities to teach the lesson[s] like that; we called Miracle Baptism, because they can't stay here for a long time, and they can't learn the lesson in China, so they come to H[ong] K[ong] or Macau to be baptized. [signed, Sister Lau; original grammar and spelling maintained][13]

Obviously, the teaching and baptisms had to be rushed—the family heard about the Church in China but had to leave that country to receive the formal missionary lessons and apply for baptism.

This family of eight, similar to hundreds of Latter-day Saint Chinese baptized in the US, Hong Kong, Germany, and many other countries, has now returned to their homeland. They may find a local Church congregation with whom to meet, but they may also drift away to one of the many Christian gatherings in that country, or they may have to practice a simple form of Latter-day Saint worship in their own homes. In this way, the Church is spreading to areas of the world where formal preaching is not now possible.

WHAT TO DO WITH MIGRANTS IN THE CHURCH

Multiple factors explain why Latter-day Saint missionaries experience surprising success among immigrants. A first and obvious reason is that many immigrants find that in joining a new religion, they can escape the marginality and alienation mentioned in the study of Chinese students who have come to the US. The Church usually provides an instant community of friends and already integrated citizens for the foreign-born convert. He or she will likely find someone who "speaks my language" because so many returned missionaries do indeed speak a foreign language. Social identity with the new group adds legitimacy; the convert often perceives the new religion as providing upward mobility in a society that appears to be very rigidly structured. In short, the convert sees a chance for more personal progress in the new church. The foreigner has also likely left behind some family bonds that existed in the home country; unfettered, he or she is now open to new ideas and spiritual feelings and can more easily embrace a new religion. Further, the immigrant has likely come to the new country with a hope for economic improvement. He or she first notices and is taught by well-dressed Latter-day Saint missionaries, then attends a neatly groomed and well-cared-for chapel and associates with stable, employed Latter-day Saints. The immigrant can visualize achieving the same circumstances with the help of these new friends.

I do not want to diminish the role of the Holy Ghost in the conversion process; the factors mentioned in the previous paragraph generally work on the individual to then allow the Spirit to touch him or her. The new environment, removed from old family ties and a traditional religion, or no religion at all, allows the immigrant to feel the Spirit more deeply. The instructions in *Preach My Gospel* place a necessary emphasis on the missionary's spiritual preparation so that he or she can guide the investigator to feel and properly respond to the powers of the Spirit. Based on the aforementioned reasons, immigrants in every country appear to experience and bask in this Spirit more easily than many nationals.

Foreign-born Latter-day Saint converts may create challenges for themselves as well as for the Church. How will they best be integrated to assure permanence and enduring to the end? What language will they speak for the first few years of their new membership? How will long-standing members relate to someone who represents a different culture? How does a mission president, stake president, or bishop provide leadership for a culture and language with which he is not familiar? How does the Church retain an Asian or African convert who returns to a homeland with no organized Church structure? What do we do about the many converts who are in the new country illegally? (As noted, Latter-day Saint missionaries do not inquire regarding the legal status of their contacts, nor is legal status a part of the baptismal interview, yet the fact that many illegal immigrants are baptized may bother or even shock long-term members.) Should foreign-speaking branches, in any country, strive for full linguistic and cultural integration, or should they maintain a separate identity in order to achieve a higher retention rate? Are we providing the proper support for diverse groups, or is it even possible to do so? Do members resent new converts who are often economically dependent on others and cannot meet their own needs? Mark Grover has shown that "in 1985, over 50 percent of the membership of the Church in Portugal had previously lived in Africa."[14] These immigrant converts are often poor and lack the means of self-support. Will their economic status indeed change once they are baptized, or will they become a constant burden to Church resources? There are more questions than answers, and there are still many more questions.

For the present, Latter-day Saints worldwide must accept the fact that 30–40 percent of baptisms in OECD countries will be immigrants. It's in our blood as descendants of past-generation converts. It's in our scriptures. It's part of the reality of the contemporary world. Just as Mosiah's people infused new spiritual life and a new language into the established culture of Zarahemla, and just as the converted people of Ammon set an example of nonviolence to the established Church, new foreign-born converts will also enrich the culture of the present-day Church.

NOTES

1. Reported openly to the Chilean ambassador to the United States in a conversation with President Thomas S. Monson, Salt Lake City, Utah, 17 April 2007.
2. Phone conversation with Cyril Figuerres, 16 March 2007.
3. Rodney Stark, email to author, 17 March 2007.
4. "Factfile: Global Migration," *BBC News*, 2009.
5. Philip Jenkins, *The Next Christendom: The Coming of Global Christianity* (New York: Oxford University Press, 2002), 43.

6. Emilio Willems, *Followers of the New Faith: Cultural Change and the Rise of Protestantism in Brazil and Chile* (Nashville, TN: Vanderbilt University Press, 1967), 83–92.
7. UNFPA, "Meeting Development Goals," 1.
8. David J. Garrow, "Images of a Growing Nation, from Census to Census," *New York Times*, 13 October 2004.
9. Garrow, "Images of a Growing Nation, from Census to Census."
10. Doctrine and Covenants 4:4.
11. Wang Yuting and Fenggang Yang, "More than Evangelical and Ethnic: The Ecological Factor in Chinese Conversion to Christianity in the United States," *Sociology of Religion* 67, no. 32 (2006): 179.
12. Yuting and Yang, "More than Evangelical and Ethnic," 179.
13. Wing Yi Lau, email to author, 28 March 2007.
14. Mark Grover, "Migration, Social Change, and Mormonism in Portugal," *Journal of Mormon History* 21, no. 1 (Spring 1995): 76.

Dome of the Rock in Jerusalem. The geographical boundaries historically shared by the Islamic world and Christendom have led to multiple conflicts between the two civilizations.

18

SOURCES OF TENSION BETWEEN THE WEST AND THE ISLAMIC WORLD

DANIEL C. PETERSON

Daniel C. Peterson, then professor of Islamic studies and Arabic at Brigham Young University, presented this essay at "'The Perplexities of Nations': Current Trends and the International Church," the International Society's eighteenth annual conference, April 2007, Brigham Young University, Provo, Utah.

There will always be some stress between the historically Christian West and the world of Islam, if only because of normal and predictable religious disagreements. But shared theological territory exacerbates the doctrinal differences between them. Just as, at least in the era before air-power, nations have traditionally needed common geographical borders or territories in order to fight each other, religions fight much more effectively and fiercely if they share theological common ground. Christians and Muslims have much to quarrel over because they share belief in the God who created the universe, placed Adam and Eve in the Garden of Eden, and revealed himself to a series of prophets—including Abraham, Moses, and Jesus. By contrast, in a sense, Buddhists and Christians have far less basis for fighting each other, for the straightforward reason that they share less theological territory and, accordingly, have fewer disputed claims over which to compete.

The geographical boundaries historically shared by the Islamic world and Christendom have led to multiple conflicts between the two civilizations, including those of the multicentury Iberian Reconquista in the West and the long struggle for Constantinople in the East. Most notable among these struggles, though, because of their continued resonance down through the years, are the Crusades. While these European invasions actually had relatively little impact upon the Near East when they were underway—Arab historians made less of a fuss about them than did their Western contemporaries, and they were fairly transient affairs in any event—the potency of the Crusades as a historical symbol and rallying cry in the Islamic world has tended to grow with the passage of time. In recent years, accordingly, 'Usama b. Ladin exhorted his audience to fight "the Crusaders and the Zionists" as if Muslims were still confronted by the aggressive Christian Europe of the twelfth century.

By contrast, modern Westerners don't think about the Crusades very much—truth be told, we don't typically think about history very much—and we only dimly remember the etymological connection between the English words *crusade* and *cross*. That link, however, is much clearer in Arabic, in which the Crusades are the *hurub al-salibiyyin*, from the word *salib* (cross). Thus, a few years ago, when President Bush innocently pledged a "crusade" against terrorism, Arabic-speaking Muslims literally heard him promise a new "war of the cross."

Another obvious source of resentment and strife is the history of European colonialism that commenced in the eighteenth century, gained strength in the nineteenth century, and continued well into the twentieth century. Britain and France, for example, came to dominate large areas of the Islamic world—with the influence of the latter (in Algeria and Lebanon) proving particularly baneful.

Related to this earlier colonialism is the very real problem of the alliances of necessity that the West, and the US in particular, felt obliged to form with many defective regimes throughout the Near East and the Islamic world in order to contain the Soviet threat during the Cold War. Although these alliances may well have been necessary, our professed commitment to democracy and freedom often rings hollow in the ears of people subjected to the autocrats whom we supported as necessary allies.

There are, moreover, two special cases where our foreign policy actions have had quite unintended, negative consequences for Western-Islamic relationships. First, our support for Israel, motivated by genuine sympathy as well as by Cold War realpolitik, has earned us hatred throughout not only the Arab world but well beyond, among Muslims of many nations. They are aware of the enormous sums of money that we have given and continue to give to Tel Aviv as aid, and they are acutely conscious of the American-made weapons used to maintain Israeli security among (or, as they see it, dominance over) hostile Muslims. Second, our support for 'Usama b. Ladin and the other *mujahideen* in Afghanistan, using them as proxies in our battle with the Soviets, trained dedicated enemies and encouraged them to believe that, just as they had successfully fought one superpower, they could eventually defeat a second. This is, of course, a misreading of the Afghan War, which, though it manifestly damaged the Soviet Union, did not, contrary to Muslim fundamentalist imaginings, bring it down. But there is no question that the Islamically motivated *mujahideen* and the Islamically motivated Iranian revolution that occurred roughly at the same time restored a sense of pride and power to many Muslims that had been lost through decade after decade of feckless and corrupt secular rule.

Despite all the contact between Muslims and the West over the centuries since the rise of Islam in the seventh century and its rapid expansion thereafter (which was itself an example of imperialism and colonialism, though typical of its times and so far in the past that it is no longer typically felt as such), both civilizations are characterized, to a remarkable degree, by mutual ignorance. Western knowledge of Islam and Islamic civilization, for instance, is minimal, even shockingly lacking, in the general population. (At least, though, thanks to more than a decade of greater or lesser military involvement, many Americans can now find the Middle East on a map; one recalls Ambrose Bierce's cynical definition of war as "God's way of teaching Americans geography.") There is still a tendency, even though we're now aware that there are Shi'ite Muslims and Sunni Muslims, to think of Islam as an undifferentiated monolith and to throw our hands up in despair before a complex of cultures, histories, attitudes, and, yes, varying beliefs that we haven't really troubled ourselves to try to understand.

On the other side, after the initial expansion of Islam in its first few centuries—which was intellectual as well as geographical—Muslim society eventually lost its once almost insatiable appetite for Greek medicine, science, mathematics, and philosophy and settled into an incurious complacency, secure in the knowledge that it was the most advanced civilization on the planet and smugly confident that it would remain so. (The historical record is an invaluable treasure house of such cautionary tales so long as we recognize that we have no immunity to the mistakes that we love to point out in others.) As Bernard Lewis has observed in books like *The Crisis of Islam* and *What Went Wrong?*, Muslims failed to notice the Renaissance, the Reformation, the Enlightenment, and the Industrial Revolution. They simply weren't paying attention.

When some of us heard that Abu al-Hasan Bani-Sadr, the first president of the post-revolution Islamic Republic of Iran, had earned his doctorate in economics at the Sorbonne in Paris, we hoped that his understanding of European culture might bode well for some kind of eventual rapprochement between Iran and the West. Disappointingly, though, we soon learned that his tenure in France had been spent entirely in lecture halls, the library, and his flat and in transit back and forth between them while he pursued a narrowly technical degree. He had experienced little or nothing of European culture and values; he wasn't interested. In this regard, he was only slightly ahead of the Muslim masses, among whom widespread illiteracy has led to an oral culture that too often feasts on rumors and, frankly, paranoia about the West and about other matters.

Unfortunately, though, not all of what many Muslims think they know about the West is actually untrue. We could wish that it were all ignorance, but it isn't. Western decadence is no myth, and many Muslims feel it powerfully in both its seductiveness and its repulsiveness. Moreover, that combination is psychologically very potent, as those who feel themselves allured by the attractions of the West hate themselves and the West for that very attractiveness.

In that light, let me comment upon the common (and, to Westerners, often rather comical) notion of the US as "the great Satan": We fail to understand that phrase, I think, if we have in mind the supernatural monster of evil who inspired Auschwitz, the Gulag, and the Cambodian killing fields. Rather, we should think of a diabolical tempter, a fallen angel, a smooth and attractive seducer. Here is the centrally relevant text, Sura 114 (the last chapter) of the Qur'an, in my rough-and-ready translation:

> Say: I take refuge with the lord of the people,
> The king of the people,
> The God of the people,
> From the evil of the lurking whisperer
> Who whispers into the breasts of the people
> Among the jinn and the people.

The reference is clearly to the devil. But now listen to the sound of the original Arabic, as nearly as I can reproduce it in Roman letters without including distracting diacritical marks. Notice the hissing *s* sounds, and think of the seductive tempter in the Garden of Eden:

> Qul: A'uudhu bi-rabb an-naass,
> Malik an-naass,
> Ilaah an-naass,
> Min sharr al-wasswaass al-khannaass
> Aladhi yuwasswissu fis-sudur an-naass
> Min al-jinna wa'n-naass.

America is dangerous not because it is loathsome but precisely because of its very attractiveness, its wealth, its comfort, and its power, which threaten to seduce believers away from fidelity to God.

And to make things worse, Muslims are frustrated because their civilization—which was for several centuries the most advanced on the planet and which was founded, according to their belief, on the final divine revelation—has become, by and large, an economic backwater, a technical and scientific consumer rather than a producer, and a political pawn. Its scholars, scientists, and philosophers were once the foremost in the world, but its schools and universities are now, on the whole, mediocre. To put the case in Latter-day Saint terms, the Islamic "final dispensation" has gone awry.

When the Ayatollah Khomeini returned to Iran from his exile in France, during which he had smuggled his messages to his followers via

Western-made cassette tapes, he flew to Tehran in a Boeing jet and climbed into a Chevrolet in order to drive into the city from Mehrabad Airport. Western hegemony is inescapable. And, from the perspective of many Muslims, the future is not especially promising. If, for instance, fossil fuels (an ever-diminishing and irreplaceable resource) and their derivatives were left out of the picture, and all the Arab nations were somehow joined together in a single country (call it "Arabistan"), the gross national product of that country would rank just below the GNP of Finland.

The result is a deep sense of humiliation among many Muslims of having been wronged and, in some circles, a sense of anger and a desire to get revenge. These feelings sometimes make it very difficult for even sympathetic Westerners and very intelligent representatives of Islamic culture to engage in meaningful conversation. There is too much baggage. There are too many psychological obstacles. And the situation isn't helped by language differences. Knowledge of Near Eastern and Islamic languages in the West is very rare; I'm told that, at the time of the Iranian revolution in the late seventies, fewer than five Americans on the staff of the huge American embassy in Tehran could comfortably read and converse in Persian. And on the other side, the state of Arabic publishing is extraordinarily weak, and there are few Arabic translations from Western languages. This is no recipe for curing an intercivilizational crisis that rests, to a very large degree, on mutual incomprehension.

And to make conditions worse still, the Near East is densely populated with failed or largely failed states whose governments have a strong interest in scapegoating and misdirection, and there is no free press to hold them accountable. Nor has there been an adequate effort on the part of the US or the West in general to tell our story. Yet, if it were well and properly told, that story would have much (including the religiosity of many of our people and a tradition of religious tolerance that allows Muslims to flourish in our midst) that could help to overcome the negative stereotypes that many residents of the Islamic world have about our society.

The rise of "fundamentalist" Islam (which comes in various flavors and goes by a number of names, including *Salafism* and *Wahhabism*) represents a new threat and source of tension. Promulgated through vast networks of schools (*madrasas*) and backed by petrodollars, this form of

Islam misreads the lessons of the past. In trying to return to the days of Islamic greatness, it fails to recognize that in those days, greatness came in large part because of the openness of Islamic society to foreign ideas (e.g., in connection with the famous translation "movement" of the eighth and ninth centuries). 'Usama b. Ladin, hiding in the mountains and caves of Afghanistan, represented a path to nihilistic irrelevancy, not to the revivification of Muslim strength and glory.

Nevertheless, Islamic fundamentalism is a genuinely powerful force, as every Western observer now realizes. Confident predictions of global secularization have been proven wrong. Religion may not move the intellectual and political elite in the West, but it continues, despite prophecies to the contrary, to exert enormous influence upon such elites elsewhere and upon ordinary people everywhere. Stalin's famous question "How many divisions has the Pope?" has been answered: The Vatican still commands the allegiance of hundreds of millions of people, as it has for centuries. The Soviet Union lasted well under a hundred years; Stalin's commissars no longer control even the Kremlin. And dreams of a renewed caliphate inspire millions and terrify many millions more.

Though, just at the time that Islam is on the rise and, in many areas, newly militant, the West appears to have lost its nerve and its faith. (With an eye strictly on the fanatics and not all Muslims, the famous line of William Butler Yeats comes to mind: "The best lack all conviction, while the worst are full of passionate intensity.") Europe seems to be dying. Or, at least, the Europeans are. Demographic trends on the continent appear to promise what some have called "Europistan" or "Eurabia." And interreligious dialogue often tends to be one-sided, with assertive Muslims faced only by apologetic and tenuously Christian conversation partners.

Such trends are or should be worrisome for the West, and, in my opinion, aren't even good for Muslims. Islam is in serious need of redefinition in a pluralistic world. Adaptation is always necessary for religions. Western tradition itself recognizes the concept of a Christian church that is *semper reformanda*, "always reforming," and Muslims commonly teach that a *mujaddid*, a renewer, is sent by God in every century to revivify Islam. But the necessity for believers to faithfully rethink their faith is surely more urgent in Islam at the moment than in any other major religious tradition. It needs to decide what the status and function of *shari'a* will be, and particularly so for Muslims of the diaspora, living outside of traditionally Islamic lands. It needs to confront the issue of what Pope Benedict XVI has called "reciprocity": Will the religious freedom of the West, which allows the construction of mosques and conversions to Islam, be matched by corresponding freedoms in the Islamic world? Will conversions from Islam remain capital crimes? Will Christian communities be as free to build churches in Islamic countries as congregations of Muslims in the West are to build houses of worship? And where are the moderate Muslims?

Reform of Islam will have to come from within, from Muslims. But it would be helpful for would-be Islamic reformers, on the issues just sketched here as on many others, if they had strong, informed, Western and Christian dialogue partners for support and encouragement and even for example and advice. It will be most unfortunate if—just at the point when some Muslims might be trying to show that Islamic belief can be reconciled with, and thrive within, a pluralistic and tolerant social order—the onetime Christian West seems to demonstrate by its own religious collapse that such hopes are illusory and dangerous.

I have, I realize, seemed quite negative. I blame this on the topic that I was asked to address, which was the sources of tension between the West and the Islamic world. It would be Pollyanna-ish and misleading to ignore such obstacles and difficulties. But I do not want to end without asserting my strong belief that these obstacles need not have the final say. There is also considerable reason for guarded optimism. Good things can be and are being done.

19

THE CHURCH AND THE GLOBAL COMMUNITY

ELDER CREE-L KOFFORD

Elder Cree-L Kofford, then an emeritus member of the First Quorum of the Seventy of The Church of Jesus Christ of Latter-day Saints, presented this essay at "The Church and the Global Community," the International Society's twentieth annual conference, April 2009, Brigham Young University, Provo, Utah.

The second-to-last verse of the book of Matthew gives what Matthew penned as the Savior's last instruction to His Apostles. You have all heard it. He said, "Go ye therefore, and teach all nations, baptizing them in the name of the Father, and of the Son, and of the Holy Ghost."[1]

The thing that draws our attention to the worldwide nature of the Church is that He didn't bother, at that moment, to tell the Apostles why they were to go into all the world and baptize everybody. If you go back to His conversations with Moses, He told him, "This is my work and my glory—to bring to pass the immortality and eternal life of man."[2] We all know that immortality is a free gift that comes from the atoning sacrifice. What is not a free gift is the eternal life part. Eternal life means life in the highest degree of the celestial kingdom. And to get that, there are certain requirements, certain prerequisites that must be met.

There are, of course, the ordinances that must be obtained: All must receive the ordinances of baptism and confirmation. They must also receive the endowment and, thereafter, the sealing ordinance of the temple. And men must receive the Melchizedek Priesthood. Without those ordinances there cannot be eternal life. In addition to those ordinances, one other important thing is needed: obedience to the covenants that you have made.

The Lord has been very gracious in His administration of the world in essentially saying, "I won't hold you responsible for something you don't know anything about." And that indicates the need to teach the people of the world. The link between the Book of Moses and the Book of Matthew is found in Doctrine and Covenants 131:1–2: "In the celestial glory there are three heavens or degrees; and in order to obtain the highest, a man must enter into . . . the new and everlasting covenant of marriage."

All of that goes together to form a course of action the Lord wants for His children. We know He wants this not only for His children on this earth but for His children on all other earths that have been formed. Christ's atoning sacrifice transcends this geographic sphere, and it brings forcibly to mind the fact that whether you and I like it or not, the Lord intends His gospel to go throughout the world. His gospel cannot effectively bless without the Church going throughout the world. When we speak of the Church and the global community, we are in reality speaking about the doctrine of the Lord. We are talking about the purpose and substance of the gospel of Jesus Christ. We are talking about why all that we do is done. And it is within that framework that we begin to understand what we know about the Church around the world.

My frame of reference for today will be taken from Asia. Asia is a fascinating place. It covers over five million square miles of the earth's surface. It has 3.4 billion people, which make up about 52 percent of the world's population. Asia is an interesting assortment of seventeen major countries. There are more than that in terms of territories and minor kingdoms, but seventeen is enough to keep your mind going. It starts in the north with a country that I was taught to love by President Richard Cook—Mongolia. We'll talk more about Mongolia later. Let your mind conjure up thoughts about that great country, and you'll understand why it is with such affection that we speak its name.

South of Mongolia, you have China and all that China is and has the potential to become. A dot on China's geographic landscape is the beautiful international city of Hong Kong, which is where the administrative offices of the Church were located and where President Richard Cook, President H. Bryan Richards, and I spent three years of our lives together in the presidency, having previously served under the direction of President John H. Groberg.

To the east lies what I consider to be the heartbeat of Asia: Taiwan. It contains the largest assembly of Latter-day Saints of any place in this massive area. It is a family-oriented place where people live in relative democracy. It is also a place where the gospel has taken root and is progressing well.

South of there, we run into a series of countries that still have an attitude about the United States and about the Church (because the Church is part of the United States), derivative of the experiences that preceded historically. I speak of Vietnam, Laos, Myanmar (Burma), and, to a lesser extent, Bangladesh. All of those countries are relatively closed and relatively challenging in which to work. There have been some minor breakthroughs, and I am sure that the work will continue there.

The day I flew to Hanoi to talk to officials about the possibility of some kind of Church presence in Vietnam, it became clear that, while we may have at one time had a congregation there and may have at one time even owned a building there, those days would not return during these officials' time. So we waited. We also have exotic countries like Thailand, Cambodia, Singapore, and Sri Lanka—which was of course bathing in the blood of a long-term civil war—and India—so massive that I am not even sure its own people understand how big it is—and Pakistan and Afghanistan—although Afghanistan is never a place we spent any time because we were excluded from being there as a church.

There are other countries equally interesting: Nepal and the mountains of Tibet, Bhutan, and, not far from there, the giant country of Indonesia. I am told there are more Muslims in Indonesia than in any place in the world. And, if I haven't forgotten any, I think I have covered most of the countries that we had responsibility for.

Lumping them together, there is a great deal we can learn about the different areas of the Church. Had I served in other areas, I am sure they could just as easily be used as a model for the comments to be made, but Asia provides an almost perfect ground from which to learn various things for the simple reason that it is so diverse. Seventeen countries plus seventeen languages made it easy to salve our consciences when we said to ourselves that there is no way we can learn all of these languages, so let's not learn any. I was so grateful for that. If I had been sent to France, I probably would have had to learn French, but in Asia it was easy to excuse my ignorance.

Asia is an area filled with countries of significantly diverse governments; some are reasonably friendly to the US; others dislike us with an intensity that borders on hatred. This is not because we are members of the Church, I think, but because we are citizens of the US.

All that I am going to tell you comes from my own observations, my own experience, and my own opinion. That makes it subject to great fallibility. If I say something that is wrong, just chalk it up to the fact that I didn't learn very well, and I'll accept that. I made no effort, except for a call to President Cook, to find out if my memory of certain things was accurate or to triangulate my thinking with that of others. This is not a committee report. It is a report of one person's time. When I talk about what the Church is doing, I have to be candid and tell you I am talking about what I know the Church has been doing. You see, I always served in an atmosphere of "need to know." I was one of those who believed that if I didn't need to know, no one needed to tell me. I found over the years there was a great deal that others thought I didn't need to know, so there is a lot that went on that I didn't know about.

In addition to that, there is an enormous amount of work being done by those who operate independently of the Church. I say "independently" in the sense that they do not function under the umbrella of the administration of the Church. I speak with great admiration of such entities—for example, the Kennedy Center at Brigham Young University. I have long admired and watched the work that they do. The closest I got to understanding how the Kennedy Center operates was watching each year as the sixty or so Chinese teachers would migrate from China to Hong Kong for what they called a summer break, which meant spending a week or so in Hong Kong. We were privileged to meet with them and feel of their spirit. I know the good they have done. Without being told of it or knowing officially what goes on, I have witnessed it and felt their presence. Yet, they are outside the pale of my knowledge. I think one of the reasons they function is because they are outside the pale. They are not perceived by the governments that allow them access to their countries as a church organization, at least not officially. The prohibition against churches coming into certain countries does not apply to organizations of this type.

Other organizations about which I know only by observation are the universities. BYU and other schools—particularly their performing groups—have had a great impact in various countries. Perhaps the most notable efforts have been those made by BYU–Hawaii; it has specialized in that part of the world and has taken the lead in a very aggressive and, in my mind, positive way in accomplishing good things in these countries. I will talk in a little bit about a time when we were with President Shumway, of BYU–Hawaii, and President Gordon B. Hinckley on a visit to Thailand to demonstrate what that university has done.

I offer these two illustrations of what is being done by the Church outside of my realm of experience and responsibility. We are grateful for what these entities do, and others could be named. I do not mention things on the legal side because they were attached by direct assignment to the area office, and we worked with them on an almost daily basis. The simple fact is that we could not have lived without them. I do not mention the humanitarian aid, although it was massive and essential. More good was done by the humanitarian aid program in the Asia Area the years I served there than you can possibly imagine. Natural disasters came with such regularity that there was no need to stage mock disasters to prepare; they could use real ones for training and learning. They were present in a large number of countries, many of which we could not get the organized Church into, and they were invited in to provide services.

I speak particularly of a country—and I am going to try to remember not to give you the names of any of the countries I speak of specifically, and that is because the Area President of Asia, upon learning I was going to address this subject, reminded me that there are many things that are sensitive in that part of the world and that it would be appreciated if I would be less than totally revealing in terms of the countries about which I am speaking. I honor that request. I was there long enough to learn that losing face is one of the cardinal sins in that part of the world. I would not want to say anything that might upset a delicate balance now in process. Nevertheless, I think we can learn well from the illustration without knowing exactly which country is being illustrated. And so it is that the humanitarian aid program had missionaries performing aid work in countries where no other activity would be allowed. And they established a great base.

I arrived in Hong Kong in July 1997, a few days after the handover of that colony by the British to the mainland Chinese government. On the lips of everyone was wonderment about what would transpire. I would later learn that there was concern about the future of Hong Kong because many Hong Kong residents had disposed of their assets and had left to take up citizenship in other countries. Most of those, I am told, were members of the British Commonwealth. What that meant was not totally apparent for some time, until one by one we learned of former leaders of the Church who had left the area and were now residing in other places.

There was a second worry that was not expressed to me in those early days but which came to my attention later. There was among some an honest fear that the mainland Chinese government would invade Hong Kong. It turns out that was an unnecessary worry. The Chinese government has done all that it said it would do, as far as I am aware. The question on everyone's mind at that time was—and if I was asked one question more than any other, it was this one—"When is China going to open to missionary work?" Everyone wanted to know, and so did I. The honest truth was that we didn't know then, and we don't know now.

The impressive thing was that the base for sending the Church into countries has usually been laid by fine men, particularly businessmen and professionals who have lived in or at least had extensive business dealings in the country. We are blessed to have some outstanding men who have done that. We benefited greatly in a number of countries from businessmen who entered into contractual relationships, which they honored with great integrity and which brought honor to them—and vicariously to us.

I believe that in many of these countries the base that will be used as a springboard for our participation in a religious sense has already been laid by people like you who are engaged there. By way of background, that tells you a little bit about these countries. They are different, government-wise. I don't think it needs to be said, but just to be certain we are communicating, one can go from places as easy to live in as Taiwan to those that are governed by brutal dictatorships.

In that area, you have countries that have been at war with each other. One of the more interesting illustrations of that is in the tiny country of Cambodia, a gorgeous country. Arithmetically, it is the fastest growing country in terms of Church membership in Asia. It's a marvelous little place of great poverty and great concern for the future of the land. The problem is that it is not far removed from the country of Laos. Some of you will know where I am heading when I say "Khmer Rouge."

For those of you who don't know the history of that area, there was a time when a renegade band of individuals operating under the name Khmer Rouge came down out of Laos, which was their home base, to occupy Cambodia. They rolled into the capital of Cambodia and rounded up all of the citizens who were educated. They took the doctors, the lawyers, the teachers, and all others who had any education or could possibly be labeled as a leader; they put them in the backs of trucks and took them to a place that a journalist later described as "the killing fields." There they were murdered systematically, one by one, leaving the country devoid of any significant top leadership or top mental capacity. I had the opportunity of meeting a young man who was a child when this happened. He went in the same truck as his parents and siblings. He told me that he watched as his mother and father were shot or beheaded, and then they turned their attention to his brothers and sisters. In the confusion of that process, he slipped away into the underbrush and walked for weeks into the hinterlands of the country, where he was ultimately discovered by someone who helped him find a distant relative. He grew up in Cambodia and lives there today. He is a member of the Church and has a strong testimony. That leads to the purpose of the story.

We were in Cambodia one time to conduct a conference. We were preparing to build a new building there. Baptisms had gone extremely well, and the people were progressing. We had rented a hall in a hotel since there were no church buildings anywhere that were near large enough to hold the several hundred members of the Church who were assembled. As we walked into the room, there was an interesting contrast. The room was divided down the center by a large aisle. On one side were all of the Cambodians, and on the other were all of the Laotians. It was very obvious that they had intended to sit that way. I wondered if there was great animosity between the two groups, but I was assured by local leaders that this was not the case, but the comfort level each had for the other was still tainted by the memory of what had happened some years before in the invasion. Our challenge, of course, was to build that diverse group into a common force, all as members of the Church. We started on that. We did not complete it before I left, but I have no doubt that in due course they will one day be sitting intermingled one with another.

That brings us to an interesting challenge in terms of the Church in the world. You see, except for during the War of 1812 and the Civil War, the US and Canada have always had a reasonably friendly relationship. About the worst that happens is that you have Democrats and Republicans talking to each other, or you have Brigham Young University and University of Utah graduates talking to each other, but aside from minor skirmishes of animosity, most of us get along reasonably well. That is not true in places like Asia. Nor is it true in other places of the world about which I know less than I do Asia. The Church, as it moves forward, has to be sensitive to these needs and circumstances. Even in the marvelous place of Taiwan there were vestiges of concern about the attitude and ambitions of the Chinese government in terms of that relationship. And so, sensitivity is needed, and sensitivity must exist.

What do we do in countries where in one place you are allowed to do missionary work and in another one you are not? The answer is simple. We do what we can. We go where we are allowed to go. We do as much as we are allowed to do, but we faithfully, scrupulously, and honestly obey the rules set down by local governments. Our opinion was that it was far better to wait and abide the time than it was to try to force a decision that was not ready to come. The Lord knows His purposes, and He knows His plan, and He said on more than one occasion: "I can do my own work."

Our responsibility was to be there to implement what needed to be implemented at the time the Lord saw fit to make it possible. And He did see fit to make many things possible. I think one of the greatest illustrations of what can happen in that circumstance is the country of Mongolia, about which only good things can be said.

Mongolia was opened to the gospel just a few years before we arrived in Asia. To my best recollection and best knowledge, we were somewhere near the first of the people to go into that magnificent country, and *magnificent* is a word that I use advisedly in the sense that I don't know that I would call it a beautiful country, unless you call rugged, vast loneliness beautiful, but it is a magnificent country. One of the first to have gone into that area is Brother Cook, about whom I have already spoken. He was the first mission president there. He did a marvelous work—actually Sister Cook did a marvelous work, and Brother Cook took care of her, but they accomplished a great deal. As a result, today Mongolia stands as a bastion of good members of the Church. They are intelligent, capable, and willing. Several beautiful buildings were built under President Cook's supervision and were dedicated by him. The gospel continues to roll forth, but to show you the challenge that we have when we go into the world, let me explain to you one problem with which we had to wrestle somewhat. It is not one you would imagine.

It had to do with missionaries. Some of you serving in other areas may have seen this situation. The question is that once you reach the point where young men and young women are prepared to serve missions, do you recommend that they serve where they can help their own people—stay in their own country and develop and go forward—or do you recommend that they be sent to foreign countries, preferably places like the US, where they can witness the full Church in action, experience living amongst a large number of members of the Church, and become better educated and better equipped to lead the people at home, with the possibility that they may not want to return home or will be dissatisfied with home when they get back? I do not presume to know the correct answer in all cases. However, I do understand the problem in all cases. That is something that must be examined by the Church, each country in turn as the Church goes through the process of spreading across the world. If it hasn't happened yet in Africa, it will. In any country where there is poverty, lack of education, or lack of opportunity, that question is going to have to be addressed by priesthood leadership and probably by the First Presidency and the Twelve in making a decision. We learn from that experience.

What about the threefold mission of the Church? How does that work? Let me explain to you what we experienced there. The first mission of the Church is, of course, to preach the gospel. That means missionary work. Where we're not allowed to have missionaries, the answer is simple: we don't do missionary work. Last year, you heard Elder Wickman stand at a pulpit like this one and talk about the man with the stamp and the need for visas. That is indeed a lifeline for missionary work. What he may not have told you was that even getting the stamp doesn't solve the problem because countries can shrink or expand the stamp almost at their whim. You may be allowed to have forty missionaries in a country this week and fourteen next week. There is a constant juggling in some areas where that is an issue. That presents challenges for the missionaries and for the missionary work. It requires constant care and concern.

We had that experience in one country, which incidentally did not allow Americans. We had a number of missionaries there, but they were from Australia, Canada, and other countries besides the United States. A local religious group became exercised. You may have read about it. They accosted tourists in the hotels, particularly Western tourists. The government became concerned about the safety of the people, particularly Americans, and we were asked to withdraw all of the missionaries. And, if my memory serves correctly, for a short period of time we did pull all of the missionaries from the country. I point this out not as a fact in terms of this country, but as a principle that these are the kinds of issues that must be addressed.

Now to point out the challenge: What do you do with fifty missionaries when all of a sudden they can't be where they were called to serve? Where do you send them? How often do you move them? There was a mission that had this problem on a regular basis; it was composed of more than one country. The visas there allowed the missionaries to stay anywhere from a few weeks to a few months. That meant a rotating complement of missionaries who would first stay in country A until their visa time ran out, then move to country B, then move to country C, then back to mission headquarters, and then start the process all over again. Try that if you are a mission president with 140 or 150 missionaries. That's a logistical nightmare, but it is a reality of life, and missionary work has the challenge of that. It is not at all unlike what the Saints experienced in Missouri. They couldn't stay in one place for very long either: Jackson County to Clay County to Caldwell County and finally across the frozen ground to Nauvoo, all in a period of a few years. I suspect they felt a little bit like some of these mission presidents, wishing they could stay in one place long enough to get the job done. That's one of the dangers, one of the challenges, and one of the characteristics of the global Church.

Incidentally, we have a good reputation in the United States. Among my early assignments, I worked in New York and Washington, DC, and saw firsthand the magnificent work of bridge building and working with ambassadors. I went to the Marriott farm picnic and shook hands with more ambassadors than I knew what to do with. I've been to the Christmas lighting ceremony at the Washington D.C. Temple Visitors' Center, where many bridges were built and foreign dignitaries were honored. I have watched the magnificent work performed by these "professionals." And I use quotation marks around professionals because they are people like you and me, graced by the Spirit and functioning in an outstanding way. Some of you will remember their names—Beverly Campbell, LaMar Sleight, Ann Santini, and the list goes on. They are marvelous people who perform a great work. The simple fact remains that while the Church enjoys a great reputation in most parts of the US and in many parts of the world, it is a fly on the wall in Asia. You take our 160 thousand members and put them up against 3.4 billion people and you can see that we do not by weight of numbers impress very much. In addition to that, we have the typical resistance from those who were there before us and who do not like the fact that we are taking people from their flocks. These all become challenges for those who serve in international areas as the Church grows more and more in the world.

Let me tell you what I consider the crux of the challenge of the Church moving out. We see ways of training people. We're a great training Church. The truth is, though, if you watch the way we train people in the North

American area, meaning both Canada and the US, we use techniques of training that work well with large groups. We use video and other mass communication means to do training. To have that work effectively, you have to have people near the same level of gospel growth so that you can teach. Admittedly, there are some places in the US where we're still teaching T-ball and others where we are teaching them how to hit a ninety-mile-an-hour fastball. But the truth is, in places like Asia, in one place we are teaching baseball, in another we are teaching soccer, and somewhere else we are teaching tiddlywinks—simply because it's that different. And so training is vastly different, and that is not understood until you have lived there and been responsible for the training. I preferred to train in the smallest possible group I could find because when you are dealing with translators, that is the only way you have any hope of knowing if the message that you said is the message that they heard. Let me illustrate the point I'm trying to make.

One of my first assignments when I arrived in Asia was to attend a week-long youth conference of young adults in Taiwan. They were holding the conference in the mountains of central Taiwan, and we were to spend a week with them. My wife, Ila, and I enjoyed a glorious week. It was absolutely marvelous. It was there that I saw my first Chinese handcart company, and they did a beautiful job of trying to emulate what the handcart pioneers would have looked and acted like. I had several spiritual experiences while there. Later in a conference in another part of Taiwan, using a translator—which was always the case—I wanted to express that experience, so I told the experience. I thought it went over very well. I watched the eyes of the audience and felt that they had received it reasonably well and that the point had been made. Months later when I went back, the translator who translated for me asked if he could see me. He said, "I need to repent." I had no idea what he had in mind, but I hoped it wasn't one or two things that quickly came to me. He proved that it wasn't. He said, "I need to tell you, do you remember the story that you told about . . ." and related the story I told. He said, "When you started to tell that story it sounded so farfetched that I didn't think they'd believe it, and I didn't want to tell them about it. So I just made up another story."

I learned something that day. Just because I said it, didn't mean they heard it. I also learned that you need to do some checking to see what people have heard. I may have given the best talk of my life, meaning the one he gave, if I just knew what it was I had said. I got to the point that I would get into a room with the people I was trying to teach, express the principle, and then stop and try to find some way to determine whether or not they had learned the principle. One way of doing that is simply to say, "Now, what did I just teach you?" and then listen as they try to return the message. That works to some extent. There are a variety of other ideas that I am sure you have, but somehow as we go into the world with the Church, we need to make sure that the messages we are delivering are the messages that they are receiving.

That challenge is compounded by another problem, and that is that words, even English words, do not mean the same in all languages. Sometimes words do not convey the thought. You have the challenge of knowing if the people you're teaching understood the principle in their minds or if they have yet to understand it in their hearts. Let me tell you another story that illustrates the point I am trying to make:

I spent a lot of time teaching about the principle of love. There were evidences in one particular country that they were having challenges with loving one another, loving families, loving husbands and wives, and so on. I taught the same kinds of things you would have taught, trying to get them introduced to the principles of love and caring. After I had been particularly eloquent at one conference, after we had finished, a contingent of sisters asked if they could see me. I thought, "Yes, certainly you may." We retired to a room off the stage of the building where we had held the meeting. What they said was, "Brother Kofford, we've heard what you have said about love, but do you realize that is contrary to the way we are culturally? We just don't go around expressing love to each other." One of them said, "For a fact, my husband has never told me that he loves me. I've never heard him say that." I later asked if she had ever told him, and she said, "No. I have never told him I love him."

So there we were. I had been teaching "love one another" and "husbands and wives loving each other" for weeks in that country—obviously, they had heard the words because I had asked them and they would say, "You have taught us to love one another and to express love." That seemed to me to be clear. *Express* means to say it, but it didn't mean "say it" to them. You see the problem? You end up in a situation where as you train, you want to take their face in your hands, look them in the eye, and say, "Now, let's be sure what I've said is what you've heard"—and don't let them get away with just the words because these people are very bright and they've learned to recite. They can tell you what you have said better than you can say it. Whether they understand it is a totally different experience. Typically, at least in my limited experience, their deductive or inductive reasoning abilities are very limited. They are masters at math and science and other such disciplines because they require heavy memorization and regurgitation. But when you try to connect the dots and analytically apply one principle in situation A to situation B, they have challenges. And that's not bad; it's just human nature. The reason I mention it is for those of you engaged in all of these things, you may want to consider worrying about that happening in your experience.

The other thing that becomes an issue in the world has to do with understanding where these people are spiritually. I think back on Joseph Smith's challenge of doing that in the Kirtland and Nauvoo era. You remember that Joseph was anxious to get a temple. The Lord was anxious to get a temple built. He kept telling Joseph, "Build me a temple." They were supposed to build one in Jackson County, and then He said, "I want one in Kirtland." Joseph was building the temple because they wanted the ordinances of the temple. Joseph, just prior to or while they were building the Kirtland Temple, had a meeting with the Quorum of the Twelve in which he said something. Keep in mind that this is the Quorum of the Twelve that presided over The Church of Jesus Christ of Latter-day Saints in the Kirtland era. These are the men who gave their lives, as well as their fortunes, to building the Church. Men who served missions when they were destitute and who were obedient and thoughtful and kind. I am trying to draw a picture of a good, faithful Latter-day Saint. Joseph said to the Twelve, "I know you are anxious about receiving the endowment"—and I am going to paraphrase here—"but you are not yet ready." What he said was, "Nor could even Gabriel explain it to the understanding of your dark minds." They were not ready.

The Twelve were not ready in the 1830s to receive the ordinance of the endowment. What makes us think, then, that there are not people in foreign countries, especially emerging countries, who do not have that same challenge? We must temper our teaching to their ability to learn.

It was not until twenty years after his first vision that Joseph finally began to unfold the principles of the temple. It was 1840 when he first gave the doctrine relating to baptisms for the dead, which the Doctrine and Covenants tells us is the welding link necessary to save the world.[3] Two years later in 1842, Joseph finally felt that they were ready as leaders—and I am talking now about Brigham Young and Hyrum Smith among others—to be taught the endowment. It was yet another year later before he announced sections 131 and 132, which are the sections relating to the celestial principle of sealing. The Lord waited in that circumstance until the people were ready. Sometimes we go into foreign countries, into areas of the world, and we dump the whole thing on them and expect them to take it and run with it. We need, as leaders, to be as wise as the Lord was with Joseph by saying, "Wait to teach until the people are ready to learn." That's not an easy thing. I think Asia is a perfect place to use as an example for what I am trying to say because we had all levels of learning, which makes it even harder. As you go out, you must teach in some countries on a significantly more elementary level than in others, and even within the same country you have the same disparity.

Let me go on now to the third mission of the Church, which is to redeem the dead. That requires sensitivity regarding the conditions of the country. In Asia we had some unusual circumstances. Among other things, the records of the dead had in some countries been destroyed, systematically and purposefully. There were no records. How then do you do family history research? You teach as much as you can teach. You teach what has to be taught. You teach them about personal histories. You teach them about working with relatives who are still alive. You teach about the temple, and you teach them about preparing themselves to hold a recommend even though the temple is so far away that in their lifetime there is little chance they will ever get to one—again, sensitivity to the needs of the people.

Now we could compound illustrations for the rest of the day, but that would be counterproductive. Hopefully, what I have done is give you enough words from which you can draw a picture of what it is like to go throughout the world with the Church. What you see working well along the Wasatch Front does not always work well along other mountain ranges in other parts of the world. Leadership and membership of the Church must be cautious not to take people beyond the place where they can be. It is our responsibility to provide the kind of leadership that will bring people along as rapidly as they can come but no more rapidly than that, with compassion, understanding, and love.

Incidentally, if I don't add one more word, I will have trouble with two good friends, John Carmack and Richard Cook. I have not said anything about the Perpetual Education Fund, which negligence is a cardinal sin. The reason is that program wasn't active when I was in Asia. They were just getting it started, so we didn't see it. But I know this: I've watched it since, and it is a powerful force accomplishing great good.

I promised I would tell you about BYU–Hawaii and the trip with President Hinckley. We were visiting a country in which relationships had been good, although there had been one incident that had seriously damaged it. President Shumway was there to distribute a series of scholarships to high school seniors who were graduating, some of whom were nonmembers of the Church. That program had been going on for several years and was extremely well received by the government. We were simply beneficiaries of the prior goodwill that someone had introduced into that country, and so again I applaud the efforts of them as I do many of you.

I have been talking about all of you in some way or another, particularly those who live in and who are involved in other lands in business, education, or other functions. Thank you for what you do. Thank you for understanding what we as General Authorities who work in these areas try to do, and thank you to those who function so beautifully who are not under the umbrella of the Area Presidency. I pray that my words, though many, may have conveyed a few simple thoughts that will let you understand and build into your lives a knowledge of what going into the world means when we talk about The Church of Jesus Christ of Latter-day Saints.

NOTES

1. Matthew 28:19.
2. Moses 1:39.
3. See Doctrine and Covenants 128:18.

"ORGANIZE YOURSELVES ACCORDING TO THE LAWS OF MAN"

Ethical Challenges in Establishing the International Church

ELDER ADESINA J. OLUKANNI

Elder Adesina J. Olukanni, then an Area Authority Seventy of The Church of Jesus Christ of Latter-day Saints, presented this essay at "Challenges in Establishing the International Church," the International Society's twenty-first annual conference, April 2010, Brigham Young University, Provo, Utah.

June 1978 ushered in the revelation that extends priesthood and temple blessings to all worthy male members of the Church (Official Declaration 2). It signified a new beginning and understanding of the fulfillment of the words of various prophets, as contained in scriptures, that God will save all His children—irrespective of race or color, whether bond or free—thereby removing all previous restrictions. It also means the restored gospel, or the establishment of the Church, could extend to areas where it has hitherto not been, including Brazil and Africa, making the Church truly international and global in coverage. The enormous scale of this work cannot be overemphasized—Africa alone has over one thousand ethnic groups speaking over one thousand languages and having diverse cultures and political structures and laws.

The revelation depicts a continuation of the fulfillment of what Joseph Smith, the Prophet of the Restoration, saw 176 years ago on a Sunday night. He stated, "I want to say to you before the Lord, that you know no more concerning the destinies of this Church and kingdom than a babe upon its mother's lap. You don't comprehend it. . . . It is only a little handfull of Priesthood you see here tonight, but this Church will fill North and South America—it will fill the world."[1] This statement further defines the establishment of the international global Church amidst geographical, political, cultural, ethnic, or tribal divisions, as opposed to a small American church in Kirtland, Ohio, envisioned by the handful of priesthood holders gathered in a fourteen-by-fourteen-foot room who represented the entire leadership of the Church at that place and time.

History has shown that establishing the true church has always been fraught with challenges—from the times of Adam to Noah, from Moses to Jesus Christ and His Apostles, and more important, in these the latter days, defined by the Apostle Paul as "perilous times."[2] Against this backdrop, the topic of this conference is timeless and of great importance. It calls for reflection upon the past in order to appreciate the present and contemplate the future in the light of truth. The topic is "'Organize Yourselves According to the Laws of Man': Ethical Challenges in Establishing the International Church." I am expected to focus on successful experiences that show how "going through the front door" at times hinders the work but ultimately blesses the work beyond what we might have expected, with specific reference to Africa.

Going through the front door in the face of ethical challenges in principle implies keeping our actions consistent with agreed-upon principles of correct moral conduct at all times and in all places and in all circumstances. This is where the "rubber" of obedience meets the road, characterized by potholes of ethical challenges, leading to a well-established church. Going through the front door is also in keeping with the African adage that says, "If lies journey for twenty years, truth will overtake them in one day." Used with appropriate stories and folklores, this adage facilitates teaching African children the art of ethics, the value of being truthful and trustworthy and virtuous, and the concept that truth will ultimately prevail against lying and deceit, no matter what.

The Lord expects us to organize according to the laws of man so we may be enabled to keep His laws and commandments, so we may be preserved, and so our enemies will not have power over us.[3] In doing this, we are expected to be honest, true, chaste, benevolent, virtuous, and of good report.[4] In other words, in the course of establishing the "international" Church, we cannot afford to be dishonest. The consequences of cutting corners, going through the back door because of expediency, or making the end justify the means portend evil and will negatively influence the work of establishing the Church.

What I have learned in my experience in the course of serving in the Church is that the issues of general interest in all countries involve a range of approvals from governmental and quasi-governmental bodies, which are required to permit the Church and its affiliates to perform the full range of gospel programs incidental to our establishing the Church. For example, some basic approvals include the rights to assemble, to become a legal entity recognized by government, to have self-governance, to declare our beliefs publicly, to worship according to the dictates of our conscience, and to travel freely. Permissions are required to enjoy those rights, such as visas for missionaries, the title documents necessary to own and enjoy assets, zoning approvals and building permits necessary to construct houses of worship, permits to perform marriages, and exoneration from taxes and duties with respect to social and humanitarian services provided by the Church. The front-door policy of the Church has helped in overcoming the challenges that face the Church in the process of establishing itself in Africa.

Beyond legal recognition lies public opinion of the Church in general. This is the summary of how we—the people and the community within which we operate—perceive our church after we have passed through the court of public opinion. This is how the media, business, government, and faith-based organizations and all the other entities see us.

In his address to this conference in 2008,[5] Elder Lance B. Wickman classified being "organized according to the laws of man" into three phases. The first, the registration phase, means that a legal entity constituting "the Church" in the eyes of the government has been organized and registered as required by law. The second phase, credibility, he said, means that the Church must always be defined on the right side of what could be called the "cult line" and is a responsible and pacific organization. The third phase, respectability, the ultimate phase of legal recognition, refers to a broad array of factors measuring the extent to which the institutions and representatives of government have recognized the Church as bona fide.

For example, the fact that the Church was legally registered did not stop the public from wanting to destroy Joseph Smith and the then-young Church. They simply ignored the law.

The goal of the established Church is to bring men unto Christ and ultimately to save them in the kingdom of God. In doing this, the Church is to preach the gospel, to help members perfect themselves in their endeavors to become more Christlike, to carry out the saving ordinances of the gospel by proxy for their kindred dead, and, lastly, to do good to all men through service and humanitarian projects—again according to the laws of man and of God. This goal is sought in various countries having different sociopolitical climates; diverse, often harsh economic conditions; varied but mostly antagonistic religious environments; and difficult-to-change traditional and cultural settings.

In order to succeed in these harsh environments and be more acceptable, the enticement of going through the back door or cutting corners, as expected by corrupt officials; of conforming to increasingly permissive polities; and of obtaining quick results becomes not only real but also almost inevitable. Herein lies the basis of the challenges facing the Church as described hereafter. An African adage is appropriate here to highlight the issues. It says, "The world abhors truth; the heavens forbid lying; yet there is no third option"—meaning you are either truthful and of the Lord or a liar and of the devil.

If I may, I wish to echo two thoughts that President Gordon B. Hinckley called the cornerstone of our responsibility: the Church's overall challenge as it rolls forth in Africa, as in other parts of the world, is to keep the Church doctrinally pure first and morally clean second. This includes keeping the doctrines, principles, and practices of the gospel unaltered and unadulterated by the traditions of humankind. Stated another way, it is to avoid being assimilated into contemporary cultures or to ensure that the traditions of humankind and their corrupt practices are not assimilated into the restored gospel culture, that is, Latter-day Saint culture.

My purpose today is not to embark on the impossible task of identifying all the challenges faced by the Church nor to state all the successes recorded by the Church in every African country, tribe, and culture. I will, however, identify a few of the challenges, and, to keep it simple, I will classify them under various headings—religious, sociocultural, political and governmental, economic, and internal (within the Church itself). I will then provide a few successful examples of how going through the front door, though somewhat difficult and more time consuming, always results in success and consequently always blesses the work and the Church.

THE CHALLENGES

Broadly speaking, the Church in Africa faces ethical challenges arising from difficulties in four major areas: first, in obtaining needed permits and visas and securing duty-free status on customs fees and tariffs on Church curriculum items and humanitarian goods and avoiding excessive property transaction fees; second, in dealing with marriage issues as they affect the family, as well as the lack of recognition for temple marriages; third, in being fully accorded the status of a church by other religious denominations and individuals in the government offices with whom we do business (difficulties may arise from these individuals' personal religious indoctrinations, widespread ignorance, misconceptions that the Church is non-Christian, and the media, whose disposition is to present sensational stories about the Church); and fourth, in navigating the interplay between LDS culture and contemporary African traditions and culture.

The challenges I will mention are not borne out of judging the customs, cultures, or traditions of the African people, which have evolved over thousands of years, but they are a statement of what hinders the teachings of the restored gospel and consequently the establishment of the Church. Similar challenges exist all over the world in various forms or shades. Even the Savior chastised the Jews because their traditions posed similar challenges to His establishment of the Church amongst them. As mentioned earlier, Joseph Smith faced the same challenges borne out of traditions of humankind in the early days of the Church.

I will now proceed to present some of the challenges experienced across African countries.

RELIGIOUS CHALLENGES

Ecumenical

In almost all cases in Africa, there is one or more dominant religious faiths (be it Christian, Islamic, or other) that exerts tremendous influence on the government of each nation. Also, all faith organizations come under ecumenical bodies, or a council of religious bodies that has political power over any faith-based organization not belonging to this body. The ecumenical body may consider the faith-based organization to be nonreligious (a cult), and, consequently, it is difficult to enjoy privileges given to religious bodies, such as missionary allocations, exceptions from taxes, etc. In addition, the ecumenical body may make things difficult for those not belonging to the body, and these other organizations are treated as cults.

Mode of Worship

The manner of worship in the other churches has become the acceptable standard of worship and has embraced local traditions, which to a large extent include drumming, loud singing, clapping of hands, and dancing. The churches also carry out large crusades and conduct all-night services and vigils, among other things. Other orthodox churches and Islamic sects have changed or are changing their modes of worship to fit this mode. In addition, some local customs are permitted in church worship, social events, and activities; hence, in most African countries, the Church, whose mode of worship differs and remains reverent, is seen as somber and boring and is perceived as an organization not friendly to local customs and traditions.

Religious Disposition

Unlike most of the Western world, Africans are very religious. Workers in many offices start their day with prayers, and government institutions often have mosques and chapels built for employees' use. Many state and government agencies use scriptures or religious messages as mottos—for example, Lagos State Waste Management Company (LAWMA), which is a government body, has "Cleanliness is next to Godliness" as its motto. Africans believe in revelations; to them heaven is not closed. Herein lies one of the secrets of the great success of the Church, manifested by its rapid growth, in sub-Saharan Africa; great numbers believe in the First Vision. The challenge this poses is that the people expect all leaders to see visions and to tell members how to conduct their personal daily affairs. Most religious organizations in Africa do this; their leaders are viewed as prophets. But this is not the way of the Church, nor is it the Lord's way. Some members think their local LDS leaders have lost their power and have become fallen prophets when they do not receive this guidance as leaders did in their former churches, and they sometimes wander away to other faiths after baptism for lack of these publicly expressed "visions."

Representation and Continuity

Almost all religious organizations in Africa have an overseer (an ecclesiastical leader) who serves as the face of the organization and who is revered and consulted on matters of religion. There is no one overall face to represent the Church because of its local and geographical organization. This nonconformity has the effect that the Church does not have representation to interact with government and religious organizations, and, hence, we have little or no contributory voice when decisions affecting us are made. We are left to rely on third parties, who know little or nothing about the Church, to represent us. In addition, institutionalized knowledge is lost in the course of characteristic periodic changes of leadership in the Church; thus, relationships have to be formed over and over again.

SOCIAL AND CULTURAL CHALLENGES

Marriages

The good news is that with the exception of one or two countries, the issue of same-sex marriage remains yet a distant worry or challenge to the Church in Africa; a vast majority of Africans still hold the traditional interpretation of marriage as being the union of man and woman. Across Africa, marriage remains a major traditional and cultural event guided by the traditions of the fathers, some of which are not in conformity with the restored gospel.

The major challenges in this area are not always the issue of bride price, or dowry, but largely the mode of marriage celebration, child paternity (patriarchy versus matriarchy), plurality of wives (polygamy is acceptable to major religious sects, including orthodox churches), caste or intertribal restrictions, and divorce issues, to mention a few. Western "family law," which has been introduced in Africa, has accommodated and incorporated polygamy, but this cannot be possible in the restored gospel culture. The expanded mode of celebration caused by the fusion of Western and local culture has become indeed very expensive and competitive, resulting in widespread delayed marriages and cohabitation, among other problems. These challenges have had a negative impact on the extent to which we are successful in establishing the Church across Africa.

Divorce proceedings also pose challenges. Even when a couple marries according to the legal laws of the land, couples wishing to dissolve their marriages often do not dissolve them legally. Most just separate and enter into other relationships and other marriages. The law and most religious organizations often turn a blind eye, and these people freely join with other religious bodies. The Church will not baptize the hundreds who desire baptism if they are not legally and lawfully married or if they are in a polygamous relationship, whereas many other churches will, so we are seen as not favorable to people or friendly to local customs, among other things.

Chastity

The advent of Western civilization and industrialization in Africa has eroded the high standard of morality that once existed among the various tribes. Whereas in the past one became an outcast for having sex outside marriage, it is no longer so. Following the contemporary Western cultures, cohabitation, trial marriages, multiple partners, sexual laxity, and promiscuity, especially in big cities, are now generally accepted by the polity. And many other churches turn a blind eye to these things, but the Church sees these practices as opposed to the teachings of the restored gospel.

Law of Inheritance

The hereditary system in some customs does not generally protect the wife and the children. At the drop of a hat, relatives of the dead husband can disown and dispossess the wife and children of all possessions and housing and throw them into the street. The teachings of the Church run counter to such customs. Even though some other sects allow or have embraced these customs, the Church will not; hence, it is perceived as not friendly to tradition.

Death

Widows face unhealthy practices in some places upon the death of their husbands. These practices are contrary to the teachings of the restored gospel.

Role and Position of Women

In many cultures, traditions have generally looked upon women as inferior and unequal to the men. This is also contrary to the teachings of the restored gospel. Some men will not sit with their wives in meetings, hug or walk with women, or allow women to teach them in classes because these practices are seen as taboo.

POLITICAL AND GOVERNMENTAL CHALLENGES

Political Neutrality

The Church remains neutral in politics and does not promote any political party or make any comment on government affairs in Africa. Sometimes, the government of the day sees us as a foe or may question where our allegiance lies. Or, in rare cases, when we have been seen as being too close to a ruling party and the opposing party comes into power afterward, we often face the wrath of such new political parties. In these circumstances, we may find ourselves between Pharaoh and the Red Sea, so to speak. It has always been helpful that we have continued to educate all comers that we are politically neutral.

Permits

It is often difficult and sometimes impossible to obtain from governmental and quasi-governmental bodies the approvals required by the Church to operate. These include visas for missionaries, title documents for owning and enjoying assets, zoning approvals and building permits to construct houses of worship, exoneration from taxes and duties, and so on. These challenges do not come from communities averse to the Church, as is the case in the Western world, but from corrupt officials who demand gratification, and things are made more difficult because of the perception that the "American" church is rich. Also, some view most churches as big businesses. Most government services cannot be obtained without offering gratification or bribes to the office or officers concerned, and the Church will not bribe nor pay gratification. This means long waits and delays that sometimes run into several years or, in a few cases, canceled projects.

Real Estate Acquisition and Tenancy

Another fundamental challenge arises from the fact that in some countries, property and rental laws are very complicated and thorny, and perfection of documents could be very expensive. In view of this, properties exchange hands without proper documentation, and often a buyer or tenant has to pay more than one person since it is easy to pay the wrong person. The problem with this is that in some cases, land purchases end up with litigations that take years to resolve. Tenancy is also fraught with excessive payments, and tenants are expected to do repairs and maintenance afterward, among other things. It is purely a seller's market.

ECONOMIC CHALLENGES

Due to the failure of governments at almost all levels and their inability to provide their citizenry with the basic necessities of life and enable them to become self-reliant, far too many Africans remain on or below the poverty line, living on less than a dollar a day. Against this backdrop, religious organizations like Catholics, Baptists, Anglican and Pentecostal churches, and a few NGOs have largely taken on the responsibilities to provide medical care for their members in church-owned and operated hospitals, clinics, and health centers;

build institutions (high schools, universities, etc.) that provide educational and vocational training for all their members;

engage the services of their own qualified members in all their professional services;

provide employment to a large number of their members by building bakeries and businesses;

network and employ each other in their personal businesses (hardly would you see such religious sects engage a nonmember to render any form of service to them when its members can provide such services); and

provide transportation for members to their worship meetings.

The Church is establishing itself in these environments. Thousands who are convinced the Church offers the true gospel will not join the Church because they cannot afford to lose all the services offered by other churches. I often receive email and text messages from investigators asking if the Church will provide them with employment, pay their school fees, or provide their Sunday-meeting transportation should they leave their current church and join ours.

Some are confused and wonder why the Church will not add this venture to its mission, due to its potential to alleviate poverty and because offering services is fast becoming the standard expected of a church.

The Church, however, took a high road by providing humanitarian services. Establishment of businesses provides its own myriad of challenges that may further exacerbate the challenges we face, part of which include the infringement of our status as a religious organization.

INTERNAL CHALLENGES

Being first-generation members, local members sometimes face the dilemma of operating the "Wasatch Front" institutions or programs. Therefore, they introduce some of what they know from their former churches. Also, in some cases, when you release a leader, it is seen as an insult and loss of face, and he or she may leave the Church with his or her family; other churches do not release their ecclesiastical leaders. Women are not supposed to teach men (yet in corollary, many question why the Church will not allow female clergy), and boys are not expected to hold the priesthood. In some cultures, husbands and wives will refuse to sit together in meetings, nor will they hold hands in public. Men do not tell their wives they love them. These are but a few of the challenging traditions and customs, and it will take some generations to remove them through gospel teachings.

The growth enjoyed by the Church poses its own form of challenges. If we desire, we may sometimes baptize a whole village, but then we face the challenge of leadership as pertaining to depth of doctrinal understanding and sometimes as pertaining to level of literacy. This is a challenge our church is currently facing in many places in Africa as people join the Church in large numbers. The branches often outgrow the root, and we experience the problem described in Jacob 5 in the Book of Mormon.

Again, while some things may be applied in general terms as the Church rolls forth, a number of issues must be localized in order to have more meaningful, effective, and lasting positive impact upon the lives of the local members and citizens as a whole. In addition, as the Church moves into the nations of the world, it must shed the image of being perceived as an American church or organization. There is need to allow the Spirit of God to be made manifest in the unfolding of this great work as it affects the peoples in each country. People understand things differently, and to the extent that misunderstandings exist, the rolling forth of the Church will be hindered.

THE SUCCESSES

"Going through the front door" sometimes looks like the work is being hindered; success looks elusive, and the smell of failure and disappointment is overwhelming. However, experience has proved that, ultimately, doing so blesses the work beyond what is expected. As people of faith, we recognize the hand of God in this work as we witness impossible situations turn into successes or miracles, great or small. Truly, when we do this work the Lord's way, impossibility becomes possible.

Before highlighting some such success, I would like to publicly thank all missionaries, couples, mission presidents, and Church officials who in no small measure have taught and lived by example in going through the front door to establish the Church in Africa over the years. Some have seen the success, while some merely lay the foundation but do not witness its fruition. Time will not permit me to list their names, neither do I know them all, but the Lord knows them, and I know that they will in nowise lose their reward from the Lord. Again, time will not permit me to record tens of situations in each of the countries from east, west, south, and central Africa in which difficult moments turned out to be blessings. The Lord continues to use them in teaching us that going through the front door—that is, operating according to the laws of man and following the best of ethics—is the only way that we can do His work. Now, I will talk about the successes.

RELIGIOUS SUCCESSES

Ghana Freeze

On 14 June 1989, the Ghana Broadcasting Corporation announced the "freeze" of all Church activities, along with those of about three other churches. All our meetinghouses were locked and placed under guard, and we were prohibited from carrying out any Church activity.

The freeze was instigated by the mainline churches due to their fear of our church's growth. Some of the reasons given for the act were that our Church was building apartheid in Ghana because blacks were not allowed to be in any leadership positions and could not enter some Church buildings, while all efforts were being put in place to end apartheid in South Africa, and, secondly, that the Church was an arm of the American CIA and was floating dollars to recruit followers.

Our Church officials held a series of meetings with government officials to clear all the allegations and show that we are law-abiding people in all our activities. After thorough investigation was extended to the other churches involved, our Church was the only one found to be duly and legally constituted and truthful in all its presentations. On 30 November 1990, after eighteen months, the freeze was lifted and the Church was cleared to continue its programs.

The freeze, though painful, proved to be a blessing in disguise. During the length of the freeze, members continued to meet in homes. Because of publicity, investigators flocked to the Church and, upon discovering the truth, joined the Church in large numbers. Faith increased, the Church was brought out of obscurity in Ghana, and membership grew exponentially. In addition, public opinion became very favorable, and goodwill increased toward our Church—a situation that continues today.

On the contrary, if the Church had in any way broken any law, it would have taken many years to wade through the problem, and the stigma would have still remained. As the Lord has revealed in Doctrine and Covenants 44:5, our enemies could not have power over us because we went through the front door in all we did in establishing the Church.

Namibia

Following a series of interfaith activities and Helping Hands service projects, the Church's friends and popularity grew among other churches and the public. We were subsequently invited to a meeting of an ecumenical body, the Namibia Council of Churches. The leader of the body, as voice, offered that our Church would be granted membership in the body if our missionaries would cease to proselyte. This offer was declined with thanks and explanation.

It was clear that the success and increasing growth of the Church was worrisome to the ecumenical body. Though we have not obtained the various permits we require from the government and its agents, we remain respected and are seen as highly credible.

Nigeria

The city of Jos, situated in the heart of Nigeria, has been in the news for some time now due to the recurring religious crises it has been experiencing. Thousands have been killed as Christians and Muslims of various sects engage in a theater of politically motivated religious strife fueled by tribal differences. The various sects are engaged in a macabre dance of supremacy.

In one such crisis in 2008, an Islamic group came to burn the only Church-owned chapel in town, but another group prevented the action, telling them that our Church is a friendly one which treated the Muslims with respect and honor; therefore, the Church was spared the touch of arsonists. This action was repeated each time the crisis erupted.

However, a year later, the church building was burned. Upon investigation, it was discovered that the arsonists were hired from the neighboring country and our protectors had to flee for their lives. This is a case of bitter success that I thought I should mention. Who knows what blessings lie in the future as a consequence of this event? The revealed word of God in similar circumstances in this dispensation, stated by Joseph Smith, declared that all things shall work together for the good and sanctification of the Church.[6]

South Africa

The first successful attempt by the Church to begin an interfaith outreach in Johannesburg in 2007 saw only three of many invited leaders of other religious organizations accepting our invitation. They were from the Salvation Army, the Methodist Church, and an Islamic sect. The outreach was a big success, and those who were invited took it upon themselves to invite other religious organizations. Today, we have relations with leaders of over twenty other faiths, including the Catholic Church, Dutch Reformed Church, Methodist Church, Salvation Army, some Islamic sects, and so forth.

Some of the successes we have experienced include the invitation to our Church to be part of a coalition of all churches in South Africa to draft a bill of religious rights. We refined, corrected, and resubmitted the bill, and it was accepted in whole. The greatest joy came one afternoon on the grounds of the area office in Johannesburg in October 2007, during the press briefing of the 2007 all-Africa Helping Hands project, when heads of about twenty-five religious organizations put on the "Mormon Helping Hands" vest and one of them said, "This is truly the Church of Jesus Christ." Such an embrace is indeed comforting, and it gladdens the heart.

SOCIAL AND CULTURAL SUCCESSES

Marriages

Following the favorable disposition enjoyed by our Church over the years, the Church has been granted permission to perform civil marriages in many countries in the Africa Southeast Area and in all countries in the Africa West Area except Benin, Togo, and Ivory Coast. This guarantees monogamy and leads to temple marriage. The ability of our Church to perform civil marriages helps to remove in part some problems associated with traditional and customary marriages. We also see this as a necessary step toward securing the recognition of temple marriage in the future. The reason for this non-recognition is that temple marriage cannot be performed in a building accessible to the public, as currently required by law.

The remaining myriad of challenges facing marriage is slowly being taken care of as members become converted to the teachings of the restored gospel and as they go into temple marriage. In truth, the teaching of the word of God has more effect on the souls of children of men than the sword does.

POLITICAL SUCCESSES

Nigeria

In 2003, the government of Nigeria decided to enforce the city ordinance of the Federal Capital Territory, which was being flouted with impunity by the high and mighty, both in government and in business. This enforcement involved the demolition of hundreds of structures built illegally in and around the capital city of Abuja without approval, including those that ignored the zoning policy. Hundreds of houses, office complexes, and hospitals were affected. Lawsuits and appeals to the government, whether overt or covert, failed to dissuade the determination of the government.

The process of demolition continued in phases for years, and on a fateful day in 2006, the demolition team, led by the then-president of Nigeria and the Federal Capital Territory minister, came to Accra Street, a stretch of about three kilometers, where the only two Church-owned buildings (a meetinghouse and an institute building) in the nation's capital of Abuja were situated. All buildings on the street, including over fifty churches and a modern private hospital, were demolished. The president used our Church premises as his field office. Only the Church buildings were left standing because all necessary permits were obtained and all legal requirements were fulfilled before the land was cleared for construction to start.

Today, the whole length of the street has been restored to its original purpose—a public park—and the Church meetinghouse and institute building stand as icons of truth and beauty and a testimony that going through the front door is the only way—the Lord's way.

Ivory Coast

In May 2009, eight missionaries went to the Ivory Coast Abidjan airport, headed for the Accra Ghana Missionary Training Center. When their luggage was scanned, an empty Kalashnikov (AK-47) cartridge case was discovered in the bag of one of the missionaries. Due to heightened national security in the country at the time, the missionary was immediately taken into police custody, and the heads of the airport police department, national police, and Ministry of the Interior were all notified.

Two hours later, a phone call came from the police headquarters asking for the release of the missionary. It seems the police chief recalled the previous fall's all-Africa Mormon Helping Hands service project, which provided cleaning of the Abobo District Police Station, where police operations are headquartered.

One of the staff officers declared, "The Latter-day Saints are the friends of the police in Ivory Coast, for they cleaned our working place and environment last year, which nobody did before them." Some police officers at the airport also attested that they were accustomed to regularly seeing Church members and missionaries travel without incident. The police officers apologized for the trouble they caused and allowed the missionaries to board their flight.

The empty cartridge case was seized after questioning. The missionary admitted he found that cartridge case in the street after the November 2004 unrest, when French troops fired on and killed young demonstrators in Abidjan. He added that he kept it as a souvenir of that event and forgot to leave it before moving from home.

Once again, the good the Church continues to do through public affairs programs has proven to be a blessing in times of need.

GOVERNMENT SUCCESSES

Kenya

In 2008, all efforts to renew residence permits for our couple missionaries proved abortive. The director and deputy involved wanted gratification, and the Church would not comply. All previous attempts to build friendly relationships failed with the director and deputy. Further explanations and communications to show what good the Church had done and continued to do in Kenya made matters worse, and we ended up alienating the two officers who were responsible for the authorization. The Church took the only option left and wrote the minister in charge, explaining the problem and requesting his intervention. He approved the permit for all seventeen couples involved. Those officers who wanted gratification then invited the press and wrote a sensational story about our Church and vilified the minister, who in consequence had to face a ministerial panel of inquiry. It was indeed a gloomy period for our Church, and we were worried for the minister, but we were hopeful that as on previous occasions we would be justified.

The media (press and TV stations) came to the Church in droves, requesting interviews for the Church to state its side. This gave the Church the opportunity to educate people on Church programs. Individuals showed up to investigate the Church, thereby keeping the missionaries busy. A member helped in ensuring that the press published a release detailing the programs of the Church, including a summary of its humanitarian activities in Kenya and around the world. The Church and the minister were vindicated; the two officers' lies earned them a reprimand, and the truth prevailed. The difficulty proved to be a blessing in disguise.

ECONOMIC SUCCESSES

Africa

Unlike other religious organizations, the Church does not establish business entities—such as hospitals, clinics, bakeries, thrift societies, or money-lending concerns—that employ its members, provide education, or provide government services. Instead, the Church provides humanitarian services, helps those in need of education, provides employment services and training, provides clean water by digging hundreds of deep wells, and provides neonatal resuscitation training, vision clinics, health services, and various relief programs, to mention a few (with no strings attached, unlike other organizations).

The Church's humanitarian projects have earned it more respectability, goodwill, friends, and admiration and have empowered more people—members and nonmembers alike. These projects continue to translate into more friendly press and free media coverage, and they also soften the hearts of people. Sometimes they also encourage people to receive the missionaries and to be less critical of the Church. To the extent that the work of establishing the Church continues to be smoother, we often see increased growth.

GENERAL SUCCESSES

Nigeria

In 2006, we received word that one newly constructed Church-owned building in Lagos had been sealed off, and our Church was warned not to come on the property and was told that if we did, we would be seen as trespassers. We later learned the group that did this had won a long and protracted court case to repossess hundreds of acres of land with hundreds of houses on the land. These people singled out the Church for reprisal and punishment.

At the time our Church purchased the land, we discovered the land was not registered in the current owner's name in the land registry, even though he had duly purchased it. The land had also gone through many hands before him. Following lengthy negotiations and at additional cost to the original owners, whose names appeared as possessing the title to the land in the land registry, we made sure all legal and due processes were completed. The land was then duly registered in our Church's name. Those who sealed off our Church building did not know this fact, and they did not care to investigate because it is not normal for people to follow due process in such matters.

When the group discovered their error, they were not only embarrassed; they feared we would draw our pound of flesh. We demanded only the minimal remedy required by the law by way of tendering their apology in writing, stating they were in error and indemnifying us from all the charges levied against us in the court that had granted them the leave to do what they did.

Once again, we were saved because the Church did not cut corners—we went in through the front door. It took nearly two years to complete the initial purchase transaction and required an additional cost to the initial owner. It looked like we would lose a choice piece of land for a future stake center. The Saints were disillusioned, and it appeared the Church was losing. Obeying the law of the land and applying the front-door policy delivered our Church from the loss of its building and investment and saved us from our enemies.

CONCLUSION

In responding to whatever challenges the Church may face, five fundamental principles have been helpful in order to be able to escape the designs of our enemies in their bid to hinder or frustrate the work. They are the following:

> 1. Our behaviors should never be specific to a region or country. When it comes to being disciples of Christ and members of the Church, respectful, consistent behaviors, wherever we are, will most likely engender respect and trust and provide the possibility of influencing societies for good. It may be essential for us to accommodate some appropriate local customs within the community as

far as doing so conforms to gospel laws and we are not required to violate our sacred covenants.

2. Going through the front door is the best and only policy. Applying this policy is often tedious, cumbersome, and sometimes apparently unproductive. However, if those who know and have covenanted to keep the law of God enter a society where it is not the norm to be honest, courteous, and evenhanded, how are we of the covenant ever to be the "salt of the earth" if we succumb to the traditions of mankind? We can make a difference, and the Lord expects us to make a difference.

3. We should always have a soft response to hard situations or roll with the punches. People generally are quick to find fault and to criticize. Some have found it a good practice to speak to all people of all walks of life kindly and with respect and to be patient and kind in the face of antagonism. This may be difficult, as many can attest, but most of the time it has the tendency to disarm the enemy, and when this is done, the tenor of some situations may change dramatically. If, however, the situation demands that we violate our covenants, we should simply walk away from it.

4. We should be proactive. Using the public affairs tools of the Church, we should continually identify the gatekeepers; lawmakers; opinion leaders in government, media, business, the community, and other religious organizations; and national icons, whose actions or inactions may hinder or help the Church. Then we should develop a friendly relationship of trust with them in order for them to understand our true beliefs and behaviors, to the end that they will not have the disposition to harm us but to assist the Church as expedient. Our humanitarian service projects in Africa have also been effective in showing the people that we are true followers of Jesus Christ and have been of help in dispelling rumors and falsity.

5. We should pray and counsel with the Lord for guidance. For Latter-day Saints, prayer and the inspiration of heaven are indispensable as we move within societies where our values may be a

> tremendous blessing to the people. Almost always, the majority of people within the community are thirsting and praying for those who can make a difference and turn the tide for the better in their lives.

Challenges will always arise. It has been so since the beginning. The story of a poor old man helps me in particular to put the challenges in the right perspective. A poor old man lived in a fort on the top of a hill with his son and horse. One day the horse did not return home, and the neighbors came to sympathize with the old man because of his loss. The old man asked how they knew it was a bad thing. A couple of days later, the horse returned with a lot of wild horses, and suddenly the old man had many horses. The neighbors came again to rejoice with him on his good fortune. And the old man asked, "How do you know it is a good thing?" In the process of breaking one of the horses so he could now own and ride it, the old man's son broke his leg. Again, the neighbors came to sympathize with the old man, lamenting again at his bad fortune. The old man asked again, "How do you know it is a bad thing?" War broke out shortly afterward, and all sons were sent to the warfront except of course the old man's son because of his broken leg. His neighbors came to him as usual, congratulating him for his good luck. He replied yet again, "How do you know it is a good thing?" In effect, persecution cannot stop the progress of truth. Every dark cloud has a silver lining; that is, a positive aspect or an unseen benefit.

There is a Chinese saying that states, "May you live in interesting times." We are indeed living in such a time, a time of temple building, a time of the winding up of all things expedient for the salvation of humankind preparatory to the coming of the Savior, a time of working under the direction of and living with living prophets. What a marvelous time to live in—a time, it is said, when the Savior is in a hurry in Africa. It is a time to earn and lay treasure in heaven by doing our very best in obedience to the Lord's commandments, being anxiously engaged in good causes and thereby bringing to pass much righteousness.

Indeed, as the Prophet Joseph Smith declared, "The Standard of Truth has been erected; no unhallowed hand can stop the work from progressing; persecutions may rage, mobs may combine, armies may assemble, calumny may defame, but the truth of God will go forth boldly, nobly, and independent, till it has penetrated every continent, visited every clime, swept every country, and sounded in every ear, till the purposes of God shall be accomplished, and the Great Jehovah shall say the work is done."[7]

In the final analysis, while dealing with challenges, our basic premise is that as Latter-day Saints we should act as the covenant people of the Lord, remembering that we are agents of the Lord, that the Lord is our leader, and that we have to do what he wants. If we do this, our enemies will not have power over us.

NOTES

1. Joseph Smith, quoted by Wilford Woodruff, in Conference Report, April 1898, 57.
2. See 2 Timothy 3:1.
3. See Doctrine and Covenants 44:4–5.
4. See Articles of Faith 1:13.
5. See chapter 5 in this volume: Elder Lance B. Wickman, "The Church in the Twenty-First Century: Public Perceptions and the 'Man with the Stamp,'" 33–49.
6. See Doctrine and Covenants 100:15; 105:40; 122:7.
7. *Teachings of the Presidents of the Church: Joseph Smith* (Salt Lake City: The Church of Jesus Christ of Latter-day Saints, 2007), 142.

Each of us must take interest in the establishment of the Church throughout the world. (Madrid Spain Temple. (Courtesy of Intellectual Reserve, Inc.)

21

CHALLENGES, OPPORTUNITIES, AND THE INTERNATIONAL CHURCH

ELDER DENNIS B. NEUENSCHWANDER

Elder Dennis B. Neuenschwander, then an emeritus member of the First Quorum of the Seventy of The Church of Jesus Christ of Latter-day Saints, presented this essay at "Challenges in Establishing the International Church," the International Society's twenty-first annual conference, April 2010, Brigham Young University, Provo, Utah.

I must say, whenever I hear the phrase "going through the front door" or some variation of it in connection with the expansion of the Church, I ask myself why the Lord or His Church would ever go through any other than the front door. Be that as it may, I hope that my remarks and observations will complement the overall discussion of the conference relating to the ethical, legal, and political challenges that confront you who are working so diligently to establish the Church in the international arena.

There is no expert quite so qualified to speak on a topic as the one who no longer has any responsibility for it. As I no longer have any responsibility for Church matters in Europe—or anywhere else for that matter—I qualify as such an expert. I hope you will forgive me if I forbear speaking of the current challenges in Europe; there are many here much more qualified and current than I to address them. However, I would like to direct some remarks to the first part of my assignment and speak of some fundamental principles that define what "going through the front door" means to me. I base my comments on the assignments I enjoyed for over a quarter of a century working with a front-door policy in helping to establish the Church in Eastern Europe. These principles guided me to the very end of my active service as a General Authority. As you consider them in light of your current responsibilities, and in the context of the conditions in which you must currently work, I hope you can benefit from them. I would like to speak about each of these principles, illustrating them with personal stories and examples.

I begin by identifying five fundamental principles I have found central to the process of expanding and establishing the Church: (1) represent the Church with integrity, (2) respect and keep the laws of the land, (3) work with government officials who have responsibility for religious matters, (4) work to the limit that conditions and situations permit, and (5) use local leaders and members of the Church as fully as possible.

REPRESENT THE CHURCH WITH INTEGRITY

The reputation of the Church is created and shaped by the behavior of those who belong to it or represent it in some official capacity. The gospel itself is synonymous with integrity—so must be its representatives. We are morally bound to act in accordance with the principles we espouse. Each of us must certainly know that a dishonest act can never lead to an honorable end, no matter how important or inevitable that end might be.

There are no shortcuts leading to the front door of establishing the Church. The road we must follow is the one Jacob describes: "Remember that his paths are righteous. Behold, the way for man is narrow, but it lieth in a straight course before him."[1]

President Kimball dedicated Poland in August 1977. Part of the agreement that allowed limited Church activity required a local presidency that would be responsible for the actions of the Church. The only three holders of the Melchizedek Priesthood in Poland at the time formed this presidency. Brother Borszczow, who lived in the western Polish city of Poznan, was a counselor in this presidency. Each time I was in Poznam to work with our microfilming project, I met with him and in one of our meetings he presented me with a question. He was righteously anxious to establish the Church, even though there were just a small handful of members in the entire country. "Do you know," he asked, "what we need in order to establish the Church?" I answered in the negative and asked his opinion. "We must understand the system," was his reply.

This was a logical approach at that time. In the late seventies, the Communist Party was still very much in power. One made his way in such a society on the basis of connection, barter, manipulation, and "understanding the system." I felt discomfort with his comment but didn't know exactly how to respond to it. After a moment, I was given an idea that helped me beyond measure in years to come. "Brother Borszczow," I said, "what the Church needs in Poland are not men who understand the system but men who understand the priesthood." As it turned out, this was a very wise answer that came as a stroke of inspiration, and I certainly take no credit for it. Within a few short years, the system collapsed. There was nothing left to "understand." Where would the Church then have been in Poland if it had been established on such an unstable foundation, even if at the time that foundation appeared indestructible? If individuals must build their own foundation on the rock of Christ to avoid misery, as Helaman taught,[2] then it only follows that the Church must be established on the same foundation.

A corollary to following the path that places the Church on a sure foundation is the knowledge that we cannot establish that path by diverging from it. After the collapse of the Soviet Union, negotiations began for Church recognition in Latvia. Our attorneys conducted time-consuming and frustrating negotiations in what seemed an endless search for registration. As it turned out, the director of religious affairs was on the verge of retirement and promised recognition if we were to give him five hundred dollars under the table. For the Church, this was not a tremendous amount of money; however, for him it was a fortune—certainly sufficient for a nice little retirement nest egg at the time. As much as we desired the recognition, we declined the offer. It was a long time before the Church finally gained official recognition in Latvia. Of course, it is well established there now, but I have often wondered how much that five hundred dollars would have cost the Church in its integrity and reputation had we accepted it. Fortunately, we never had to find out.

I know very well the desire to see that important things are done "on my watch." This can easily lead to impatience. In *The Brothers Karamazov*, Dostoevsky gives a fictional account of the Grand Inquisitor's confrontation with Christ. At least twice, the inquisitor tells Christ, "We have corrected Thy work."[3] We can never put ourselves in the position of the inquisitor. We can neither correct nor improve upon Christ's work. On the other hand, when our timetable coincides with the Lord's timetable, patience becomes our ally. Time really is on our side. After the first missionaries were introduced into Kyiv, we ran into all kinds of difficulties with their visas and their presence in Ukraine. The relationship with the government was strained, at best. From day to day, sometimes from hour to hour, I did not know whether or not the missionaries would be permitted to stay in Ukraine. The pressure was immense, and, quite frankly, I worried about myself. I was concerned that I would "lose" our opportunity in Ukraine before it ever got started and that "my watch" would be remembered as such.

Elder Dallin H. Oaks came to our area for a mission presidents' seminar and consented to visit with me early one morning about the situation in Ukraine. I began a description of the challenges and problems. It was immediately clear that he was not nearly as concerned as I was. After a few moments, I slowed down. Elder Oaks looked at me and gave me perhaps the best advice I ever received about establishing the Church: "This is the Lord's work; why don't you let Him do a little of it?" I did, and matters have worked out pretty well over the last twenty years in Ukraine.

Here are three ideas concerning establishing the Church with integrity: (1) there are no shortcuts; (2) don't diverge from the path in an effort to establish it; and (3) work with patience, try to stay in harmony with the Lord's timetable, and permit Him to do a little of His own work.

RESPECT AND KEEP THE LAWS OF THE LAND

The Lord set the pattern of respecting and keeping the laws of the land when He revealed, "Let no man break the laws of the land, for he that keepeth the laws of God hath no need to break the laws of the land."[4] Even though the Church is to "stand independent above all other creatures,"[5] it still must work within the context of law, respect for the society in which it operates, and fidelity to the principles that distinguish it as a religious society. Neither representatives of the Church nor its members can flout the law and hope to be known as peacemakers or be considered as a valuable, influential, and respected member of society.

I speak of respect in the sense of "obey" or "comply," but I also suggest that respect for law and the rule of law calls for contributing to its development and improvement. Many countries, including the US, are currently considering legislative enactments or interpretations relating to the relationship between church and state. Countries that are now emerging from long years wherein law, educational curricula, economic policy, and social tradition existed to support a single party, dogma, or system, must now deal with diversity, religious freedom, and matters of individual conscience.

In addition, the weakening or outright disappearance of political borders, resulting in a significant migration of people who bring their religious and cultural heritage with them; the expanding global economy, with all of its tangential requirements; and increasing access to online information create a rich opportunity for us to be an influence for good in a cauldron of development and change. It is essential for the establishment of the Church across the world that its representatives participate in defining the issues and framing the laws that affect them. When the definitive history of Eastern Europe is written, some of its most critical chapters will be devoted to the work of the International Center for Law and Religious Studies, located in the BYU Law School. Cole Durham and his colleagues have made a contribution that very few recognize and, in my view, have framed the debate on critical issues that have direct bearing on the establishment of our Church and others, especially in the so-called emerging or developing areas. Their work has touched on the well-being and security of people who look to faith as the basis of their lives. The contribution made by their worldwide symposia and its annual conference each fall can hardly be measured. The creation of a forum in which people of goodwill may discuss and learn of such important issues is its greatest achievement. The center has, in a very real way, created the context in which ecclesiastical leaders may do their work.

What I have said thus far works well over time, but what of an opportunity that requires immediate or quick action? Speaking of Eastern Europe, the political and social changes of the eighties and nineties occurred so rapidly that laws defining or permitting Church activity lagged far behind the reality of the situation. In order to take advantage of such immediate situations, we must rely wholly on principle. Those who work to establish the Church have good access to the Holy Ghost. His guidance is like an inner gyroscope of good judgment. It has always been my advice to our attorneys and to others that in the absence of clearly defined law, we must follow the moral and ethical standards given to us in the gospel itself. I felt that if we would do so, with respect and with the knowledge of the right people, we would be all right when the laws finally do catch up to us. To my knowledge, this has always been the case.

Here are three ideas concerning respect for the law: (1) obey it, (2) participate as fully as possible in the drafting of laws relative to the establishment of religion and individual conscience, and (3) use good judgment and rely on the inner gyroscope provided by the Holy Ghost and gospel principles themselves.

WORK WITH GOVERNMENT OFFICIALS WHO HAVE RESPONSIBILITY FOR RELIGIOUS MATTERS

The Church cannot be established in a religious, social, or political vacuum. Many countries, not unlike those in Central and Eastern Europe, have offices and governmental appointments that look after matters relating to religious activity. Countries that do not have a tradition of religious freedom or laws that are conducive to religious activity are naturally suspicious and wary of religions, particularly foreign ones. I cannot emphasize enough the importance of building bridges and relationships with these officials and departments.

I am grateful I learned very early in my assignments in Eastern Europe to build relations with those who had political and legal influence on the course of Church development in any given country. Building such relationships was not always easy, pleasant, or fast, but it always paid great dividends. These relationships provide opportunities for the gatekeepers and opinion makers to know us, to learn not to fear us, and at times to (begrudgingly) respect us. During the initial years of the Church in Bulgaria, I tried to meet regularly with the director of religious affairs. He was a well-educated and fair man, but he was also suspicious and cautious. I often felt he met with me only because it was his job. Nonetheless, I persisted, and, through time, we built a cordial relationship. In one of our meetings, he candidly said that he liked meeting with "the Mormons." He remarked that we never brought him problems and spoke only of solutions. He compared us favorably to other groups who were always badgering him for favors and intervention. He also told me he appreciated that we never spoke evil of other religions. His comment opened a wonderfully receptive opportunity to discuss the Church and the principles it espouses. It allayed his fears that the Church would somehow be a disruptive problem for his office and brought us latitude in our activities.

Good relations with the government offices permitted us to solve problems that otherwise would have turned detrimental and may have had disastrous consequences. In the developing missions of Russia, we tried to build our missionary force slowly. However, as sometimes happens, the missionaries arrived much too quickly for the comfort of other churches. One such example occurred in Novosibirsk. There, the other churches complained to the director of religious affairs, who called me into his office. In preparation for this meeting, the Area Presidency and mission president had determined that twenty-six missionaries in that city of somewhat over a million inhabitants were about the right number. During the meeting, the director asked that we limit the missionaries to twenty-six, saying that such a move would bring some peace to his office. The problem was easily defused as we worked out a schedule to reduce the number of missionaries to the suggested complement.

Building solid relations and bridges takes time and persistent effort. Progress may not always be immediately obvious. The director of religious affairs in Armenia asked us to be conservative in our work, thus permitting the Armenian Church time to right itself after long years of suppression. This seemed a reasonable request. We respected his direction. It built good relations, provided the Church some protection and privilege, and, in the long run, did not harm the establishment of the Church at all.

Regarding the building of bridges, I cannot speak highly enough of the significant work the public affairs staff accomplished in Eastern Europe. In this connection, President Packer has recommended each area establish a government relations council. This council may include the Area Presidency, the director for temporal affairs, legal counsel, and representatives from public affairs, Church education, and family history. These men and women work directly with the challenges of the legal establishment of the Church.

They are the decision makers and problem solvers, particularly in newly developing areas. In Eastern Europe, I found open, frank, and candid discussions in such a council may anticipate and resolve many problems before they seriously jeopardize the expansion and establishment of the Church.

Humanitarian work also fulfills a very important role in the development of Church visibility and reputation. Humanitarian projects bring the Church into close contact with governmental offices and officials and provide invaluable opportunity to establish a positive and lasting reputation for the Church.

Here are my suggestions for productive work with local and general governments: (1) identify and build relations with individuals and offices that are responsible for or influence religious activity in a given jurisdiction, (2) be willing to work with patience in a cooperative and respectful manner, and (3) use the internal resources of the Church effectively.

WORK TO THE LIMITS THAT CONDITIONS AND SITUATIONS PERMIT

Even though the Lord has revealed that His word will extend to the ends of the earth and to each individual in it, there are still mortal challenges and limitations that must be addressed. I would like to say a word about limitations, both external and sometimes internal to the Church.

Unfavorable local conditions and situations can and do affect the process of establishing the Church. There are times when we have no other option than to understand them, do what we can to change them, and then be patient in accommodating our work to them. The Austria Vienna East Mission was charged in 1987 with taking the gospel into the countries of Central and Eastern Europe. The political openness of those years and the unbounded curiosity of the people toward spiritual values and Western ideas were a huge advantage in the initial stages of establishing a Church presence. On the other hand, the political, economic, and legal structures were simply not equipped to cope with the kind of missionary activity we have come to expect in the Church. There was also the matter of social convention that greatly limited door-to-door contacting or open conversations on the street. The mission was simply forced to recognize many kinds of external limitations in the accomplishment of its objective.

One of the fundamental rules I had set for the mission was that we would work to the full extent that the law would permit. The missionaries soon discovered that even with imposed limitations, they could do far more than they initially thought possible. Even more surprising, at least to me, was that when we reached and gently touched the limits, they quite often—though not always—expanded to meet our needs.

Limitations internal to the Church include lack of materials in local languages, lack of adequate training of missionaries to serve in areas where external limitations may be quite severe, and a sophisticated Church administrative structure. Some of the most difficult limitations are the ones we, often unwittingly, impose on ourselves through unrealistic expectations. We expect a certain and familiar pattern in the establishment of the Church. When we are restricted in establishing that pattern, we feel we are not establishing the Church. For example, we think missionaries should be allowed to do what missionaries do. If reality does not reflect our expectations, we may feel we are not making progress or the Church is not being established. However, if we focus on limitation to the exclusion of all else, we miss opportunity. In reality, establishing a Church presence is very much a matter of attitude on the part of those who are charged with this responsibility. We may lament the imposition of limitations where we are struggling to establish the Church, which may result in frustration and disappointment, or we may focus on what we are permitted to do and pursue it with full purpose and energy.

Belarus is a good example in this discussion of limitations. The Church has been present in Belarus for almost twenty years. Though the government permits the presence of missionaries, it does not permit them to proselyte openly or to initiate gospel conversations. They cannot serve in branch leadership positions or teach or speak in Church meetings. They may perform some limited humanitarian service, but the overall missionary experience in Belarus certainly differs from the traditional expectation of missionary work. But that difference does not mean their work is any less important. The Church is doing quite well in Belarus—even under very stringent limitations. Should we give up simply because we don't have the same latitude we may have elsewhere or because the pattern differs from the expected norm? The answer is "No." We must learn to focus on what we can do and let the limits expand as they will in the course of time.

Closely connected with recognizing limitations and working within them is the idea that we don't need to have everything in order to have something. I have come to the conclusion that if any part of the Church is present in a given place, the Church is there. The establishment of the Church is a process that continues to unfold as time progresses. It is not an end station. The work is never done until the Savior says it is. No single event or piece of the Church may be identified as the one piece that confirms the Church is "established." The Church, even in its most mature expression, continues to change, develop, and grow according to the circumstances that surround it. Perhaps this is why we call it a living Church or why we believe that God has not yet revealed everything. Consequently, just because one area of the world does not have quite as much Church as another area, it does not mean the Church is any less present or established. The Church—not unlike our testimonies, faith, and knowledge—is built "line upon line, precept upon precept, here a little and there a little."[6]

Simply put, we must at times be content with less than we desire in order to attain in time our plans. I worked for many years with the Czech national archivist, Dr. Sykora. The Church had been successful in filming genealogical sources in almost all the countries of Central Europe, including Slovakia, but not in the Czech portion. On one occasion, Dr. Sykora offered to produce and make available to us some fifty rolls of film each year. I turned him down, saying that it was not much and we wanted more. He asked how long we had been talking about filming, and I told him, "Four or five years." He smiled and asked me how many films we had in our collection from Prague; I then realized that fifty rolls per year were fifty more than we had previously been receiving. If I had been satisfied with fifty per year over a five-year period, we would have already collected 250 rolls of film. I failed to realize fifty was the place to begin. An agreement for fifty rolls would have brought me back to the archives more often, because we would have had something productive to speak about; it would have opened doors of cooperation that were otherwise closed. In retrospect, I think we could have increased that amount each year. But no, I wanted everything. And in wanting everything, I had received nothing.

These lessons of patience, limitations, and small steps may easily be applied to the Middle East. In fall 1987, Egypt was assigned to the Austria Vienna East Mission. I soon was told that the registration of the Church in Egypt was imminent. Much good work had been done, and we had every indication we were making good headway. In 2008, twenty-one years later, I was assigned to what is known as the Middle East/North Africa desk, an assignment that brought me back in touch with the Middle East. Imagine my delight when I heard registration in Egypt was imminent. As of today, it is still imminent. Does this mean no progress had been made in twenty-one years? No, of course not! Missionary couples and members of the Church have done much good; we are still there and still doing significant work. Does the fact that we can't do everything we wish, even over a long period of time, mean we shouldn't do what we can? We must take satisfaction in the small steps or interim successes that come our way.

Please remember that though limitations are inevitable in establishing the Church, they don't mean we are powerless to act or we are not making progress. Focus on what you can do and be content with some things so that in time you may have all things and be happy for small steps and interim successes.

USE LOCAL LEADERS AND MEMBERS OF THE CHURCH AS FULLY AS POSSIBLE

One of the most frequently voiced criticisms from government leaders in Eastern Europe was that ours is an American church. As it was primarily the Americans they saw in their offices, I can see why they came to such a conclusion. The only way to put a local face to the Church is to use local faces. Let us never underestimate the conviction, abilities, courage, faith, and desire of our local members, even if they have been a short time in the Church. The long-term value of their participation may hardly be overemphasized. The Church is best established when local leaders and members carry their share of the responsibility. We may know the Church culture, policies, and procedures better than they, but they know the intricacies of their own culture into which the Church must fit.

Necessity taught me the importance of engaging local leaders and members in the process of establishing the Church. Obtaining recognition in Ukraine was very difficult. The government officials did not want to negotiate with an American. Using a local member was really the only option. Consequently, we created a council in Ukraine. Its members consisted of the presidency of the Ukraine Association of the Church, the two mission presidents, legal counsel, and the Area President. The purpose of our monthly meetings was to discuss the challenges, chart a course of action, and then give instruction to Alexander Manzhos, the association president, prior to sending him off to visit with government officers. Once I conquered my ego and recognized that my presence in the eyes of the government was not nearly as important as was Alexander's, the Church moved ahead just fine.

The participation of local leaders and members in Church recognition is important for the members themselves. Their personal engagement permits them to learn. For example, Elder Manzhos has served as a mission president and now as an Area Seventy. His intimate participation in solving the challenges and problems that faced us years ago played a very important role in his administrative education and increased monumentally his ability to serve.

Member participation does not come without cost to them. But it is a cost that every Latter-day Saint must, sooner or later, be willing to pay. When we were gathering signatures from the few Church members in Romania for the submission of required petitions to the government, I met with each individual member to explain the process and, as best I could, the danger they might face. After I had done so with one dear older sister, a very recent convert to the Church, she looked at me and said, "But this is my Church too." I have never forgotten her words or the rebuke that came with them. This dear sister taught me I could not hand the gospel or the Church to the members like some gift-wrapped package for them to enjoy at no cost to themselves. Not only did they want to be part of the process, they needed to be part of it.

The long-term well-being of the Church will always be in the hands of local leaders and members. I share with you two accounts of wonderful, courageous, and faithful local leaders who fulfilled exceptional roles in establishing the Church in their respective countries. Without them, I think the Church would not be what, or where, it is today. The Church was introduced into Vyborg, Russia, very early in its expansion into the Soviet

Union. Andrey Semyonov was among the first converts. He soon became the president of the local religious association and eventually the district president. The first chapel in Russia was built in Vyborg. President Semyonov faced intense and vicious personal opposition through the whole process of finding a site and constructing the chapel. Nonetheless, he faced his difficulties with courage and in good spirit. Elder Dallin H. Oaks and I visited the site while the chapel was under construction. In passing, he told me he would like to have me dedicate the building, but the closer the dedication crept, the more uncomfortable I became. I finally called Elder Oaks and asked him whether someone other than the presiding officer could pronounce the dedicatory prayer. He said that no one had ever asked the question and wanted to know why I had. I told him that after all the trouble President Semyonov had faced, he, not a foreigner, should dedicate the building. Permission was given. He wrote the beautiful prayer of dedication and pronounced it flawlessly. I can still see President Semyonov in front of the people, some of whom had been his most vicious detractors, exercising his priesthood with equanimity and confidence. Personally, I am forever grateful that the first Church building in Russia was dedicated by a Russian.

I would now like to tell you of Ivan Valek, district president in Zagreb, Yugoslavia. Without his courage and spiritual sensitivity, I think the Church would have been delayed significantly in its registration in Slovenia. He had come to Ljubjana from Zagreb to meet with the minister of religious affairs, who was in the process of leaving his position on the day President Valek called on him. He was packing up his office, and President Valek's request for registration was flatly denied. This man had previously threatened to have President Valek thrown in jail or exiled or to have his business confiscated. President Valek came out of that meeting very distressed and downtrodden. He walked with the missionaries some distance, then stopped and asked them whether he should return to the office. They told him to follow the Spirit; twice more he stopped to ask them the same question. Finally, he said he must return—an act of great courage in the face of terrible threats from one who could see them through. President Valek reported that when he returned to the office, he bore a strong testimony and asked that the Church be recognized. The man pondered for some time, took out a piece of paper, and prepared an official document granting the Church its registration. I assume that at some point the Church would have been registered, but President Valek's courage and spiritual sensitivity moved the process forward very rapidly.

What, then, is my counsel to you regarding local members and leaders? Counsel with them, teach them, and trust them. They are capable and courageous. They have testimonies and are willing servants in difficult circumstances. Their engagement in the process of establishing the Church is not only vital to the long-term well-being of the Church but to them personally.

CONCLUSION

By way of review, I commend to you five fundamental principles in establishing the Church: (1) represent the Church with integrity, (2) respect and keep the laws of the land, (3) work with government officials who have responsibility for religious matters, (4) work to the limit that conditions and situations permit, and (5) use local leaders and members of the Church as fully as possible.

Each of us must take interest in the establishment of the Church throughout the world. Please be assured that your prayers and good work make a significant contribution to that end. You are engaged in the most important work any person can do. Do it well, learn from it, and love it! I express my testimony of the divinity of Jesus Christ, of His Atonement, and of the veracity of His words.

NOTES

1. 2 Nephi 9:41.
2. See Helaman 5:12.
3. Fyodor Dostoevsky, *The Brothers Karamazov* (New York: Farrar, Straus, and Giroux, 2002), 237–40.
4. Doctrine and Covenants 58:21.
5. Doctrine and Covenants 78:14.
6. 2 Nephi 28:30.

Appendix 1

"WHEN THE WORLD WILL BE CONVERTED"

SPENCER W. KIMBALL

From an address delivered at a Regional Representatives Seminar on Thursday, 4 April 1974. (Published as Spencer W. Kimball, "'When the World Will Be Converted,'" *Ensign*, October 1974, 3–14.)

My beloved brethren and sisters, this is a momentous time. I am sure that you know how weak I feel in this place that Brother Lee had filled so admirably. No one expected what has happened less than I. I felt absolutely certain that I would die, when my time came, as president of the Twelve. I had no idea that this could ever happen. But since it has happened there is only one thing for us to do and that is to move forward and this is our purpose today.

I said at President Lee's funeral that no one had prayed harder than Sister Kimball and I for his restoration when he was ill and for his continuation while he was well. He was such an admirable leader, and so I approach this new responsibility with fear and trembling.

Now, all of you have much to do with the missionary work of the Church in stakes or missions. May I now discuss with you some of the things which have been uppermost in my mind.

Every area of the Church must properly feel that its work is of greatest value, but let me quote the Lord in a revelation to the Prophet Joseph Smith:

"And if it so be that you should labor all your days in crying repentance unto this people, and bring, save it be one soul unto me, how great shall be your joy with him in the kingdom of my Father!" (D&C 18:15.)

If there were no converts, the Church would shrivel and die on the vine. But perhaps the greatest reason for missionary work is to give the world its chance to hear and accept the gospel. The scriptures are replete with commands and promises and calls and rewards for teaching the gospel. I use the word *command* deliberately for it seems to be an insistent directive from which we, singly and collectively, cannot escape.

I ask you, what did he mean when the Lord took his Twelve Apostles to the top of the Mount of Olives and said:

". . . And ye shall be witnesses unto me both in Jerusalem, and in all Judea, and in Samaria, and unto the uttermost part of the earth." (Acts 1:8.)

These were his last words on earth before he went to his heavenly home.

What is the significance of the phrase "uttermost part of the earth"? He had already covered the area known to the apostles. Was it the people in Judea? Or those in Samaria? Or the few millions in the Near East? Where were the "uttermost parts of the earth"? Did he mean the millions in what is now America? Did he include the hundreds of thousands, or even millions, in Greece, Italy, around the Mediterranean, the inhabitants of central Europe? What did he mean? Or did he mean all the living people of all the world and those spirits assigned to this world to come in centuries ahead? Have we underestimated his language or its meaning? How can we be satisfied with 100,000 converts out of nearly four billion people in the world who need the gospel?

After his crucifixion the eleven apostles assembled on a mountain in Galilee and the Savior came to them and said:

". . . All power is given unto me in heaven and in earth.

"Go ye therefore, and teach all nations, baptizing them in the name of the Father, and of the Son, and of the Holy Ghost:"

(He said "all nations.")

"Teaching them to observe all things whatsoever I have commanded you: and, lo, I am with you alway, even unto the end of the world. Amen." (Matt. 28:18–20.)

Again the word *power* and the word *command* and the promise of continual support.

In 1830 when the Lord sent Parley P. Pratt, Oliver Cowdery, Peter Whitmer, and Ziba Peterson to the Lamanites he added:

". . . I myself will go with them and be in their midst; and I am their advocate with the Father, and nothing shall prevail against them." (D&C 32:3.)

Did he mean all the nations then extant? And then he said,

". . . And, lo, I am with you alway, even unto the end of the world. . . ." (Matt. 28:20.)

Do you think he included all the nations that would be organized up until that time? And as he commanded them to go forth, do you think he wondered if it could be done? He reassured us. He had the power. He said, "All power is given me in heaven and in earth . . . and I am with you alway."

Again as Mark records the events after the resurrection, he upbraided those who had some doubts about his resurrection; then commanded them:

". . . Go ye into all the world, and preach the gospel to every creature." (Mark 16:15.)

And this was just before the ascension. Do you think he meant Egypt and Palestine and Greece? Do you think he included the world of 33 AD or the world of 1970, 1980, 1990? What was included in his phrase "all the world" and what did he mean by "every creature"?

And Luke records the event—

". . . That repentance and remission of sins should be preached . . . among all nations, beginning at Jerusalem." (Luke 24:47.)

Again, his last command. Surely there is significance in these words! There was a universal need and there must be universal coverage.

As I remember the world as Moses saw it—it was a big world.

". . . And Moses beheld the world and the ends thereof, and all the children of men which are, and which were created. . . ." (Moses 1:8.)

I am constrained to believe that at that time the Lord knew the bounds of the habitations of man and the areas that would be settled and already knew his people who would possess this world.

Still impressing Moses with the magnitude of his works and glory, the Lord showed him more.

". . . Moses cast his eyes and beheld the earth, yea, even all of it; and there was not a particle of it which he did not behold, discerning it by the spirit of God.

". . . And their numbers were great, even numberless as the sand upon the sea shore.

"And he beheld many lands; and each land was called earth, and there were inhabitants on the face thereof." (Moses 1:27–29.)

Remember also that Enoch, the prophet, beheld the spirits that God had created. (See Moses 6:36.) These prophets visualized the numerous spirits and all the creations. It seems to me that the Lord chose his words when he said "every nation," "every land," "uttermost bounds of the earth," "every tongue," "every people," "every soul," "all the world," "many lands."

Surely there is significance in these words!

Certainly his sheep were not limited to the thousands about him and with whom he rubbed shoulders each day. A universal family! A universal command!

My brethren, I wonder if we are doing all we can. Are we complacent in our approach to teaching all the world? We have been proselyting now 144 years. Are we prepared to lengthen our stride? To enlarge our vision?

Remember, our ally is our God. He is our commander. He made the plans. He gave the commandment. Remember what we have quoted thousands of times as told by Nephi:

"And it came to pass that I, Nephi, said unto my father: I will go and do the things which the Lord hath commanded, for I know that the Lord giveth no commandments unto the children of men, save he shall prepare a way for them that they may accomplish the thing which he commandeth them." (1 Ne. 3:7.)

And as I read the scripture I think of the numerous nations that are still untouched. I know they have curtains, like iron curtains and bamboo curtains. I know how difficult it is because we have made some efforts. Surely the Lord knew what he was doing when he commanded. And like Nephi we can say:

"For the fulness of mine intent is that I may persuade men to come unto the God of Abraham, and the God of Isaac, and the God of Jacob, and be saved." (1 Ne. 6:4.)

And certainly the command to the original apostles of this dispensation followed the command of the others of earlier years, and you Twelve have that same command.

The 112th section of the Doctrine and Covenants was addressed to Thomas B. Marsh, the President of the Twelve in 1837, and concerns the Twelve Apostles. The keys of the kingdom were given to the Presidency and the Twelve. Apparently President Marsh had been praying for his brethren and the Lord listened:

". . . Thine alms have come up as a memorial before me, in behalf of those, thy brethren, who were chosen to bear testimony of my name and to send it abroad among all nations, kindreds, tongues, and people. . . ." (D&C 112:1.)

Further:

". . . Thou shalt bear record of my name, not only unto the Gentiles, but also unto the Jews; and thou shalt send forth my word unto the ends of the earth." (D&C 112:4.)

He was commanded:

". . . Let not the inhabitants of the earth slumber, because of thy speech.

". . . Thy path lieth among the mountains, and among many nations." (D&C 112:5, 7.)

You, the Twelve, today inherited that command.

My brethren, why did the Lord continue to repeat and repeat these phrases if he did not have meaning for them? To President Thomas B. Marsh, and to you, the Twelve, the Lord said:

". . . I have chosen [you] to hold the keys of my kingdom . . . abroad among all nations—

"That thou mayest be my servant to unlock the door of the kingdom in all places. . . ." (D&C 112:16–17.)

I introduced to you Brother David Kennedy. I have a vision that probably Brother Kennedy and others may assist the Twelve in finding the keys that have apparently been lost to many nations wherein we can open those worlds.

As to Brother Marsh, the promise came to you and me regarding the opening of the doors:

"Wherefore, whithersoever they shall send you, go ye, and I will be with you; and in whatsoever place ye shall proclaim my name an effectual door shall be opened unto you. . . ." (D&C 112:19.)

When I read Church history, I am amazed at the boldness of the early brethren as they went out into the world. They seemed to find a way. Even in persecution and hardship, they went and opened doors which evidently have been allowed to sag on their hinges and many of them to close. I remember that these fearless men were teaching the gospel in Indian lands before the Church was even fully organized. As nearly as 1837 the Twelve were in England fighting Satan, in Tahiti in 1844, Australia in 1851, Iceland 1853, Italy 1850, and also in Switzerland, Germany, Tonga, Turkey, Mexico, Japan, Czechoslovakia, China, Samoa, New Zealand, South America, France, and Hawaii in 1850. When you look at the progress we have made in some countries, with no progress in many of their nearby countries, it makes us wonder. Much of this early proselyting was done while the leaders were climbing the Rockies and planting the sod and starting their homes. It is faith and super faith.

These men of valor began to walk the earth with dignity and honor, with mantles on their shoulders and keys in their hands and love in their hearts.

To the Twelve the Lord said,

"You have a work to do that no other men can do. . . . There will be times when nothing but the angels of God can deliver you out of their hands. . . ." (*History of the Church*, vol. 2, p. 178.)

Now let me speak of the expansion which I think is necessary and, may I add, which I think is possible. The Lord said again:

". . . All power is given unto me in heaven and in earth." (Matt. 28:18.)

The Lord gave to Thomas B. Marsh and Joseph and Sidney and Hyrum power "to hold the keys" of the kingdom and that they would be the servants who could "unlock the door of the kingdom." (See D&C 112:16–17.)

To those intrepid leaders the command came:

". . . And in whatsoever place ye shall proclaim my name an effectual door shall be opened unto you, that they may receive my word." (D&C 112:19.)

The Twelve have the keys and those they send have the command to open doors. Today we are blessed with many strong, trained men, in government, in foreign service, and with much prestige and "know-how." Perhaps we can bring to our call men like these who can make new contacts with emperors and kings and rulers and magistrates.

Somehow I believe the Lord meant what he said through the centuries.

Again to the apostles through their president, Thomas B. Marsh:

"Contend thou, therefore, morning by morning; and day after day let thy warning voice go forth; and when night cometh let not the inhabitants of the earth slumber, because of thy speech." (D&C 112:5.)

"For verily the voice of the Lord is unto all men, and there is none to escape; and there is no eye that shall not see, neither ear that shall not hear, neither heart that shall not be penetrated.

"And the voice of warning shall be unto all people, by the mouths of my disciples, whom I have chosen in these last days." (D&C 1:2, 4.)

Somehow, brethren, I feel that when we have done all in our power that the Lord will find a way to open doors. That is my faith.

"Is any thing too hard for the Lord?" he asked, when Sarah laughed when she was told that she would have a son. When she heard this in the tent door, she knew that both Abraham at 100 years and she at 90 years were past the age of reproduction. She could not bear children. She knew that, as well as it has been known that we could not open doors to many nations.

"And the Lord said unto Abraham, Wherefore did Sarah laugh. . . .

"Is any thing too hard for the Lord? At the time appointed I will return unto thee, according to the time of life, and Sarah shall have a son." (Gen. 18:13–14.)

Brethren, Sarah did have a son, from Abraham, the father of nations.

"Therefore sprang there even of one, and him as good as dead [and that was Abraham, 100 years old], so many as the stars of the sky in multitude, and as the sand which is by the sea shore innumerable." (Heb. 11:12.)

Is anything too hard for the Lord?

Also to Jeremiah he had said:

"Behold, I am the Lord, the God of all flesh: is there any thing too hard for me?" (Jer. 32:27.)

If he commands, certainly he can fulfill.

We remember the exodus of the children of Israel crossing the uncrossable Red Sea.

We remember Cyrus diverting a river and taking the impregnable city of Babylon.

We remember the Lehites getting to the promised land.

We remember the Revolutionary War and the power of God that gave us triumph.

I believe the Lord can do anything he sets his mind to do.

But I can see no good reason why the Lord would open doors that we are not prepared to enter. Why should he break down the Iron Curtain or the Bamboo Curtain or any other curtain if we are still unprepared to enter?

I believe we have men who could help the apostles to open these doors—statesmen, able and trustworthy—but, when we are ready for them.

Today we have 18,600 missionaries. We can send more. Many more! Eight thousand, nine hundred went through the mission home in 1973.

I believe it was John Taylor who said, "God will hold us responsible to the people we might have saved, had we done our duty."

When I ask for more missionaries, I am not asking for more testimony-barren or unworthy missionaries. I am asking that we start earlier and train our missionaries better in every branch and every ward in the world. That is another challenge—that the young people will understand that it is a great privilege to go on a mission and that they must be physically well, mentally well, spiritually well, and that "the Lord cannot look upon sin with the least degree of allowance."

I am asking for missionaries who have been carefully indoctrinated and trained through the family and the organizations of the Church, and who come to the mission with a great desire. I am asking for better interviews, more searching interviews, more sympathetic and understanding interviews, but especially that we train prospective missionaries much better, much earlier, much longer, so that each anticipates his mission with great joy.

Not that I had much influence on it, but when I came into the Council of the Twelve in 1943 there were less than one million members; today there are 3,353,000. We then had 146 stakes and about 40 missions, and we now have 633 stakes and 107 missions. We have grown from 937,000 in 1943 to 1,116,000 in 1959, and 3,300,000 in 1973. That means approximately a 19 percent increase in the 16 years between 1943 and 1959 and approximately a 196 percent increase from 1959 to 1974. This is phenomenal growth.

It may be of interest to you brethren, some of you, to know that of the 17,564 missionaries, as of last week, 9,560 are teaching the gospel in English, which is about 55 percent of all the missionaries, and these are in the United States, Canada, Great Britain, Australia, New Zealand, and the Philippines. About 8,000 missionaries are learning languages in the language training missions. These 45 percent are training in the three language schools—about 17 percent or 3,000 in Spanish, about 1,000 in German, about 1,000 in Japanese, about 400 in French, and about 600 in Portuguese, and substantial numbers in Danish, Finnish, Dutch, Norwegian, Swedish, Chinese, Italian, Korean, Thai, Samoan, Afrikaans, and Navajo.

It is interesting to me that some statistician told us that in 33 A.D. when the Savior himself was stressing so strongly "every nation, kindred, tongue, and people" that there were on the earth possibly a quarter billion people (250,000,000).

Eighteen hundred years later, when the command came through Joseph Smith to proselyte the world, our experts estimated that there were one billion people (1,000,000,000), or about four times as many as in the meridian of time. And now as we renew the injunction to cover the earth with the gospel, it is estimated that there are probably almost three and a half billion (3,400,000,000).

The question is frequently asked: Should every young man fill a mission? And the answer has been given by the Lord. It is "Yes." Every young man should fill a mission. He said:

"Send forth the elders of my church unto the nations which are afar off [He said elders—we have been talking about elders]; unto the islands of the sea; send forth unto foreign lands; call upon all nations, first upon the Gentiles, and then upon the Jews." (D&C 133:8.)

He did not limit it.

The answer is "yes." Every man should also pay his tithing. Every man should observe the Sabbath. Every man should attend his meetings. Every man should marry in the temple and properly train his children, and do many other mighty works. Of course he should. He does not always do it.

We realize that while all men definitely should, all men are not prepared to teach the gospel abroad. Far too many young men arrive at the missionary age quite unprepared to go on a mission, and of course they should not be sent. But they should all be prepared. There are a few physically unfit to do missionary service, but Paul also had a thorn in his side. There are far too many unfit emotionally and mentally and morally, because they have not kept their lives clean and in harmony with the spirit of missionary work. They should have been prepared. Should! But since they have broken the laws, they may have to be deprived, and thereon hangs one of our greatest challenges: to keep these young boys worthy. Yes, we would say, every able worthy man should shoulder the cross. What an army we should have teaching Christ and him crucified! Yes, they should be prepared, usually with saved funds for their missions, and always with a happy heart to serve.

The Lord says:

"And that every man"—(Did you catch the words, "every man"?) "should take righteousness in his hands and faithfulness upon his loins, and lift a warning voice unto the inhabitants of the earth: and declare both by word and by flight that desolation shall come upon the wicked." (D&C 63:37.)

Note that he said *every man*; but we must find a way to have every man prepared.

Now, how can we do this? We see that there are these elements to be considered: the breaking down of resistance of the nations of the world to receive our missionaries; a greatly increased missionary force (greatly, I emphasize); a better trained missionary army; and better and additional methods and approaches.

Now here we will consider each one in its turn. We need to *enlarge our field of operation*. We will need to make a full, prayerful study of the nations of the world which do not have the gospel at this time, and then bring into play our strongest and most able men to assist the Twelve to move out into the world and to open the doors of every nation as fast as it is ready. I believe we have many men in the Church who can be helpful to us, who are naturally gifted diplomats. I believe we should bring them to our aid and as stated before, I have faith that the Lord will open doors when we have done everything in our power.

Second, I have already discussed and will discuss a little further, an enlarged army of missionaries.

Third, I believe that the Lord is anxious to put into our hands inventions of which we laymen have hardly had a glimpse.

The Prophet Joseph Smith declared: "The truth of God will go forth boldly, till it has penetrated every continent, and sounded in every ear, till the purposes of God shall be accomplished."

A significant revelation states: "For, verily, the sound must go forth from this place into all the world, and unto the uttermost parts of the earth—the gospel must be preached unto every creature. . . ." (D&C 58:64.)

I am confident that the only way we can reach most of these millions of our Father's children is through the spoken word over the airwaves, since so many are illiterate. We have proved the ability of our young men to learn other languages.

President David O. McKay, speaking in the October 1966 conference of the Church, said of the scientific discoveries of recent years which will make possible the preaching of the gospel to every kindred, tongue, and people: "They stagger the imagination."

And further: ". . . discoveries latent with such potent power, either for the blessing or the destruction of human beings as to make men's responsibility in controlling them the most gigantic ever placed in human hands. . . . This age is fraught with limitless perils, as well as untold possibilities."

King Benjamin, that humble but mighty servant of the Lord, called together all the people in the land of Zarahemla, and the multitude was so great that King Benjamin ". . . caused a tower to be erected, that thereby his people might hear the words which he should speak unto them." (Mosiah 2:7.)

Our Father in heaven has now provided us mighty towers—radio and television towers with possibilities beyond comprehension—to help fulfill the words of the Lord that "the sound must go forth from this place unto all the world."

Even though there are millions of people throughout the world who cannot read or write, there is a chance to reach them through radio and television. The modern transistor radio can be mass produced by the thousands in a size that is small and inexpensive. We can preach the gospel to eager ears and hearts. These should be carried by people in the marketplaces of South America, on the steppes of Russia, the vast mountains and plains of China, the subcontinent of India, and the desert sands of Arabia and Egypt. Some authorities claim that this tiny miracle will be recorded by future historians as an event even greater than the invention of the printing press. The transistor is an eloquent answer to the illiteracy and ignorance which reign supremely over the earth. The spoken voice will reach millions of hearers who can listen through a $3 or $4 transistor but could not read even an elementary treatise.

There are over 7,000 AM and FM radio stations in the United States, with thousands more in other parts of the world. There are innumerable opportunities for us to use these stations overseas, if we only prepare the message in the native languages.

Also, missionaries could be supplied with small portable cassette tape players and go into the homes with prepared messages to humble family groups all around the globe. Millions of people are anxious and willing to learn, if only they can hear the "sound" in their own language and in a manner that they can grasp and understand.

Just think what can be accomplished when we broadcast our message in many languages over numerous radio stations, large and small, around the world, and millions of good people listening on their transistors are being indoctrinated with the truth.

The Lord has blessed the world with many Early Bird satellites. They are stationed high in the heavens, relaying broadcast signals back to almost every corner of the earth's surface. Today there are 67 earth receiving stations operating in 50 countries of the world. Certainly these satellites are only the genesis of what is in store for the future of worldwide broadcasting.

With the Lord providing these miracles of communication, and with the increased efforts and devotion of our missionaries and all of us, and all others who are "sent," surely the divine injunction will come to pass: "For, verily, the sound must go forth from this place into all the world, and unto the uttermost parts of the earth—the gospel must be preached unto every creature. . . ." (D&C 58:64.) And we must find a way.

We are happy with the people of Hong Kong, but according to our records only 1,000, or less than 1 percent of the people, have accepted the gospel.

We have a stake in South Korea and a mission there, with about 7,500 members. What must be done to reach the other 37,000,000? There must be a way, for the Lord does not talk in riddles. He must have anticipated that something could be done so that his word might be fulfilled.

The millions of people in the Philippines would receive the gospel in large numbers if it were properly presented to them. We have two missions and a stake there. We should use their own young men as missionaries and then every facility that is available to bring them to a knowledge of the true church.

There are 14,000,000 people in Taiwan, 2,000,000 in Singapore, 119,000,000 in Indonesia, 31,000,000 in Korea, 40,000,000 in Thailand, and 103,000,000 in Japan, and all these 300,000,000 people are sons and daughters of God and have a right to hear the gospel, and we have not only the right to give it to them but the obligation to do so.

We mention Australia with its over 13,000,000 people, and we have been doing missionary work there since 1851. Now, after 123 years, we still have only 29,000 members, for which we are grateful, with 13,000,000 yet to touch, and for 123 years we have been sending missionaries from this land to that land and today have more than 600 missionaries in Australia. Of this 600 plus missionaries, only a relatively small handful, about 5.5 percent, are Australians. Where have we failed to help these good people to see their duty in this pivotal matter?

In Mexico we have around 54,000,000 people with about 92,000 members. We have 489 full-time missionaries now serving in that country, only 122 of which are native Mexicans. We have had some difficulty getting missionaries from the United States into Mexico or we would have far more. There has been a limitation of about 360 American missionaries that could get visas. We are unable to send a new elder from the United States until another elder is released and has surrendered his visa. In addition to this problem, the cost of placing missionaries in Mexico has greatly increased, and so for both these reasons there is ample argument that Mexico, with its nine stakes and five missions, should furnish its own missionaries, or the equivalent.

Suppose that South Korea with its 37,000,000 people and its 7,500 members were to take care of its own proselyting needs and thus release to go into North Korea and possibly to Russia the hundreds who now go from the states to Korea.

If Japan could furnish its own 1,000 missionaries and then eventually 10,000 more for Mongolia and China, if Taiwan could furnish its own needed missionaries plus 500 for China and Vietnam and Cambodia, then we would begin to fulfill the vision. Suppose that Hong Kong could furnish its needed missionaries and another 1,000 to go to both of the Chinas; suppose the Philippines could fill its own needs and then provide an additional 1,000 for the limitless islands of southeast Asia; suppose the South Seas and the islands therein and the New Zealanders and the Australians could furnish their own and another several thousand for the numerous islands of south Asia and for Vietnam, Cambodia, Thailand, Burma, Bangladesh, and India.

With this movement of missionaries who would be traveling north and west, the lands of the world could begin to be covered with the gospel as the lowlands of the world are covered with the oceans.

Now in another part of the world, suppose that Mexico and Central America provided far more missionaries than they needed themselves and the people of South America had reached the point where they could export numerous fine missionaries and then suppose that the United States and Canada awakened to their real responsibility, sending thousands of missionaries to join them, going east and north so that Iceland, Scandinavia, southern Europe, Germany, and Europe could be covered.

Great Britain, with seven missions and 14 stakes now but numerous others later, should join that army and all together the army of the west would move across western Europe and central Europe and Arab lands, and in a great pincer movement join their efforts with the missionary army from the east to bring the gospel to millions in China and India and other populous countries of the world. You will note the size of the men on the map which is intended to represent the relative population size—our problem in those areas.

May we emphasize again that numbers are incidental and secondary to our main purpose, which is the same as that of our Heavenly Father—to bring to every soul the gospel which can open the doors to eternal life for man. Our objective is not for power or domain, but totally spiritual. And to every nation and people which opens its borders to the gospel will come unbelievable blessings.

It must be realized, too, that the directions of the assignments are, as indicated by the arrows, merely suggestive. The individual assignments could be merely an expansion of the present-day coverage. The missionaries would be sent where the most good could be accomplished—something like this:

The sharing of the gospel often requires us to cross language and cultural barriers and the arrows you see on the screen are representative of what needs to happen and will not, in every case, represent a perfect match of which country could best supply the missionaries to preach the gospel in another country. The basic point is, where the land masses of the world are, there, also, are the populations masses to whom we must bring the gospel of Jesus Christ.

This would be difficult. It would take some time. Sometimes it might seem impossible but again remember the little stone cut out of the mountain without hands which was destined to roll forth and fill the whole earth. It has gone a long way but it must go farther.

Using all the latest inventions and equipment and paraphernalia already developed and that which will follow, can you see that perhaps the day may come when the world will be converted and covered?

If we do all we can, and I accept my own part of that responsibility, I am sure the Lord will bring more discoveries to our use. He will bring a change of heart into kings and magistrates and emperors, or he will divert rivers or open seas or find ways to touch hearts. He will open the gates and make possible the proselyting. Of that, I have great faith.

Now, we have the promise from the Lord that the evil one will never be able to frustrate totally the work that He has commanded us to do.

"This kingdom will continue to increase and to grow, to spread and to prosper more and more. Every time its enemies undertake to overthrow it, it will become more extensive and powerful; instead of decreasing it will continue to increase; it will spread the more, become more wonderful and conspicuous to the nations, until it fills the whole earth." (President Brigham Young, April conference, 1852.)

Further, Brigham Young wrote:

"We believe, as the time draws near, the Lord will hasten his work, and nations will soon be gathered into the fold for Christ.

"The work urges and is becoming very much enlarged and extended, and requires a commensurate accumulation of men and means, and expansion of mind and energy, ability and perseverance. The Lord, our God, is our strength, and under this accumulation and weight of care and business, has hitherto given in grace and strength, according to our day and generation, has sustained us in every time of need and preserved and delivered us from the hands of our enemies. Blessed forever be his holy name; great and wondrous are his ways. Let all nations give heed to his servants, for they are preparing the way for his coming; yea, when he shall come in power and great glory, to take unto himself a kingdom, prepared and made ready in the due time of the Lord; for this is the Lord's work; woe be unto him who putteth forth his hand, his influence, his energies, or any of his powers to oppose it." (From a letter written by President Brigham Young to Elder Samuel W. Richards, who was presiding over the European Mission. The date of the letter is October 29, 1852. It is found in the *Millennial Star*, vol. 15, pp. 106–7.)

You are acquainted with the statement of the Prophet Joseph Smith in the Wentworth Letters written March 1, 1842. (*History of the Church*, vol. 4, p. 536.) I am sure the Prophet Joseph looked ahead and saw many problems with national animosities and fears with war and commotions and jealousies, and I am sure that he saw all these things would happen and yet in spite of everything he said with great boldness and assurance:

"No unhallowed hand can stop the work from progressing; persecutions may rage, mobs may combine, armies may assemble, calumny may defame, but the truth of God will go forth boldly, nobly and independent, till it has penetrated every continent; visited every clime, swept every country and sounded in every ear; till the purposes of God shall be accomplished, and the great Jehovah shall say the work is done."

The immensity of the work before us is emphasized as we consider the population of the world as it approaches the four billion mark.

I am under no delusion, brethren, to think that this will be an easy matter without strain or that it can be done overnight, but I do have this faith that we can move forward and expand much faster than we now are.

As I see this almost impossible demand, I believe that you brethren, our representatives, can immediately accept the challenge and in your stakes and missions explain to the people how they must increase their missionaries, how they can finance their missionaries, how they can indoctrinate and train these additional missionaries, and how, through all the agencies of the Church, they can move ahead. Here is where you come in.

A year ago now I was in Japan and Korea, and as I saw the many handsome young men joining the Church and giving leadership to its organizations, I seemed to envision a great movement when there would be thousands of local men prepared and anxious and strong to go abroad. As I have been in Mexico since that time, I seemed to envision again Mexican youth and Latins from Central and South America in great numbers qualifying themselves for missionary service within their own country and then finally in other lands until the army of the Lord's missionaries would cover the earth as the waters cover the mighty deep.

I have stated the problem. I believe there is a solution. I think that if we are all of one mind and one heart and one purpose that we can move forward and change the image which seems to be that "We are doing pretty well. Let's not 'rock the boat.'"

In all the countries I have ever visited I have found many intelligent and qualified people who give leadership in their countries, and I also remember numerous people from deprived countries enjoying benefits from the gospel.

In our stake missionary work at home we have hardly scratched the surface.

Brother T. Bowring Woodbury told us of 93 cooperating families in one Utah stake who were working with 93 non- or part-member families. Clifford Johnson told us of bringing five of 26 non-members into the Church in a few months.

It can be done.

We can change the image and approach the ideals set out by President McKay, "Every member a missionary." That was inspired!

I know this message is not new, and we have talked about it before, but I believe the time has come when we must shoulder arms. I think we must change our sights and raise our goals.

When we have increased the missionaries from the organized areas of the Church to a number close to their potential, that is, every able and worthy boy in the Church on a mission; when every stake and mission abroad is furnishing enough missionaries for that country; when we have used our qualified men to help the apostles to open these new fields of labor; when we have used the satellite and related discoveries to their greatest potential and all of the media—the papers, magazines, television, radio—all in their greatest power; when we have organized numerous other stakes which will be springboards; when we have recovered from inactivity the numerous young men who are now unordained and unmissioned and unmarried; then, and not until then, shall we approach the insistence of our Lord and Master to go into all the world and preach the gospel to every creature.

Brethren, I am positive that the blessings of the Lord will attend every country which opens its gates to the gospel of Christ. Their blessings will flow in education, and culture, and faith, and love, like Enoch's city of Zion, which was translated, and also will become like the 200 years of peaceful habitation in this country in Nephite days. There will come prosperity to the nations, comfort and luxuries to the people, joy and peace to all recipients, and eternal life to those who accept and magnify it.

Someone gave us this:

> "To walk with God, no strength is lost.
> Walk on.
> To talk with God, no breath is lost.
> Talk on.
> To wait on God, no time is lost.
> Wait on."

I pray the blessings of the Lord will be upon us as we approach our great responsibilities, in the name of the Lord, Jesus Christ. Amen.

Appendix 2

PAST LDS INTERNATIONAL SOCIETY CONFERENCES, 1990–2015

"Global Changes and the Church," 1990

"BYU's Role in Assisting the International Mission of the Church," 1991

"Post-Cold War Environment: Challenges Facing the International Church," 1992

"Cultural Challenges Facing the International Church," 1993

"Development and Relief Efforts of the LDS Church in a Troubled World," 1994

"The Global Church in a World of Ethnic Diversity," 1995

"Religious Liberty and the Global Church: The Challenge of Sharing," 1996

"Out of Obscurity: Public Affairs and the Worldwide Church," 1997

"Family and the Church: Cultural and Political Challenges," 1998

"The Challenge of Sharing Religious Beliefs in a Global Setting," 1999

"Development Assistance and Humanitarian Aid: The LDS Perspective," 2000

"Education, the Church, and Globalization," 2001

"Muslims and Latter-day Saints: Building Bridges," 2002

"The Gospel, Professional Ethics, and Cross-Cultural Experience," 2003

"Church Development in the Developing World," 2004

"Joseph Smith and the World," 2005

"International Challenges Facing the Church," 2006

"'The Perplexities of Nations': Current Trends and the International Church," 2007

"Meet the Mormons: Public Perception and the Global Church," 2008

"The Church and the Global Community," 2009

"Challenges in Establishing the International Church," 2010

"The Erosion of Religious Liberties—Impact on the International Church," 2011

"In the Public Eye: How the Church Is Handling Increased Global Visibility," 2012

"The Church and International Diplomacy," 2013

"The Church and Humanitarian Assistance: In the Lord's Way," 2014

"'Blessed Are the Peacemakers': Peace Is Possible," 2015

The full proceedings of these conferences can be accessed from the LDS International Society's website at http://ldsinternationalsociety.org.

INDEX

A

B

D

G

H

K

L

M

N

O

P

S

T

U

V

W

Y

Z